Disciplining gender

John M. Sloop

Disciplining gender

Rhetorics of Sex Identity in
Contemporary U.S. Culture

UNIVERSITY OF MASSACHUSETTS PRESS
Amherst and Boston

LC 2003024581
ISBN 1-55849-437-5 (cloth); 438-3 (paper)
Designed by Sally Nichols
Set in Janson Text by Binghamton Valley Composition
Printed and bound by The Maple-Vail Book Manufacturing Group

Library of Congress Cataloging-in-Publication Data

Sloop, John M., 1963–
  Disciplining gender : rhetorics of sex identity in contemporary U.S.
culture / John M. Sloop.
      p. cm.
Includes bibliographical references and index.
  ISBN 1-55849-437-5 (cloth)—ISBN 1-55849-438-3 (paper)
  1. Sex role. 2. Gender identity. 3. Gender identity—Case studies.
I. Title.
HQ1075 .S576 2004
305.3—dc22   2003024581

British Library Cataloguing in Publication data are available.

Contents

ACKNOWLEDGMENTS vii

INTRODUCTION
Critical Rhetoric, Public Argument, and Gender Trouble 1

ONE
Re-membering David Reimer
Heteronormativity and Public Argument in the John/Joan Case 25

TWO
Disciplining the Transgendered
Brandon Teena, Public Representation, and Normativity 50

THREE
"So Long, Chaps and Spurs, and Howdy—er,
Bon Jour—to the Wounded Songbird"
k.d. lang, Ambiguity, and the Politics of Genre/Gender 83

FOUR
The Disciplining of Female Masculinity
Janet Reno as "the Lesbian Swamp Monster" 104

[v]

[Contents]

FIVE
In Death, a Secret "Finally and Fully Exposed"
Barry Winchell, Calpernia Addams, and the
Crystallization of Gender and Desire   123

CONCLUSION
Bringing It All Back Home   142

NOTES   151
WORKS CITED   167
INDEX   183

Acknowledgments

Like all book projects, this one could have only been brought to completion with the support of numerous colleagues and friends. The first (and perhaps most important) group of people I want to thank are the members of the Working Papers in Gender and Sexuality Group at Vanderbilt University and the Fellows of the 2002–2003 Robert Penn Warren Center for the Humanities. I never dreamed that I would be fortunate enough to work and party with such extraordinary colleagues. I am in debt to each of you: Brooke Ackerly, Katie Crawford, Carolyn Dever, Lisa Duggan, the fabulous Lynn Enterline, Jose Medina, Chuck Morris, Diane Perpich, Kathryn Schwarz, and Holly Tucker. In addition, Mona Frederick, executive director of the Warren Center, saw me begin this project in my 1998–1999 stint at the center and complete it in the 2002–2003 academic year while I was at the center. Mona makes everything work better and continues to be one of the best benefits of being at Vanderbilt. Thanks to Gaylyn Martin, Sherry Willis, and Paul Burch, each of whom helped the Humanities Center function smoothly.

I owe thanks to each of my colleagues in Communication Studies: Lynn Clarke, Anne Demo, Kass Kovalcheck, Chuck Morris (about whom I cannot say enough—thank you for everything), and Brad Vivian. I sometimes wonder how I got so lucky.

Generous research support was supplied by the University Central Research Scholars Grant Program at Vanderbilt. I wish especially to thank Dennis Hall.

An early version of portions of chapter 1 originally appeared as "'A Van with a Bar and a Bed': Ritualized Gender Norms in the John/Joan Case," *Text and Performance Quarterly* 20 (2000): 130–49. Permission to use this material is courtesy of the National Communication Association. An early version of portions of chapter 2 originally appeared as "Disciplining the Transgendered: Brandon Teena, Public Representations, and Normativity," *Western Journal of Communication* 64 (2000): 165–89. Permission to use this material is courtesy of the Western States Communication Association.

Colleagues at other institutions who have been especially helpful to this project through argument, support, and inspiration include Karen Shimakawa (extra special thanks, for being there in the very beginning and urging me to be careful in my tone and analysis), Sarah Projanksy (continuing thanks), Kent Ono, Judith Halberstam, Kristin Brown, Tom Nakayama, Michelle Holling, and Celeste Condit.

The students in my "Rhetorics of Gender Trouble" courses helped push the ideas in these chapters and put together some pretty magnificent dossier material. I am in the debt of everyone in those courses, but especially Tara Lynn, who also worked as a research assistant.

Jennifer Gunn is the most generous ex-spouse that I can imagine. My son, Christopher Sloop, has been forgiving when I've dragged him back to my office after school yet again. He has also inadvertently kept me abreast of interesting transformations in contemporary music. He's a great kid in every way.

Lambchop has produced music that has moved me emotionally and intellectually in ways that continue to surprise me. I owe them a massive debt.

Thanks to all my friends at FIBS, especially phs, shuggie_ii, snowflakes, and lewscannon.

Thanks to the departments who asked me to present various versions of chapters from this work and the people at each presentation who challenged my ideas: the Department of Speech Communication at the University of Georgia; the Cultural Studies Program at the University of California, Davis; the Department of Communication Studies at Syracuse University; and the Department of Speech Communication at Northwestern University.

Calpernia Addams was generous with her time, meeting me on several occasions to discuss issues when she had rightly tired of pursuing these topics with strangers (especially people who wanted to write about them). I want to thank her publicly for trusting me.

I am especially indebted to Bonnie Dow, one of my all-time favorite people and the best media critic (and parallel parker) I know. Bonnie absolutely hated the first draft of the Brandon Teena analysis and forced me to rethink it in ways that ultimately made the entire manuscript better (this could mean, I suppose, that her sometimes loud laughter at the very idea of my next project ultimately bodes well for me). Not only has Bonnie been a supportive colleague and friend as I worked through each chapter, but she has also been wicked good fun. Simply put, I adore her.

INTRODUCTION

Critical Rhetoric, Public Argument, and Gender Trouble

Constraint calls to be rethought as the very condition of performativity.
Judith Butler, *Bodies That Matter*

Gender ambiguity, in and of itself, answers to many different political masters.
Julia Epstein and Kristina Straub, "The Guarded Body"

This "politics of home" would analyze the persistence of sexual difference for organizing identity categories. It would highlight the costs to the subject of not being clearly locatable in relation to sexual difference.
Jay Prosser, *Second Skins*

It is evident to any observer of popular culture that the 1990s were a decade in which sexual and gender norms, and the popularly understood "morals" underlying these norms, were challenged and battled over on multiple fronts. From *20/20* to *Jerry Springer*, from medical journals to *South Park*, from country music to retro glam, from Clinton's White House to www.whitehouse.com, from editorial pages to ballpark conversations, a wide variety of ambiguously gendered and/or alternatively sexualized individuals were poked, prodded, presented, re-poked, re-prodded, and re-presented. In each representation of, and conversation about, gender trouble, or gender ambiguity, cultural critics could of course find an ongoing cultural negotiation over what the dominant meanings of gender, sex, and sexuality should be. It is in these public representations and the ways individuals interpret and struggle over them that ideological transition and change can take place. Indeed, an optimistic critic might look at these representations and their interpretation in order to note—and reify—particular ways in which public understandings of gender, sex, and sexuality have changed "for the better."

While a case could indeed be made that the last few decades have

[1]

witnessed interesting, politically "messy" changes in the borders between male and female, hetero- and homosexual, I want to argue in this
work that (or I want to put my focus on the ways in which), rather than
each case acting as an example of "gender trouble" that encouraged
reassessment of cultural assumptions about human bodies and sexual
desire, such cases were more often positioned within the larger body of
public argument as aberrations in nature's plan and hence worked to
reify dominant assumptions about human bodies and sexual desire.[1]
That is, while cases of gender ambiguity were "talked about" in ways
that encouraged an undermining or questioning of the very notion of
"aberration" as related to sexuality and gender, bi-gender normativity
was for the most part underlined and reemphasized. Significantly, one
finds assumed (and not necessarily spoken) within these discourses a
series of binary roles and behaviors which ultimately constitute the very
notions of male and female, masculinity and femininity, hetero- and
homosexual. These public discussions all work in part, in Lauren Berlant's words, as keys "to debates about what 'America' stands for, . . .
how citizens should act," at least in terms of their gendered and sexual
behavior (1).

In the most general sense, the purpose of this book is to provide
critical readings of several contemporary cases of sexual/gender ambiguity in order to emphasize, and ultimately struggle with, the gender
and sexual norms that "America" stands for, that each of us learns to
protect through our language and our behavior toward one another and
toward our "selves." To see how those norms are protected through
public arguments and public discussions, I investigate five cases, a few
of which might be considered exotic and others that might initially
appear mundane and invisible. I move from cases of surgical alteration
of bodies to metaphorical and ideological rearticulations of bodies and
desires. To peek ahead:

In the early 1960s, a pair of twin boys was born in Canada. In a freak
circumcision accident, the penis of one of the two boys was completely
excised. After a year and a half of attempting to come to terms with how
to raise the injured child, his parents were given the option, an option
they cautiously took, of having the child surgically "reassigned" as female. While the child was raised as the twin sister of her brother, stories

about her life were employed over the next decade as evidence of the social constructedness of gender, as evidence that anyone could have his or her gender "reassigned" successfully on both a physical and a mental level if the reassignment occurred early enough in life. In medical journals, popular culture magazines, and newspapers, sexologist John Money frequently reported on the success of the "John/Joan" case, as it came to be called, and its support for his theories of the social constructedness of gender. Moreover, and consequently, the case was employed in numerous textbooks and college courses which assumed that gender had meaning only as a social construct. Repeatedly and publicly, then, the gender reassignment was portrayed as a success and the reassigned child identified as a happy and well-adjusted young woman. In the early 1990s, however, numerous articles in medical journals, in the popular press, and on television revealed that the child had never been comfortable as a woman, that he had in fact had another series of surgeries as a teenager in order to rebuild a penis and reassign himself again as male. Contradicting earlier claims, the young man's reassignment was now said in public argument to be conclusive proof that gender was essential, naturalized to the body. Furthermore, the case was offered in many reports and editorials as evidence of the wrongheadedness of feminism and women's studies. Finally, with the publication of a book titled *As Nature Made Him*—which included the voluntary "outing" of "John" as David Reimer—the "natural link" between sex and gendered behavior was proclaimed and strongly reiterated on talk shows and news programs.

In late 1994, a young woman who was "living as a man" in Falls City, Nebraska, using the name Brandon Teena, dated several local women, who would later refer to Brandon as the "dream man," one who "knew how to treat a woman." After Brandon was arrested on a check fraud charge and identified by the arresting officers as a woman, Brandon's local circle of friends discovered that he was "really" a she. A few days after the arrest and Brandon's release on bail, two of Brandon's male friends stripped him in front of his girlfriend at a Christmas party, forcing the girlfriend to acknowledge that Brandon did not have a penis. The pair then drove Brandon to a remote area and took turns raping him. A week later, after Brandon had reported the crime to local law enforcement officers, the two rapists murdered Brandon and two others living in a house with Brandon. The murder case and the subsequent trials received voluminous local and national news coverage and became a crystallizing site for transgender activism. In addition to the news reports and programs, the case was covered in a documentary film (*The Brandon Teena Story*), a play, a true crime book, a Guggenheim art project, multiple Web sites, and, finally, the critically acclaimed and financially successful film *Boys Don't Cry*. Within the assumptions of this body of discourse lurk cultural norms concerning gender/sexual–appropriate and inappropriate behavior. In effect, the case surrounding Brandon Teena's murder, like the murder itself, provides a case study of the disciplinary power of rhetoric and gender norms.

During the mid- and late 1980s, country singer k.d. lang emerged as something of an enigmatic star, especially within traditional country music circles. While her music, especially her collaboration with legendary producer Owen Bradley, clearly aligned her with the "Nashville tradition," there was persistent speculation about her sexuality and her "fit" with country music and the Nashville aesthetic, given her masculine (and assumedly lesbian) appearance. When lang eventually did come out as lesbian, the way she was marketed—her style—and the genre of music she was recording were altered. More important culturally, however, is that the way lang's music was talked about publicly and the way her "masculinity" was configured as an object of discourse were also altered. In many respects, the conversation before and after lang's having come out tells us a great deal about the trouble gender ambiguity can cause culturally and the very different type of trouble caused by the erasure of such ambiguity.

Almost immediately upon being named attorney general of the United States, Janet Reno's sexuality, owing to her masculine appearance, became a topic of discussion and humor in "mass mediated" texts. On television shows such as *Ally McBeal* and *Saturday Night Live*, for example, a good deal of the humor centering on Reno was derived from representing her as a highly sexualized heterosexual woman "behind the scenes" of her professional duties. Like much humor, this depiction created an ironic representation, one supposedly far from "the truth" of Reno's behavior. At best, such humor seems to imply, Reno is either a dyke behind the scenes or frigid and asexual. Similar themes appeared repeatedly in television, magazine, and newspaper discussions of Reno's capacities as attorney general—the way she was described in regard to the standoff at Waco, Texas, her unwillingness to appoint new counsels to investigate Democratic fund-raising, her general confrontations with Republican congressional leaders, her struggles with Parkinson's disease, and her handling of the Elian Gonzalez case. Again, an investigation of the discourse "about" Janet Reno, someone who did not make her sexual desires or identity a matter of public debate by choice, once again tells us something about the ways "gender trouble" is handled in dominant culture.

On July 5, 1999, Private Barry Winchell was murdered at Fort Campbell, near Clarksville, Tennessee. Investigators soon discovered that Winchell had been killed at the hands of two fellow soldiers, Calvin Glover and Justin Fisher. After several days, U.S. Army officials acknowledged that Winchell was the victim of an evident hate crime since Glover and Fisher had committed the crime in large part because of their belief that Winchell was gay. While the crime itself was sufficient to garner a good deal of public attention, when it was revealed that Winchell had been dating "female impersonator" Calpernia Addams, whom he had met at a gay nightclub in Nashville, the attention grew far more intense. Moreover, given that Addams referred to herself as a "preoperative" transsexual, the public arguments over the gender and sexuality of both Addams and Winchell became a primary focus of the case. While some gay rights groups insisted that Addams and Winchell were gay men (as did the conventions of newspaper editing), others framed the two as a heterosexual couple. Coverage of the case focused directly on both overt gender behavior and the supposed "internal" motivations of both victims and perpetrators of the crime, again providing a great deal of fodder for discussions of the meaning of gender and sexuality at the level of popular culture.

These are, of course, not the only cases of gender ambiguity and gender trouble that have been fought over at the level of popular culture in recent years. Moreover, these five cases do not, and indeed cannot, cover every aspect of public argument over gender, sex, and sexuality. I have chosen these five cases, however, precisely because they point out just how ubiquitous concerns about "proper" gender and sexuality are; they allow us so many different entryways into an investigation of how gender and sexuality are implicated in every realm of discourse—scientific debates, debates about popular music, political candidates, military legislation, moral behavior. While these cases, then, do not cover every aspect of political argument, each one forces us to think through particular domains of public discussion, and each provides one piece of the larger mosaic of dominant popular culture. In addressing these cases, I hope to provide both specific instances of gender trouble and gender discipline and a wider picture of the more stable meanings of gender and sexuality in contemporary U.S. culture.

THEORY MAKING TROUBLE

In interdisciplinary studies of gender and sexuality since the mid-1980s, it has become, if not chic, at least more comfortable to make the focus of one's study gender and sexual ambiguity and/or *to be* gender/sexually ambiguous. In my experience, this degree of comfort has increased in part because of an *assumed* articulation between such ambiguity and liberatory transgression. What Nicola Evans notes of drag within gay/lesbian circles—"Once regarded as an embarrassment, the practice of drag has moved into the vanguard of cultural politics, celebrated as a performance that denaturalizes gender and subverts essentialist views of sexuality" (199)—can be said of numerous marginal, off-center, ambiguous, or queer sexual/gender performances and representations.

In 1990 the general discussion of gender and sexuality took a "performative" turn as a result of the publication and celebration of Judith Butler's *Gender Trouble*. Drawing in part on the discourse theories of Michel Foucault, Butler posited gender as performative, "where 'performative' suggests a dramatic and contingent construction of meaning" (139); in short, gender is what we *do* rather than what we *are*.[2] But given how heavily policed gender norms are in popular culture, Butler observed, bi-gender heterosexual norms become materialized, naturalized, as if they were essential rather than contingent. As a result, individuals "perform" gender to a great extent without reflection, simply behaving in ways that "make sense," given their own gender identification.

After laying out this theory of gender performativity, Butler noted that the task of gender critique needed to expand beyond its historical boundaries: "To expose the contingent acts that create the appearance of a naturalistic necessity . . . is a task that now takes on the added burden of showing how the very notion of the subject, intelligible only through its appearance as gendered, admits of possibilities that have been forcibly foreclosed by the various reifications of gender that have constituted its contingent ontologies" (33). Specifically, Butler argued that her intention was to "think through the possibility of subverting and displacing those naturalized and reified notions of gender that support masculine hegemony" and "to make gender trouble . . . through the mobilization, subversive confusion, and proliferation of precisely those constitutive categories that seek to keep gender in its place" (34). In that book at least, Butler posited one vital function of gender critique to be the pursuit of various activities that initiate "gender trouble," subverting reified structures of identity. As a result, Butler investigated such actions and identities as drag and butch/femme and argued that such practices could (and should) be read as ones that encourage "viewers" to understand gender as performative, as something not to be found in any notion of a "true" body.[3] In short, Butler saw her purpose, and that of gender criticism more generally, as being the notation and critique of gender performance, as well as the provision of critical readings that could work to undermine bi-gender normativity.

By the time of the publication of her subsequent book, *Bodies That Matter*, Butler found herself in the position of having to curtail the more celebratory claims of her earlier work (or, rather, the more celebratory *readings* of her earlier work).[4] Here Butler highlighted some of the ways that performances she had earlier taken as gender-troubling did not persistently or completely work to de-naturalize gender, and did not work subversively in all cases and for every audience. Rather, a practice such as drag could quite often work as a hyperbolic confirmation of gender norms; that is, in noting the ways men can "perform" femininity, we simultaneously essentialize masculinity (e.g., "that's a man acting like a woman") and tie femininity to females (i.e., "that is how women should act"). Hence, in more general terms, Butler asked that we carefully delineate the ways that gender as performative should be positioned neither as a theory of pure freedom nor as a theory of pure constraint:

> Performativity cannot be understood outside of a process of iterability, a regularized and constrained repetition of norms. . . . This repetition is what enables a subject and constitutes the temporal condition for the subject. This iterability implies that "performance" is not a singular "act" or event, but a ritualized production, a ritual reiterated under and through constraint, under and through the force of prohibition and taboo, with the threat of ostracism and even death controlling and compelling the shape of production, but not, I will insist, determining it fully in advance. (95)

In this way, Butler suggested that critics must carefully seek out the ways in which, while gender ambiguity may indeed work subversively, it can quite often work complicity with dominant culture and dominant representations. Jay Prosser points to these two contradictory impulses in critical work and in popular culture concerning cases of gender trouble (for Prosser, transgenderism in particular) as either understanding cases of gender ambiguity or transgenderism as literalizing gender, and hence working hegemonically, or as de-literalizing it, and working subversively (13–15).

Indeed, to a large degree, differing perspectives on, and studies of, gender ambiguity and transgenderism work variously to highlight either the literalizing or the de-literalizing aspects of such transgressions (or assume a literalizing or de-literalizing understanding of gender).[5] An example of what I would see as an argument that either urges de-literalization or sees positions or subjectivities that encourage it is Gayle Rubin's classic essay "Thinking Sex," often posited as a precursor to much of the current discussion of transgenderism.[6] Rubin positioned this essay as an attempt to cultivate what would now be called a "sex-positive" orientation—to think of sexual practices and sexuality as being organized into systems of power that must be transgressed if we are to undermine the constraining dimensions of culture on our behavior.

Hence, Rubin wanted to challenge laws and attitudes in order to "allow" culturally a variety of sexual practices, including S/M, cross-generational sex, transgenderism, transvestitism, and so on, on the principle that such sexual practices should ultimately be articulated as creative and positive rather than conservative and immoral.

A more contemporary articulation of a liberatory position is Kate Bornstein's *Gender Outlaw*, a fascinating personal and cultural account of what it is like to exist as a male-to-female (MTF) transsexual while claiming to experience oneself as neither male nor female. Bornstein notes that whereas she had earlier defined herself, and was defined by others, in bi-gender terms (a female who lived in a male body, and then as a female after surgical reassignment), she ultimately discovered "that gender can have fluidity, which is quite different from ambiguity. If ambiguity is a refusal to fall within a prescribed gender code, then fluidity is the refusal to remain one gender or another" (51–52). Throughout her book, Bornstein questions the reader as to how he or she identifies himself or herself in this miasma of gender and sexuality. Hence, the reader finds herself/himself queried into conundrums such as: If Kate Bornstein is an MTF and is in a partnership with an FTM and you, the reader, find her attractive, what does that make you? For Bornstein, at least in this phase of her writing, we can all choose to become gender outlaws, sidestepping or utilizing the boundaries of masculinity and femininity, creating an identity inside or outside those categories. As Bornstein puts it: "A more universal and less depressing definition of passing would be the act of appearing in the gender of one's *choice*. Everyone is passing: some have an easier job of it than others" (125, emphasis added). Even while noting the existence of "gender defenders"—people who work to keep gender boundaries rigid and segregated—Bornstein has an optimistic view of how fluid and ambiguous gender can become.

Similarly (though not chronologically), others have articulated a variety of positions on gender and sexuality with varying degrees of optimism and fluidity. For instance, Sandy Stone coined the term "posttranssexual" in her now well-known "Posttransexual Manifesto" (a response to Janice Raymond's *Transsexual Empire*, which literalized gender to a transsexual's pre-reassignment sex) in order to encourage an understanding of gender and sexuality as categories that could be worked within rather than as being binding. That is, one did not have to have an "essential" body or essential experiences in order to perform a given category. Gordene MacKenzie's call for the creation of a "transgender nation" rid of all clear gender categories is on similar ground, as is Alan Hyde's critical legal study of gender laws, in which he posits the body as ontologically unstable and physically mutable to such a degree that one can with seeming ease "proliferate so many discursive representations of the body that none might ever be understood as natural, all instead understood as strategic interventions, self-conscious metaphors" (235).

Further, Susan Stryker, in an introductory essay to a special issue of *GLQ* focusing on transgender issues, aligns transgenderism and transgender theory with queer theory to the degree that each makes "visible heteronormativity's occluded structures and operations" (149). For Stryker, transgender theory and transgender performance "have achieved critical importance (and critical chic) to the extent that they provide a site for grappling with the problematic relations between the principles of performativity and a materiality that, while inescapable, defies stable representation, *particularly as experienced by embodied subjects*" (147). Judith Halberstam, in her brilliant exposition of the concept of female masculinity, notes that she wants to explore the concept in part because it is a "queer subject position that can successfully challenge hegemonic models of gender conformity" (*Female Masculinity* 9). Indeed, Halberstam notes that she wants to encourage people not to follow the futile path of "saying no to power," but instead to assert an "I don't care" to power (9). Halberstam envisions the potential of female masculinity to operate as a challenge to heteronormativity. Similarly, Leslie Feinberg argues that the very existence of transgendered individuals and their representation in works such as Feinberg's own as "warriors" can highlight queered subjectivities and ultimately encourage a freer expression of sexual and gender fluidities (x, 92). Finally, in the introduction to *Body Guards*, an anthology dealing with historical cases and theoretical statements of sexual and gender ambiguity, editors Julia Epstein and Kristina Straub assert that "transvestism, transsexualism, and intersexuality offer a point at which social pressure might be applied to effect a reevaluation of binary thinking" (4), and they posit their collection as one of the means by which this pressure may be applied.

In each work of this sort, what we find is an attempt to build an argument in which the critic or theorist investigates cases of queerness, transgenderism, or transvestism as spaces within which the heterosexual normativity of dominant culture can be critiqued. Although none of these essays or arguments ignores how gender or sex is ideologically disciplined and policed (how these categories are ideologically literalized and hegemonic, in Prosser's terms), each of them leans toward underlining the ways in which transgenderism or gender ambiguity can work to subversively de-literalize. This is clearly a vital task for critics interested in opening up the barriers to a variety of ways of expressing both gender and sexuality, to encourage a de-literalization and denaturalization of gender and sexual categories, to encourage each of us to think of gender and sexualities as "styles," for example, as Kate Bornstein suggests (e.g., butch-femme, biker, masculine, aggressive) rather than on the basis of sex and its accompanying bi-gender sexual categories (i.e., male-female and, hence, heterosexual, homosexual, and bisexual). While such positions do not generally attempt to completely eradicate existing gender categories as a starting point of identity for some,[7] they do work to focus on *queering* gender and sexual differences or highlighting how these differences are erased through cases of gender trouble.

While I share with Bornstein the goal of achieving a range of gender and sexual identities that are potentially fluid or flexible, I also share with Jay Prosser—at least at this stage of the cultural game—a concern that the de-literalization impulse works in part by encouraging people who have never been granted the right to attain a chosen identity to undermine these very identity categories. Moreover, there may be good reasons to maintain what Prosser calls "home" identities as places "in" which one feels safe, and that movement within gendered spaces could become one of many options.[8] In short, while I support in part theoretical de-literalization, I maintain that one important aspect of deliteralizing gender/sexuality is understanding clearly the ideological mechanisms that keep it literalized, the ways in which gender/sexuality difference is persistently reaffirmed and returned to "gender normality" on a mass cultural and ideological level. As Prosser notes of a "politics of home," one of its functions is "to highlight the costs to the subject of not being clearly locatable in relation to sexual difference" (204).

GENDER DISCIPLINE

One of the problems with an attempt to highlight the de-literalizing aspects of gender ambiguity, then, is that it implicitly encourages critics to celebrate de-literalization at the expense of critiquing the very persistent ways in which cultural expectations and mechanisms continue to discipline each of us to practice "proper" gender behaviors. Again, as Evans wisely observes about drag, to suggest that it subverts "gender ideologies by exposing gender as a culturally prescribed performance does less than justice to our appetites for the inauthentic. Once we know that a 'real woman' is a cultural fiction rather than an ontological birthright, have we thereby . . . reduced at all the rewards of continuing to be feminine in ways that society will recognize and approve?" (203). Although drag and other forms of ambiguity and transgression clearly work to subvert gender normativity, it is also true that multiple facets of culture powerfully stress traditional gender normativity.

Gender trouble is always limited in its deconstructive potential because representations and public arguments involving cases of gender trouble are persistently "disciplined," contained within the realms of gender normativity. That is, while particular audiences (some academic communities, some transgendered communities) may have become skeptical of sex as an ontological category, this is clearly not a fully hegemonic perspective. Resistance to the blurring of gender categories and norms at a "dominant" level is strong indeed.

It is in the classes I teach that I learn and relearn the lesson of just how powerfully ideology works to re-literalize and re-normalize gender norms. Semester after semester, my students' comments illustrate just how actively they (or "we") serve as agents in keeping the categories rigid. For the last several years, for instance, I provided students in my "Rhetoric of Mass Media" and "Rhetoric of Gender Trouble" courses a dossier of public documents (newspaper and magazine articles) dealing with the twins case mentioned earlier and discussed in chapter 1. In both of these classes I have given the students the dossier only after providing them with an adequate understanding of theories of performativity as they relate to gender. The day before they are scheduled to read the dossier, I ask them to examine each document very carefully through the lens of gender performance, encouraging them to criticize the discourse for the ways in which it literalizes gender. Yet in each class, once the discussion begins, I find that, almost to a person, the students' readings of the case are tightly bound within the parameters of gender normativity and are extremely protective of traditional norms. Rather than reading the dossier as a case study of the cultural boundaries for gender performance, and rather than highlighting how these boundaries are protected through the language and images employed in mass mediated discussions and public argument, my students consistently and vigorously accept and employ these very parameters, arguing that the case in fact serves as *proof* of gender's direct tie to sex and of the "political problems" of contemporary feminism. That is, while I am attempting to use the case to create gender trouble in the classroom, the *overall* result is a reification of gender norms.

Of course, the classroom experience is somewhat messier than this synopsis would indicate: the students are forced to understand that a binary is at work, they have to struggle with their use of pronouns in discussing the subject of the case, and so on. And critical thinking is a long-term acquisition. I draw on this example only to indicate at what a powerful and *commonsensical* level heteronormativity works. The more similar experiences I have had with my classes, the more sure I have become that I can be more successful in creating gender trouble with my students by providing critical illustrations of the ways that drag, gender ambiguity, and transgenderism are disciplined, metaphorically beaten back into place, than by looking for the liberatory potential of these same examples and cases. As much as both impulses must be at work, for many audiences, recognition of the power of ideology as constraint must come first.

Examples of work that focuses on mass mediated or medical discipline of gender/sexuality are also widespread. In looking at how gender/sexuality is tightly constrained, such criticism ultimately serves to loosen those constraints while leaving room for particular individuals to continue to adhere to certain identities with which they feel comfortable at given stages of their life; that is, if we recognize how gender/ sexuality is constrained, we recognize the ultimate untenability of these constraints but can still work within them. First, recent histories concerning the meaning of sex and gender as articulated in literary, medical, and public texts have pointed out the variety of ways in which different historical and discipline-specific texts have understood the body differently and hence have read sex and gender off the body in different ways. For example, Thomas Laqueur's well-known history of bodily sex illustrates the contingency of the ways in which the body has been read and the relationship between male and female bodies has been understood. As Laqueur argues, in certain historic periods (e.g., much of the nineteenth century), the body was understood through the template of one gender (male), with the body parts that we now think of as female being seen as an inversion of the male body (and, hence, inferior to the male body). Although individual bodies were understood as potentially alterable over a lifetime, all bodies were understood and categorized under this one-sex model. Similarly, Alice Dreger's history of hermaphrodites indicates that there have been historical breaks in the perception of hermaphrodites. In what she terms the "age of gonads," physicians identified the body as male or female but never as a mix of both, never as fused. Such a categorization was based solely on the physician's identification of the presence or absence of a set of gonads. Joanne Meyerowitz's more recent history of transsexuality works through multiple case studies, carefully noting the multiple constraints that shape how individuals are restricted in self-identification and how mass mediated outlets necessarily work as ideological containers. Laqueur, Dreger, and Meyerowitz all implicitly and explicitly observe that bodies, even transgressive bodies that do not fit existing categories, are forced, or disciplined, into those categories. Finally, work such as Jennifer Terry's *American Obsession*, Robert Brookey's *Reinventing the Male Homosexual*, and Lisa Duggan's *Sapphic Slashers* also illustrate the interconnections between gender, sexuality, class, and race throughout the history of the United States.

Furthermore, work on *contemporary* medical understandings of sex/ gender illustrate the ongoing and inevitable ways in which sex/gender is created by physicians using particular models. Both Emily Martin and Bonnie Spanier have investigated how metaphors and representations in medical textbooks encourage the positing of women's bodies, especially their reproductive systems, as passive and receptive while men's are posited as active and aggressive. Suzanne Kessler's work on contemporary cases of intersexed children shows that physicians who treat such children attempt as early as possible to reassign them surgically to either male or female categories so that they may grow up without any gender confusion. Further, both Judith Shapiro and Sandy Stone have noted that transsexuals attempting to get approval for sex change surgery find themselves in a rhetorical bind that forces them to represent themselves to the doctors who are evaluating them as a man or woman "trapped" in the body of the "other" gender. That is, the physicians have created a situation in which they give approval for surgery only to those who clearly "fit" particular gendered mannerisms and meanings. As a result, "the gender conservatism of transsexuals is encouraged and reinforced by the medical establishment on which they are dependent for therapy" (Stone 294). Moreover, once having changed genders through surgery, transsexuals often adopt a "natural attitude" toward the two-gender system so that they can effectively "pass" as a member of the "opposite" gender. The consequences of this dilemma are of course nothing if not constraining; as Stone puts it, "It is difficult to generate a counterdiscourse if one is programmed to disappear" (295).[9]

At the level of narrative analysis, while Marjorie Garber is interested in showing how transvestism can open up a variety of activities and sexualities, she also notes that because transvestism disrupts and threatens gender norms, transvestites are efficiently contained within cultural and mass mediated representations. For example, transvestism is commonly contained and normalized though a narrative she calls "the transvestite's progress." With this narrative, which ultimately soothes readers' tensions by reinstating the male/female binary, the reader or audience of the story about a given transvestite is provided with a good reason for his or her cross-dressing, for instance, the need to get a job (69).[10]

Numerous writers have shown how mass mediated reports work to discipline bodies into "true" male or female categories. For example,

Meyerowitz notes the assumption in the popular press that sex change surgery unveils "a true but hidden physiological sex and thus tie[s] the change to a biological mooring that justifie[s] surgical intervention" ("Sex Change" 164). Similarly, in the introduction to *Gender Reversals and Gender Cultures*, Sabrina Ramet suggests that it is difficult to transgress bi-genderism because the structures that hold it together are so powerful within any given culture, even those that allow gender reversals, that postsurgical transgendered persons are expected to fully play the stereotypical role expected of their new gendered position. Thus, a male-to-female transgendered person is expected to perform traditional femininity flawlessly as both a precondition for surgery and a result of the surgical transition.

C. Jacob Hale, in a brilliant essay concerning the Brandon Teena case, finds that such acts of containment occur not only at the level of the mass media but also at the level of the interests of small communities and subcultures, including those of some transsexuals. Hence, just as some media reports might rhetorically contain a transvestite within conventional gender roles based on the existence or nonexistence of the penis, some "essential" transsexualists would contain that same person's gender based on the individual's identity as "man" or "woman" or the person's desire to be a "man" or a "woman." In neither case do we find an exploration of a multiplicity of new or different subject positions that could be created or adopted. Similarly, in a forum conversation with Hale, Judith Halberstam, whose primary interest is in how transgression can work to loosen the traditional moorings of gender and the meanings clustered around femininity and masculinity, notes that critics cannot afford to underestimate the fact that "desire and gender and sexuality tend to be remarkably rigid" in popular culture—that gender trouble is persistently contained ("Transgender" 139).[11]

Finally, in an essay concerning transgenderism and embodiment, Patricia Elliot and Katrina Roen claim that work focusing on transgendered subjects and critical work focusing on transgenderism as it functions discursively are not necessarily in opposition. That is, while critical work dealing with subjectivity focuses on how given individuals come to constitute themselves, discursive studies look outward to see how mass culture legitimizes or delegitimizes (articulates, defines) what transgenderism means. A similar distinction is made by Jacob Hale in his informal on-line "rules" for writing about transgendered subjects.[12] Here, Hale suggests that people who are not transgendered should feel encouraged to write about transgenderism provided they do so in terms of investigating what the public discourse about transgenderism tells us about cultural ideologies concerning gender and sexuality rather than what it tells about transgendered identity (which, Hale argues, should be left to overtly transgendered people to investigate). In this book I investigate how a number of cases of gender ambiguity are discussed and contained at the level of public argument and what these public discussions tell us about how each of us is interpellated by particular specific notions of gender and sexuality.

From here I move on briefly to a discussion of the ways in which my approach is shaped by rhetorical criticism within the particular tradition of rhetorical and cultural theory. Because some of the essays and ideas may not be familiar to all readers, I first spend some time underscoring certain assumptions and showing how they influence my readings of these cases.

RHETORIC, MATERIALITY, HEGEMONY, AND CRITICISM

Since the early 1980s, as was the case to some degree throughout the humanities, rhetorical studies witnessed an increased interest in post-structural theories, studies of discourse, and other work emerging from critical and cultural studies. Given the rhetorical studies' tradition of investigating public argument and public meanings, rhetorical criticism and discourse studies have proved to be a compatible fit. In the most general terms, one could label this turn in rhetorical studies "critical rhetoric," a name derived from an influential metatheoretical and meta-critical essay by Raymie McKerrow in which McKerrow catalogued a number of theoretical developments that had taken place within and outside rhetorical theory. Relying heavily on the works of Michel Foucault, as well as Ernesto Laclau and Chantal Mouffe, McKerrow reversed the phrase "rhetorical criticism" to "critical rhetoric," a twist that linguistically helped refocus the mission of the rhetorical critic—and one that clearly influenced how I have carried out this project.[13] There are three implications of this move to critical rhetoric that I want to highlight.

First, critical rhetoric places its focus on *doxastic* rather than *epistemic* knowledge. That is, rather than being concerned with knowledge of the essence of objects (e.g., the "truth" about sex) or philosophical discussions about meanings, critical rhetoric is concerned with public argument and public understandings about these objects. For example, even if one held that "sex" had a particular nature in and of itself that could be known outside of culture—an extremely questionable proposition at best—a critical rhetoric study would be interested in how gender and sexuality are culturally understood. Second, and this is where the reversal of terms is most pertinent, critical rhetoric views its own writing as a political practice, an attempt to alter or shift public knowledge by illustrating how that knowledge has been constructed. By reversing "rhetoric" and "criticism," critical rhetoric focuses on the critic's function as a rhetorician and on criticism's role as a political performance (McKerrow 108). Finally, an interrelated point, critical rhetoric is concerned with the materiality of discourse, viewing the discourse of power itself as material and as working within public debate. It is this thesis of materiality embedded in discourse theory in general and critical rhetoric in particular (and the understanding of hegemony that is implied by it) to which I turn next, because it is this understanding that drives my interactions with public texts and shapes the ways I ultimately write about them.

In an influential 1982 essay, Michael McGee provided what he termed "a materialist's conception of rhetoric." To a large degree, McGee was specifically arguing that rhetorical critics and theorists needed to think about "rhetoric"—its meaning, purpose, and function— from the bottom up rather than as an abstraction. In a certain sense, McGee was offering something of a Forrest Gump theory of rhetoric: with a grounding theory of "X is as X does," McGee argued that we can understand "rhetoric" only by understanding the term "rhetoric" in use. That is, if we want to know what rhetoric is, we do not start by theorizing it; instead, we look to see how it has been employed, how it has been theorized colloquially. While McGee referred to a good deal of emerging poststructural thought in that essay,[14] the idea, now quite common-place, was compelling because he was claiming not only that a theoretical concept has meaning only in how it is used but also that the concept has a materiality, that is, it resists change, and that once a term has a meaning grounded in common usage, it resists easy transition.

McGee's claims were perhaps most significant when one was focusing not on terms like "rhetoric" but instead on words used in everyday life and public argument that have political implications for how people organize identities, hierarchies, and understandings of the human condition. That is, the significance of the "materiality of discourse" thesis was in some ways more important when one thought through the cultural politics of everyday life and everyday meanings than when one thought through arguments over disciplinary boundaries. Indeed, as Foucault's work and assumptions were disseminated and assumed by a variety of critics, almost every aspect of identity and politics was slowly subsumed under the study of discourse. In the most general sense, one of the vital implications of this observation is that those interested in political change came to think more in terms of slow rhetorical transition than in terms of overnight revolution. Lasting change is always a slow process, if only because it requires changes in meaning, and such changes are intergenerational rather than intrapersonal. In Raymond Williams's terms, meaningful revolutions are by necessity long revolutions.[15]

This move to think through discourse as material is of course linked to discussions of discourse and gender or other categories of identity. That is, it assumed that people take on their understanding of their "selves" and their worlds from available discourses and, once taking on their identities and cultural meanings, can only work change within those meanings. Of course, just as with gender studies and cultural studies of gender, such an understanding of culture led to two critical impulses: on the one hand, it led to an impulse to investigate the multiple ways that people can function in their everyday lives to overturn meanings, to resist through a manipulation of meanings, and on the other hand, there was an alternate impulse to investigate how transition or change is persistently curtailed or contained within an overall dominant cultural ideology. Even though these positions were rarely if ever carried out in the extreme in any single argument, there were clear critical efforts in either direction.

As I have said, my interest here is mainly in understanding how changes in meanings, or transitions through transgression, are contained by a variety of institutional and ideological practices.[16] Indeed, drawing on Göran Therborn, I have carried out case studies illustrating that oftentimes in matters of public controversy, those people who are articulating a transgressive position, whether on the left or on the right, whether radically inclusionary or radically exclusionary, find themselves "disciplined" economically (people boycott them, they lose jobs), physically (they suffer actual or threatened physical harm), and ideologically (they are labeled "loony," intellectually bankrupt, abnormal). Regardless of the fact that audiences can rework meanings on their own and can work with transgressive texts, my interest has been in how these transgressions are contained in public controversy. While as critics we may see our project as aiding some transgressions and cultural changes, we need to understand clearly the difficulties we face, beginning with the multiple ways in which transgression is persistently contained.[17]

In rhetorical studies and theory, Ronald Greene's articulation of materialism productively places a number of rhetorical and critical theorists into conversation and provides a rich understanding of materialism that underscores the disciplinary impact of culture while simultaneously allowing for transgression at the level of usage and articulation. That is, Greene understands both the liberating and disciplinary sides of the ideological coin while emphasizing the latter. In encouraging a move beyond representational politics, Greene looks at how that discourse acts materially as part of a process of public-ity in which people become visible with various attributes articulated "on" them, allowing them, in a sense, to be "governed in advance." Drawing in a significant degree on the well-known Althusserean division of the Ideological State Apparatus (ISA) and the Repressive State Apparatus (RSA), Greene posits rhetoric as having a function in a non-conspiratorial process of invention that nonetheless has a role in governance. He notes: "Invention concerns itself with how a 'way of life' becomes an object for social change. Of course, the forms in which this act of publicity takes place can include speeches, documentaries, photographs, movies, newscasts, white papers, statistics—the list is nearly infinite. An articulation of a governing apparatus requires that particular behaviors and populations become visible so that a program of action can intervene to improve the happiness, longevity, and material welfare of a population" (31).

For Greene, the very idea that a way of life becomes a rigid object of discourse, that it works as part of a visible public-ity effect, means that the materiality of rhetoric forces people into Foucault's "fields of stability," making them, in advance, *understandable*. In this way, Greene notes, "rhetoric is not epiphenomenal to a governing apparatus but absolutely crucial to its organization since the ability to make visible a population in order that it might calibrate its own behavior is depending on how rhetoric contributes to a panopticism as a technology of power" (31). Greene is arguing that while discourse and rhetoric must be taken seriously in terms of their material constraints on meanings and subjectivity, we should first understand how those material discourses merge with a vast array of mass mediated, educational, and governmental discourses that ultimately work in the interests of the governing (and economically powerful). When Joanne Meyerowitz observes that "transgendered people used the language available to them to identify their condition" (*How* 36), she is making the same point. That is, because there are historically only a limited number of medical and institutional terms with which to describe one's body and one's desires, one is partially a product of preexisting public-ity regarding one's "condition." Indeed, Meyerowitz suggests that in cases of "marginalized" identities, like those of transgendered people, existing public-ity is even more important in providing individuals with ways to understand their own subjectivities. Meyerowitz notes that the fact that so many transgendered individuals created scrapbooks about the Christine Jorgensen case in the 1950s offers evidence of the impact of the popular press: "[It] provided material resources that could give isolated readers a sense of community as well as a sense of possibility" (*How* 93). As with Foucault, while this does not exclude space for transgression or alternate readings, the very discourses from which change must take place emerges from sites that articulate dominant interests. Hence, the very starting point for "material" discourse serves the interests of governance.

While Greene's argument provides us with an understanding of the materiality of discourse and the links between this materiality and governing interests, Celeste Condit offers a rethinking of "hegemony" in a mass mediated society that is clearly, though not intentionally, complementary to Greene's argument and provides useful support for the disciplinary function of public argument. The fit between the two is not necessarily a comfortable one, in that Condit begins by trying to disarticulate what she sees as a careless contemporary link between hegemony and the thesis of a "dominant interest" ideology. Condit argues that in the critical community we have slowly equated hegemony with pure "dominant ideology" rather than seeing hegemony as, in her rereading of Gramsci for mass mediated societies, an articulation of meanings that have been agreed on by a plurivocal public. Hence, for Condit, hegemony indicates the overall agreed-upon concordance of meanings negotiated by a large public, and in this way she ensures a more subtle understanding of hegemony and of the "materiality of rhetoric" thesis. For Condit, even while rhetoric allows people to be judged in advance, there is some small degree to which that judgment is partially agreed on by all groups and hence partially represents their interests, although "some groups have disproportionate rhetorical advantage and some groups are not invited by the mediators into the concordance at all" ("Hegemony" 226).

If we consider her thesis along with Greene's, we can understand that while meanings are negotiated and "agreed upon" by large groups of people—that they can in fact be read transgressively—the meanings presented in mass mediated texts are ones that place "governing" interests at the center, making visible the meanings that most clearly fit the interests of those in the strongest positions of power. Though not a dominant ideology thesis, this is one that recognizes that concord is biased toward certain interests and that those interests have the advantage of making visible certain ideas and images, critiquing and disciplining all cases that work against that vision. Thus when Judith Butler stresses that performativity is neither free play nor theatrical self-presentation, that it cannot be understood outside a process of iterability or a repetition of norms, she is working with a similar, more disciplinary sense of discourse and materiality. As Butler claims (clearly in line with Greene's thesis), "performance is not a singular act or event, but a ritualized production, a ritual reiterated under and through constraint, under and through the force of prohibition and taboo, with the threat of ostracism and even death controlling and compelling the shape of the production" (*Bodies* 94). Reading Butler through Greene's claims and this branch of rhetorical studies, we can see that she is advancing the thesis of the governmentality of performance while granting that governmentality is never fully determined in advance.

These theses—of rhetoric as material, of hegemony as a matter of an unbalanced concord, of performance as an ongoing production of governmentality—are key in the study of cases of gender ambiguity and transition because the subjectivities being represented in such cases are not visible as transgressive; rather, they are disciplined in advance to be understood through particular heteronormative understandings of the human condition. Hence, a transgendered child growing up in a small community may encounter few similar cases other than that of Brandon Teena, and in encountering this case, the child sees transgenderism not as "natural" but as an instance of "deception." Or a youth who thinks he might be gay may encounter the "John/Joan" case, only to discover the "natural" link assumed between proper gender behavior and heterosexuality. Or a person who is a masculine female, to borrow from Judith Halberstam, will not see her masculinity as "normal" but instead, through the multiple discourses surrounding the body of Janet Reno, will understand that such masculinity is punished through ridicule. While those in multivocal communities and academics "in the know" might be able to look at these as cases of transgression and liberation, those without community, as Alfred Kielwasser and Michelle Wolf have pointed out in their discussion of televised representations of adolescent homosexuality, are most at risk precisely because the images they see of themselves are disciplined in advance by a hegemonic understanding that "holds them in place," judging them. When the only transgendered model one has was killed for "deception," one has understood transgenderism only through the way it is policed.

In sum, looking with a critical eye shaped by the rhetorical studies tradition and by contemporary work in gender studies, this book provides readings of five different cases of gender ambiguity. Although I acknowledge that each could be read "against the grain," that transgressive readings assuredly do occur and meanings are "messier" than my discussions might indicate, I am most interested in the ways in which the dominant closes off alternatives, reiterating norms that lead to exclusion and punishment. There is clearly a critical need to highlight transgression and alteration, but there is also a vital need to note discipline and containment. This book is an attempt to highlight the disciplinary side of the equation, the way in which transgression is shut down, altered, stopped, and to do so in the context of other critical readings that emphasize transgressive, gender-troubled readings. Significantly, in highlighting the discursive elements of ideological discipline, I would argue that we are simultaneously deconstructing it.

ONE

Re-membering David Reimer

Heteronormativity and Public Argument
in the John/Joan Case

There is a tendency to think that sexuality is either constructed or determined; to think
that if it is constructed, it is in some sense free, and if it is determined, it is in some sense
fixed. These oppositions do not describe the complexity of what is at stake in any effort to
take account of the conditions under which sex and sexuality are assumed. The
"performative" dimension of construction is precisely the forced reiteration of norms.
Judith Butler, *Bodies That Matter*

We define bodies in the first place only when we are conflicted,
as a society and often within ourselves.
Alan Hyde, *Bodies of Law*

In mid-March 1997, a radio report told the story of a male infant whose
penis had been excised as the result of an accident during a circumcision
procedure. In consultation with physicians, the parents requested that
the child, after additional surgery and ongoing hormone therapy, be
"reassigned" as female.[1] The news reporter observed that the case,
which came to be known as the John/Joan case after the child's female
and male pseudonyms, was especially interesting because the child—
then reassigned as a young girl—had a twin brother and hence had been
used by medical psychologist John Money as a case study in the social
constructedness of gender.[2] Indeed, because Money frequently reported
in both the popular and the medical press on the success of the reassignment, the case had been pointed to for years as key evidence for the
social construction view of gender.

Nevertheless, the report went on, a recent article in a medical journal
was claiming that the child had never comfortably accepted the reassignment and had in fact actively resisted living as a girl. Finally being
told as a teenager that "she" was originally a boy, the youth made an
immediate decision to be surgically and socially reassigned once again,
this time as a male (now known as David Reimer).[3] The report implied

that because the John/Joan case had been lauded for years as compelling evidence of the constructedness of gender, the revelation of the eventual outcome of the case proved that the theories of the constructionists were wrong: gender was instead essentially determined by the body. Indeed, over the next several days and months, reports in numerous publications, with headlines such as "Sexual Identity Not Pliable After All, Report Says" (Angier, "Sexual" A1), "Rethinking Gender Identity" (31), and "The Basis of Sexual Identity" (Roan E1), drew the conclusion that gender is not primarily a matter of social condition but rather a matter of biologically determined impulses. The case was said to illustrate that "the experts had it all wrong" (Gorman 83). As *Time* put it, gender is a product of the "brain" rather than of cultural conditioning, a matter of natural imperatives rather than of cultural roles and social conditioning.

As the story continued to unfold in academic and trade journals, finally culminating in the publication of John Colapinto's *As Nature Made Him*, the arguments consistently illustrated the lack of complexity that Judith Butler points to in the epigraph to this chapter. Indeed, what debate there was on the case posited it in the starkly contrasting terms of gender as purely social versus gender as essentially tied to the body's given sex, with the "latter" side clearly winning the day. The tension illustrated by this case around gender reveals what Lauren Berlant has called "a desire for identity to be ontological, dead to history, not in any play or danger of representation, anxiety, improvisation, desire or panic" (72).

In her well-known deconstruction of the sex/gender (essentialism/constructionism) binary, through the understanding of gender as performative, Judith Butler provides a lens through which to complicate the scientific and public arguments that took place around the body and activities of John/Joan. As she notes, the problem with the sex/gender division is that it establishes the sexed body as "natural," existing prediscursively, prior to culture, "a politically neutral surface on which culture acts" (*Gender* 7). While Butler argues that "sex" can never be prediscursive and therefore can never be either apolitical or determinate, she also argues against seeing gendered behavior as freely open for play by any individual. Rather, to posit gender—and gender behaviors—as performative is to see it as "a ritualized production, a ritual reiterated under and through constraint, under and through the force of prohibition and taboo, with the threat of ostracism . . . compelling the shape of the production, but not . . . determining it fully in advance" (Butler, *Bodies* 95). As a result, the project of a political genealogy of gender becomes one of noting the forces that turn contingent acts into naturalistic necessities and the ways in which possibilities for different gender behaviors "have been forcibly foreclosed by the various reifications of gender that have constituted its contingent ontologies" (Butler, *Gender* 33).

As I will show, the public discussion of the John/Joan case (or what we might refer to as the public re-membering of the body and life of David Reimer)—a case that had the potential to cause "gender trouble" by "subverting and displacing those naturalized and reified notions of gender that support masculine hegemony and heterosexual power" (Butler, *Gender* 33)—illustrates the disciplinary power of the ritualized production of gender *regardless* of the "gender theory" held by those arguing. That is, while some observers and figures involved in the case treat John/Joan's physical appearance and behaviors primarily as biological signs of sex and others treat these same appearances and behaviors as contingent signifiers, both rely so uniformly on the same signifier-signified relations that they become crystallized as natural signs. In short, even if one deconstructs the sex-gender differentiation with Butler on a *theoretical* level, arguments over the case provide a body of public and scientific discourse that consistently offers ritualized reiterations of a binaristic system of sex-based, male-female differences. To put this in the words of Judith Halberstam, rather than naïvely celebrating gender fluidity, we need to begin to talk again "about the ways in which desire and gender and sexuality tend to be remarkably rigid" ("Transgender" 290).

Hence, rhetorically and culturally, the public discussion of the case creates a complex body of discourse that calls for critical attention, especially by gender critics who hold a performative position. This case, a case that held the potential to problematize naturalized categories that tie gender to sex, consistently worked instead to reify binaristic expectations of gendered behavior. In effect, both those who posit gender as constructed and those who posit sex as natural (or at least primarily determinate) used the same set of signifiers to support their arguments about John/Joan's success/failure in fitting his/her gender role. These signifiers make up a portion of what Sabrina Petra Ramet refers to as gender culture: "a society's understanding of what is possible, proper, and perverse in gender-linked behavior" (2).[4] Moreover, these signifiers represent the same "forced reiteration of norms" (Butler, *Bodies* 94) that we all face—the same reiterations that impel and sustain our own gender performances.

In this chapter I provide a reading of the John/Joan case as it was reported in "scientific" and mass media print outlets.[5] By reviewing both medical journals and popular discourse from 1969 to the present, I was able to develop a critical reading of the evidence of proper gender behavior utilized in medical journals and then trace out the types of evidence that signal key public understandings of gender behavior as they become translated and crystallized in popular news magazines and newspapers. I argue, first, that for both those who discuss the case publicly from a constructivist position and those who hold that gender is primarily an expression of the body's sex,[6] gender is seen as being successfully or unsuccessfully behaved or expressed through particular clothing, hairstyles, body orientation (notably during urination), and physical activities. It is these activities that make up in large part the reiteration of gender norms. Second, I discuss the specific ways that the case articulates a link between successful gender behavior and heterosexual desire. Third, I discuss the social and moral implications of the bio-basic gender ideology implied by contemporary public arguments regarding the John/Joan case (i.e., one cannot successfully work against one's biological gender impulses). Finally, as a related issue, I discuss the problematic ways in which feminism and women's studies are constructed by observers of the case, how "feminism" is itself articulated with a particular view of gender. In short, I am interested in investigating and "troubling" the way gender signifiers are re-naturalized (resigned) in discussions of the John/Joan case and in exploring the possible implications of this re-naturalization of gender, given that the cultural prescriptions of gender influence each of us, subtly and overtly, on a daily basis.[7]

RE-SIGNING GENDER

In a celebrated essay, Suzanne Kessler ("Medical") illustrated the "medical construction of gender" by investigating the logic physicians use in making decisions on the case management of intersexed infants (hermaphrodites).[8] By looking at both the medical research that has proliferated on the topic and the practices of physicians (e.g., their "talk" about intersexed children both among themselves and when advising parents of possible options), Kessler makes a number of observations about the medical construction of gender. First, in line with Judith Butler's observation of the always already discursive body, Kessler notes that physicians make decisions about which gender the child should be assigned based on heteronormative cultural factors, even though they claim a biological basis for gender in the decision-making process. That is, while physicians might note in conversation and in their research that biological factors (such as chromosomal makeup) should be the major ones in determining gender assignment, "biological factors are often preempted in their deliberations by such cultural factors as the 'correct' length of the penis and capacity of the vagina" (3). That is, in making decisions on how to surgically reassign the intersexed child, physicians make the primary determinant of their decision the child's ability to fit in socially with whatever body can best be constructed. Furthermore, while an intersexed body is arguably a "natural body" in that it developed without intervention, doctors *construct* gender rather than discover it in the case of hermaphrodites by deciding which "bad" genitals need to be removed and which "good" genitals need to be repaired or made "normal." Hence, Kessler argues, doctors conceive of male and female as natural gender categories and attempt to create male or female bodies out of ambiguous genitalia.[9] As Kessler notes, "Language and imagery help create and maintain a specific view of what is natural about the two genders, and, I would argue, about the very idea of gender—that it consists of two exclusive types: female and male" (25).[10]

While I intend to draw on Kessler's insights, the case of John/Joan provides a different arena for the study of gender both because of its public nature and because it involved a child who was born with unambiguous genitalia. That is, by investigating both medical and public discussions of the John/Joan case, paying attention to the evidence from the medical literature that is crystallized in mass mediated discourses, we are provided with a view of broad cultural articulations of gender signifiers and gender behaviors. Again, as the case unfolds, the gender-specific constraints on behavior are seen to be parallel, regardless of whether the descriptions come from a constructionist or essentialist position. Moreover, the behaviors are said to be visible both as markers "on" the body (e.g., clothing, hairstyles) and as markers that reveal impulses "in" the body (e.g., body orientations, personality traits).[11] Although the arguments I examine posit the behaviors in either primarily constructionist or primarily essentialist terms, we may ultimately see these markers, gestures, and acts as "performative in the sense that the essence or identity that they otherwise purport to express are fabrications manufactured and sustained through corporeal signs and other discursive means" (Butler, *Gender* 136). Further, to see these markers, gestures, and acts as performative exposes a politics that is occluded by the constructionist and essentialist positions that have been taken up around the case.

The representation of the case as an example of gender constructedness begins when John Money, the physician who carried out John/Joan's reassignment and observed the case for years, writes about it or is quoted by others in its early stages in the mid-to late 1960s.[12] Milton Diamond and Keith Sigmundson (and others who would take up their position in the 1990s), representing the "natural" position, suggest that "the brain" or body determines gender and that individuals have impulses as male or female that outweigh social upbringing.[13] Whether John/Joan is viewed as being successfully reassigned as female or as having struggled against the reassignment, what Money sees as the signifiers of what it means to act male or female are identical to what Diamond and Sigmundson see as the signs of maleness or femaleness. Hence, when their discussions are made public, the signifiers of dominant gender performance are again reified and naturalized as signs of the body's gender/sex. Whether constructed or essential, the markers of gender behavior are reified on binary grounds; identical iterations of gender behavior are stabilized.

In Money's early comments on the case in *Man and Woman, Boy and*

Girl, he notes that John/Joan's parents implemented the change of sexual assignment of the child initially (pre-surgery) with a change of name, clothing, and hairstyle. Relying on letters from the child's mother reporting success, Money notes that the effects of these changes helped feminize the child. For Money, signs of this success could be found in the child's "clear preference for dresses over slacks" and her pride "in her long hair" (119). Money quotes John/Joan's mother as saying that Joan "just loves to have her hair set; she could sit under the drier all day long to have her hair set" (120). Significantly, when *Time* initially reports on the case, the anonymous author employs the statements concerning John/Joan's love of having her hair set and her predilection for "frilly" clothes as the primary and convincing evidence that the child had successfully become a girl ("Biological" 34).[14] As time passes and Money provides updates about the case in trade books such as *Sexual Signatures*, he continues to emphasize the child's interest in feminine clothing and hair as a powerful sign of the success of the gender change. When John/Joan reached age five, Money notes, the child preferred "dresses to pants, enjoyed wearing her hair ribbons, bracelets and frilly blouses, and loved being her daddy's little sweetheart" (97). In short, taking constructivist positions on gender, Money and those who write about the case from Money's position present the child's use of common gender signifiers as evidence that gender is purely a matter of how one is socialized (in short, "Because John/Joan likes dresses, she acts/is female").

By contrast, when the case is reported as a failure in 1997, Diamond and Sigmundson employ these same signifiers as evidence that the reassignment had in fact always been a failure, that John/Joan [David] rejected "feminine" clothing and hairstyles because "she" had in fact always been a male. In Diamond and Sigmundson's report, John/Joan's mother is quoted as admitting that, for multiple reasons, including her desire for the reassignment to be successful, she did not tell Money the truth about John/Joan's behavior. What is significant here is not that Diamond and Sigmundson get closer to "the truth" of John/Joan's behavior as a child but instead that the gender signifiers used in their reports of the case's failure are the same ones employed by Money in his descriptions of the case's success. For example, John/Joan's [David's] mother notes in Diamond and Sigmundson's essay that she "put this beautiful little dress on him . . . and he immediately tried to rip it off; I think he knew it was a dress and that it was for girls and he wasn't a girl" (300). She also notes that John/Joan showed more desire to shave with her father than to use makeup or set her hair with her mother (300).

In mass mediated articles that draw upon Diamond and Sigmundson's report, this evidence is crystallized as illustrating the case's failure, as if these gender signifiers were linked naturally with sex. In effect, this position reverses Money's causal link to argue, "She doesn't like dresses because she is male." Thus the *New York Times* reports that John/Joan's "new identity never took. Joan would tear off her dresses, reject dolls and seek out male friends. Her mother would try to get Joan to imitate her makeup ritual; instead, she mimicked her father shaving" (Angier, "Sexual" A12). The shaving story is repeated in articles in *Maclean's*, the *Los Angeles Times* (Roan), and *Time* (which also repeats the clothing story) (Gorman 83).[15] Colapinto's *Rolling Stone* essay and his *As Nature Made Him*, the lengthiest and most substantial retelling of the case (and one supportive of Diamond and Sigmundson's position), go into great detail about many of these signifiers of gender. For example, the reassigned adult male David Reimer is described as "a wiry young man dressed in a jean jacket and scuffed work boots" (Colapinto, *As Nature* xi). David's brother, Brian, retells the story of Joan's desire to shave, and his mother recounts Joan's [Brenda's] attempt to tear off the dress. In general, the family notes that John/Joan never revealed any desire to wear makeup and showed little concern for hair care (*As Nature* 49–63). Colapinto consistently emphasizes that John/Joan [David] was never comfortable with her feminine hairstyle, her clothing, or feminine toys. Indeed, the *Rolling Stone* article includes an enlarged quotation from John/Joan's mother: " 'It was a pretty, lacy little dress,' Linda [Janet Reimer] says. 'Joan [Brenda] was ripping at it, trying to tear it off. I thought, 'Oh my God, she knows she's a boy" (64). Later, when John/Joan [David] is reported to have decided to live according to his/her own desires, Colapinto reports that Joan began wearing a jean jacket and work boots, and "her hair was unwashed, uncombed, and matted" ("True" 73). Moreover, after meeting and interviewing the reassigned male John/Joan in a Hard Rock Café, Colapinto translates John's [David's] physical behavior as unequivocal evidence of John's "natural" sex: "The strongest impression I was left with . . . was of John's intense, unequivocal masculinity. His gestures, walk, attitudes, tastes, vocabulary—none of them betrayed the least hint that he had been raised as a girl" ("True" 95).

Again, I am not suggesting that there is no significance to John/Joan's preferences in clothing and hairstyle. What is more significant, however, is that the authors who see the case as a success and the ones who see it as a failure do not provide two different interpretations of the same incident but instead see two different responses surrounding the same specific set of signifiers. Money's assumption is that the appropriate enactment of these signifiers is evidence of successful gender reassignment, while for those taking up the biological position, John/Joan's rejection of these signifiers is a sign of the natural link between sex and gender. The articulation between signifiers and gender performance is so tightly bound, so "naturalized," that John/Joan's rejecting or embracing "girlish" hair and clothing is evidence of her rejecting or embracing a gender identity. Both Money on the one hand and Diamond and Sigmundson on the other, articulating the constructionist and essentialist positions on gender, "read gestures as expression of 'authentic' selves, performances as identities" (Phelan, *Mourning* 3). In either case, the signifiers themselves are reified. Furthermore, not only are these signifiers important to the researchers involved in the case, but also, perhaps more significant, they are repeatedly employed in mass mediated reports of the case, a fact that illustrates their continuing importance in the public's understanding of gender performance and the overall contours of gender culture. It is not insignificant that the strong claims of stark difference between the masculine and the feminine in this case (e.g., Colapinto's claims of David's "unequivocal masculinity," without a hint of femininity) can be found historically in U.S. culture. For example, Joanne Meyerowitz quotes journalists writing about the Christine Jorgensen case in the early 1950s observing that Jorgensen was "without a trace of masculinity," always putting "the conventions of gender into sharp relief" (*How* 63, 65). The materiality of contrasting and separate gender signifiers is strong indeed.

In addition, John/Joan's behaviors are judged as masculine or feminine on the basis of a number of issues dealing with bodily containment or excess, with the tendency toward containment (neatness, gentleness, seated urination) associated with femininity and tendencies toward excessiveness (loudness, rough-and-tumble play, standing urination) associated with masculinity. While my first examples dealt with signifiers or signs "on" the body, this section deals with signifiers "in" the body. In Money's earliest "popular" report on the case (Money and Ehrhardt), he makes a number of observations about containment of the body, many of which are highlighted in the *Time* article that extracted portions of the report ("Biological"). Money notes: "Related to being dressed nicely is the sense of neatness. The mother stated that her daughter by four and a half years of age was much neater than her brother. . . . 'She likes for me to wipe her face. She doesn't like to be dirty, and yet my son is quite different.' 'I've never seen a little girl so neat and tidy as she can be when she wants to be'" (Money and Ehrhardt 119). Further, John/Joan is said to enjoy helping keep the house and kitchen clean, while the twin brother has no interest in the same activities (Money and Ehrhardt 121; "Biological"). Three years later, in *Sexual Signatures*, Money notes that while John/Joan is an aggressive child, her aggressiveness is expressed "in fussing over her brother . . . like a mother hen" (Money and Tucker 97). She is described as "neat and dainty," often attempting "to help in the kitchen" (Money and Tucker 97).

The issue of neatness and containment carries over to the restroom, where, as Money reports, while John/Joan had tried "standing up" to urinate at age two, "as many girls do," she learned to urinate sitting down after discovering that when she tried copying her brother's urination style, she made "an awful mess" (Money and Ehrhardt 120). As I will illustrate, the issue of how John/Joan urinates or desired to urinate becomes more significant in the 1997 retelling of her life story. In this way, the case illustrates Marjorie Garber's employment (13–17) of Lacan's notion of "urinary segregation." Accordingly, despite all other differences men and women may have with other men and women, the act of urination, as symbolized by restroom doors, acts culturally as an imperative tie between all men and between all women.

Although such claims for gender might not be surprising, given the

early to mid-1970s dates of some of these publications, the same signifiers are employed in articles pointing to the failure of the reassignment.
For example, Milton Diamond summarizes a BBC documentary that
focused on the case, noting that from what the reporters had been able
to discover about John/Joan, the reassignment had been a failure; the
girl (John/Joan) was living unhappily and showed signs of being masculine. In the documentary, one of the psychiatrists familiar with the
case describes the way John/Joan moved: "The child . . . has a very masculine gait, er, looks quite masculine" (Diamond, "Sexual Identity,
Monozygotic" 183). Diamond and Sigmundson, in their later report on
the failure of the case, make a number of observations about John/Joan's
early life, many of which again focus on the lack of bodily containment
John/Joan showed as a child. The two note that "Joan [Brenda] did not
shun rough and tumble sports" (300). Moreover, they quote her mother
observing that while John/Joan may have looked like a girl, "when he
started moving or talking, that gave him away, and the awkwardness and
incongruities become apparent" (301). In articles in *Time* and the *Los
Angeles Times*, we find repeated the claim that John/Joan was clearly
masculine because she enjoyed the rough-and-tumble play of climbing
trees (Gorman 83; see also Roan E8; Diamond, "Sexual Identity and
Orientation"; Fletcher; Guernsey). In Colapinto's book, John/Joan's
brother, Kevin [Brian], observes: "When I say there was nothing feminine about Joan, I mean there was nothing feminine. She walked like a
boy. She talked about guy things, didn't give a crap about cleaning
home, getting married, wearing make up. We both wanted to play with
guys, build forts, and have snowball fights and play army" (57). In an
interview on *Nova*, David Reimer draws a clear distinction between all
things female and all things male: "I didn't like dressing like a girl; I
didn't like playing like a girl; I didn't like behaving like a girl" ("Sex:
Unknown").

In parallel fashion, David Reimer's adult occupation is cited repeatedly as anecdotal evidence of his "true" masculinity: while Colapinto
often refers to Reimer's "blue-collar" job and neighborhood (*As Nature*
xii) and others note his current status as a factory worker (Boodman),
Natalie Angier observes that as an adult, David "has the most masculine
sort of job imaginable, working in a slaughterhouse" ("X + Y"). Finally,

in two 2001 television reports on the case, images of David work to reassert his masculinity through his behavior. On *NBC Dateline*'s "The Mirror Has Two Faces," David is shown getting out of a pickup truck and checking the oil while his adult life is discussed in voice-over. On *Nova*'s "Sex: Unknown," an entire portion of an interview with David takes place while he is driving and another segment shows him barbecuing steaks for his family on an outdoor grill.

The issue of urination is again employed here (and in almost all of the mass media reports concerning the case) as an important sign of John/Joan's gender and its natural link to sex. Diamond and Sigmundson note that John/Joan began urinating standing up, despite the disapproval of others: "At school, at age 14 years, she was caught standing to urinate in the girls' bathroom so often that the other girls refused to allow her entrance" (300). As John Colapinto quotes the adult male David: "It was no big deal; it was easier for me to do that. Just stand up and go" ("True" 73).[16] Indeed, Colapinto notes that as an assertive, dominant kindergartner, Brenda had attempted to stand up to urinate, puzzling the girls in the class (*As Nature* 83). The same evidence is raised in the *New York Times* (Angier, "Sexual" A18), *Time* (Gorman 83), and the *Los Angeles Times* (Roan E1; see also "Boys Will").

Just as with the child's clothing and hairstyle, then, a single set of signifiers (gait, gestures, body movements, rough-and-tumble play, and the stance for urination) are used to illustrate masculinity and femininity in binary fashion regardless of whether gender is posited as a product of socialization or of the materiality of the body, that is, its sex. In terms of gender culture, we clearly see in the argument over John/Joan's body the signifiers that are employed in the judgments people make about one another and themselves in their evaluations of gender performance.

GENDER AND ASSUMED HETEROSEXUALITY

Paralleling Judith Butler, Elspeth Probyn asserts that "personhood is always gendered" (2). One of the reminders that this case brings to the fore is that as we are gendered (or "sexed," to use Probyn's term), so are we simultaneously situated in relation to a "compulsory heterosexuality" (Rich).[17] In perhaps clearer terms, Butler notes that "the institution of a compulsory and naturalized heterosexuality requires and regulates gender as a binary relation in which the masculine term is differentiated from a feminine term, and this differentiation is accomplished through the practices of heterosexual desire" (*Gender* 22–23). In this case, both predicted and performed heterosexual desire (and the rejection of homosexual desire) operate rhetorically as evidence of John/Joan's "real" gender. For Money and the reports that articulate his position, Joan is "truly" a girl when she desires boys as partners; for those holding "sex" as essential, John is proved "truly" to be a male when he aggressively pursues heterosexual relations with women.

Despite the fact that both Money and Diamond argue that sexual desire is somewhat autonomous from "sex" (that is, neither suggests that males absolutely must be attracted to females and vice versa), both of them actively utilize evidence of heterosexuality *in this case* as strong evidence of John/Joan's proper gender behavior. Moreover, as I illustrate in this section, the nature of John/Joan's heterosexual desire is drawn in aggressive terms and becomes among the most often repeated evidence in scientific reports about the case. Indeed, from the time that John/Joan was first reassigned as female until his chosen reassignment as male, the question is raised of sexuality and its significance within the debate over the constructedness versus the naturalness of gender. In short, as in the discussions of the physical signifiers of gender, the question of what John/Joan does (or will do) with his/her body sexually is utilized rhetorically as evidence for the success or failure of the reassignment.

When Money first writes about the case in 1972 in *Man and Woman, Boy and Girl* (Money and Ehrhardt), he assumes the importance of heterosexuality and future motherhood for the child's proper gender behavior when he notes the importance of informing John/Joan early on that while she could not have children naturally, "she *would* become a mother by adoption, one day, when she married and wanted to have a family" (119; emphasis added). When the child's mother goes on to say in this same work that she had explained to the twin brother that he would someday become a daddy "and grow muscles so he could take care of mommy and baby, and go to work in a car like daddy does . . . I've explained to each what their function will be as a grown-up" (120), Money adds that the mother consistently gave the twins good examples

[Chapter One]

of the "wife" and "husband" roles (121). Similarly, Money notes with approval that the twin son would sometimes smack John/Joan on the fanny as a sign of affection (121), illustrating that each was learning proper gender behavior. In an intriguing twist in which Money assumes that John/Joan will become interested in a male sex partner, he notes that cases like this one "represent what is, to all intents and purposes, experimentally planned and iatrogenically induced homosexuality. . . . Postsurgically, it is no longer homosexuality on the criterion of the external sex organs nor of the sex of replacement hormonal puberty" (235). The assumption Money is making here is that, given a female body and raised as a girl, John/Joan would naturally choose a male partner.

This same theme continues in Money's popular as well as scientific reports and is crystallized in mass mediated accounts of the case. Both Money's and the mass mediated reports of John/Joan's heterosexuality also point to other cases to reify the articulation of heterosexual desire and proper gender behavior. For example, *Time* magazine quotes Money making note of a case of two hermaphrodites who were reassigned, one as male and one as female: "The girl therefore reached preadolescence expecting to marry a man; in fact, she already has a steady boyfriend. The boy by contrast has a girl friend and 'fitted easily into the stereotype of the male role in marriage' even though 'he and his partner would both have two X-chromosomes'" ("Biological" 34). In an account of the case in 1975, Money says that the decision about John/Joan's reassignment as a girl had to be made early enough in the child's life so that her "erotic interest would almost certainly direct itself toward the opposite sex later on" (Money and Tucker 94). In each example, the assumption is that a successful gender reassignment would be signified in part by heterosexual desire, and in the persistent reiteration of this link its disciplinary strength is maintained.

In discussions of the case during and after 1997, in which we learn that John/Joan chose to be reassigned as male [as David], heterosexual prowess is again emphasized. This time, however, the focus is on his desire for, and attractiveness to, women. As in the arguments made by, and in support of, Money's position, heterosexuality again serves as evidence of proper gender behavior despite the fact that Diamond's

[38]

position does not necessarily entail it. In its most basic form, his position on gender identity is that the hormones specific to a child's gender, both while the child is in the womb and after birth, create a gender identity that cannot simply be reassigned. (For Diamond, this is true of hermaphrodites as well as those cases, like this one, in which the need for reassignment results from an accident.) While it is clear at times that Diamond sees sexual preference as somewhat autonomous from gender (see, e.g., Diamond, "Sexual Identity and Orientation" 207), he also persistently provides examples that imply compulsory heterosexuality (e.g., a case of males with ambiguous genitalia who were raised as females but develop male genitalia and sexual desire for females as they go through puberty). Diamond's assumption is a reiteration of what Alice Dreger points to as the historical position of those who study cases of "doubtful sex" (hermaphroditism). As she notes, at the turn of the twentieth century, it was an unstated assumption that a body's natural sex would reveal itself through heterosexual desire: "The assumption that true males—even those with mistaken identity—would naturally desire females, and true females males, pervaded the medical literature on doubtful sex" (88). Indeed, Diamond and mass mediated reports sympathetic to his position persistently characterize John/Joan as aggressively heterosexual.

Diamond and Sigmundson's report on the case establishes a heterosexual theme that becomes the most often repeated piece of evidence in the mass mediated reports. The two authors note that after John/Joan chose to be reassigned as male at age fifteen, he began to make other changes: "At 16 years, to attract girls, John obtained a windowless van with a bed and bar. Girls, who as a group had been teasing Joan, now began to have a crush on John" (300). This signifier of the use of a van— a windowless van with a bar and a bed—to pursue heterosexual activities clearly resonates with popular cultural notions of gender and sexuality. It appears repeatedly in articles about the case. It is as if in bed, hidden by the lack of windows, John's "true" sexual desire can finally express itself. For example, in a *New York Times* article that elaborates on the aggressiveness of this heterosexual desire, the reporter notes that after Joan became John, "he got himself a van with a bar in it. Dr. Diamond said in an interview, 'He wanted to lasso some ladies'" (Angier, "Sexual"

A12). The article goes on to discuss John/Joan's marriage to a woman and adoption of her children, emphasizing John/Joan's ability to have intercourse and orgasm with his newly constructed penis (A12; see also Roan E1). Similarly, during an interview on ABC's *Prime Time Live*, the adult John [David] is asked if he is able to have normal sexual relations with his wife using his reconstructed penis—a question that should be irrelevant to John's "true" gender ("Boy"). *U.S. News and World Report's* John Leo similarly writes that after John/Joan's surgery, "at age 16, he bought a van with a bed and bar and started to pursue girls. At 25, he married a woman with three children" (17).[18]

Finally, John Colapinto's *Rolling Stone* essay, which looks back in John/Joan's life to seek out early signs of the child's sexual desire, in addition to recounting the same stories about John/Joan's coming out as a heterosexual, reports that despite the fact that Money described John/Joan as heterosexual in his published reports about the case, he had asked John/Joan's parents if they would have trouble raising a lesbian (70). Colapinto thus implies that John/Joan had *always* been attracted to women sexually and hence, using a heterosexual logic, had *always* been male. The van reappears in Colapinto's book, again in aggressively heterosexual terms: "Equipped with a wet bar, TV and wall-to-wall carpeting, it was quickly dubbed 'the Shaggin' Waggon'" (*As Nature* 187). Just as Money employs John/Joan's heterosexuality as a sign of the success of the child's reassignment, Colapinto employs "John's" (or David's) heterosexuality—and "Joan's" (or Brenda's) potential heterosexuality—as evidence of its failure. In both cases, heterosexuality is signified, indeed emphasized, as a norm in the performance of gender—or, from the biological position, as an expression of the body's sex.[19]

RE-NATURALIZING GENDER: THE BRAIN AS SEX ORGAN

It has become something of a commonplace to note that "the brain is the most important sexual organ" as a way of suggesting that one's beauty, one's ultimate sexual attraction, lies more in how one presents oneself, how interesting one is "as a mind," than in the superficialities of the body. In the case of John/Joan, this same phrase is repeatedly invoked, albeit to different ends. In the 1997 reports about the case, the resignifying of the brain as the basis for gender and gender impulses implies that gender is natural (i.e., gender is sexed)—a product of the development of brain, body, and identity as the result of the action of hormones and chromosomes. As Marjorie Garber notes of this type of argument, gender essentialism is alive and well in scientific and popular culture, it has simply moved from being "on" the body to being "in" the body (108). Indeed, despite the fact that Diamond and Sigmundson posit gender as determined by both nature (the body, the brain, hormones) and nurture (cultural pressures, influence),[20] the case is presented repeatedly as if it provided evidence for a complete reversal of any argument for social pressures on the shaping of gender and gender performance. Much as will be seen in the articulation of feminism later in this chapter, the totalizing of positions in mass media outlets turns this case into one in which the "brain" is the sole determinant of gender.

In his article accompanying Diamond and Sigmundson's update on the John/Joan case, William Reiner writes that "the organ that appears to be critical to psychosexual development and adaptation is not the external genital but the brain. If the brain knows its gender independent of social-environmental influences, then we need to be able to predict what that gender is" (225). While neither Reiner nor Diamond and Sigmundson are arguing that sexual identity is completely determined and "unpliable," the mass mediated representation of their position transforms their arguments into an all-or-nothing proposition in which "nurture" is displaced. For example, the *New York Times* article, titled "Sexual Identity Not Pliable After All, Report Says," declares that the follow-up on the John/Joan case "suggests the opposite" of Money's theory: "A sense of being male or female is innate, immune to the interventions of doctors, therapists and parents" (Angier, "Sexual" A1). Similarly, *Maclean's* notes of John/Joan that "despite everyone telling him constantly that he was a girl, . . . his brain knew he was a male" ("Rethinking" 31). According to *Time* magazine, the follow-up study shows that Money's experiment was "a total failure," that gender is determined by the brain (Gorman 83).[21] *Prime Time Live*'s Nancy Snyderman declares that the lesson of the case is that gender identification "comes from the brain, not the genitals," and suggests that continued belief in the constructedness of gender in the wake of the failure is "bad science" ("Boy"). The *Los Angeles Times* observes that the case "provides stark evidence that a person's brain predetermines sexual identity—not one's anatomy or social environment" (Roan E1), while Nigel Hawkes reports in the *Times* that the case shows "that gender really is all in the genes." Finally, Colapinto's *Rolling Stone* essay, significantly titled "The True Story of John/Joan," argues that the "case was a failure, the truth never reported . . . the most important sex organ is not the genitals; it's the brain" (97).

Such comments assume that scientific studies use singular cases to prove particular theories and disprove others, rather than offering support for particular theories or the falsification of others. In this way, these publications produce a gender theory through a reading of only one study—a study that is said to "prove" that gender is not pliable, that the brain is the organ that determines gender.

The argument that the brain is the primary sex organ also implies an interesting moral equation. Toward the conclusion of Colapinto's analysis of the case, John/Joan [David] makes this observation about what his life has taught him about being a man: "From what I've been taught by my father,' John says, 'What makes you a man is: you treat your wife well, you put a roof over your family's head. You're a good father. Things like that add up much more to being a man than just bang bang bang—sex. I guess John Money would consider my children's biological fathers to be real men. But they didn't stick around to raise the children. I did. That, to me, is a man'" ("True" 97). While I have no desire to put committed fatherhood in a negative light, what is interesting about this comment, in combination with the way in which gender is constructed throughout the discourse surrounding the case, is the link made between the naturalization of gender behaviors and the moralizing of these behaviors. In effect, gender behaviors, from the activities one performs to the clothes one wears to the way one urinates, are configured here as being determined by the brain. Hence, our impulses to act in particular ways are posited as totally determined: men take wives, have children, and then provide homes for them. But not every "man" takes a wife or has children, as David Reimer seems to think, and not every woman needs a roof put over her head by a man. Our inability to enact these roles, however, gets recast as an unwillingness to perform gender correctly, including physical activities and erotic interests, an unwillingness that is then posited as immoral. The case constructs a situation in which the more closely one follows traditional gender politics, the closer one comes to behaving morally. Hence, discourses like those seen in this case that supposedly link gender behavior "scientifically" to a particular sex work to reify the "prohibitions and taboo[s]" (Butler, *Bodies* 95) that discipline and mark gender performances. A discourse that constructs gender behavior as scientifically proved to be natural turns "good" or "bad" performances according to patriarchal rules into moral or immoral behaviors and strengthens the ritualized iterations of proper gender behavior.

JOHN/JOAN AND THE ARTICULATION OF FEMINISM

While the John/Joan case clearly calls for a critical reading of the way the discourse surrounding it continues to reify gender binarism and heteronormativity, an ancillary but related articulation in this case concerns public representations of feminism and the way in which it is rhetorically linked to the case in theory *and* in actuality. From the first popular culture reports of the John/Joan case in *Time* ("Biological"), discursive links were forged between the assumptions of the case and those of feminism and women's studies. Regardless of how often "women's studies" texts or feminist theory actually drew on the case, whenever it is discussed the claim is consistently made that the case has been used in women's studies to support feminism.[22] Certainly this view was due in part to John Money's alignment of his claims with theories he saw as supportive of "women's liberation." Despite the irony of the fact that Money's discourse ultimately reifies disciplinary gender signs, the case is used early on by Money and others as evidence for many of the claims of feminism (again, feminism here is an uncontested terrain). Even while such claims are used to support feminism, however, the effects are complicated because, as I have noted, first, the "feminism" or "women's lib" articulated with the John/Joan case is a particular type of feminism that gets totalized as feminism as a whole, and second, once the case is articulated as evidence for feminism, the subsequent refutation of the success of the case is also seen as a refutation of feminism as a whole.

In the 1973 article in *Time*, "Biological Imperatives," the author notes that the case "provides strong support for a major contention of women's liberationists: that conventional patterns of masculine and feminine behavior can be altered" (34). While some scientists might argue that the biological differences between men and women limit the flexibility of sex roles, "Money is convinced that almost all differences are culturally determined and therefore optional" (34). This passage in *Time* is referred to repeatedly as the case unfolds publicly over the next two decades, illustrating a cultural need to come to grips with the claims of feminism. Milton Diamond, in one of his brief refutations of the case in 1982, notes the *Time* passage and argues that the John/Joan case requires more scrutiny both because it has been used as the basis on which other children have had sex reassignments and because it has been utilized in "numerous elementary psychology and social texts" as well as by Masters and Johnson to assert that "it is basically nurture, not nature, that determines sexual identity as male or female and the attendant gender roles" ("Sexual Identity, Monozygotic" 182). Later, Diamond and Sigmundson quote the same passage from *Time* and assert that "sociology, psychology and women's studies texts were rewritten" to fit Money's argument, as were many "lay and social science writings" (300). On a *Dateline NBC* broadcast, anchor Keith Morrison, after stating that the idea of turning a boy into a girl "sounds absurd," explains that the idea could have made sense during the 1960s, when the women's liberation movement was challenging the basis of gender. His claim is made as a voice-over while the viewer sees the iconic image of "women's liberationists" preparing a pile of bras for burning; the articulation between this case and feminism is made clear through this image ("Mirror").[23] As a whole, then, Money's arguments and their distillation in *Time* become the basis on which the case is said to provide evidence for "women's studies" as a whole, rather than for a particular argument about gender.

After Diamond and Sigmundson released their updated findings about the case, renewing interest in the meaning of "Joan's" reassignment as "John," the link to feminism became problematic. Once again, the passage in *Time* that notes the connection to women's studies is referred to or quoted directly in 1997 articles in *Time* (Gorman), *Rolling Stone* (Colapinto, "True"), and *U.S. News and World Report* (Leo). Each of these articles asserts that the case has been cited in numerous women's studies texts, and was used, as Colapinto puts it, to "buttress the feminist claim that the observable differences in the tastes, attitudes and behaviors of men and women are attributable solely to cultural expectations" ("True" 66). [24] In an essay that trades extensively on this connection, John Leo in *U.S. News and World Report* (who also quotes the same passage from *Time*) begins by observing that the case "has been cited over and over in psychological, medical and women's studies textbooks as proof that, apart from obvious genital differences, babies are all born as sexual blank slates—male and female attributes are invented and applied by society. Now all those texts will have to be rewritten" (17). Leo does not stop at arguing that women's studies must now be rethought; rather, he reinserts feminism at the outset of the case, making it liable for the very decision to perform the surgery: "Why was this disastrous experiment undertaken? One reason is that it's easier to construct a vagina than to reconstruct a penis. But another reason is just as obvious: It was a chance to prove a rising academic and feminist theory about gender . . . that almost all sex differences are culturally determined" (17). Leo declares that the John/Joan case made possible the creation of gender studies, which saw all differences between men and women as "socially constructed by men to oppress women" (17). After positing feminism as the rationale for the surgery and using the case as evidence that feminism is a failed ideology, Leo, borrowing from Daphne Patai, goes on to state that the case won't mean much to "campus feminists," who will "just shrug it off": "The whole point of being an ideologue is that new information doesn't disturb your worldview" (17).

While it is certainly true that a great many versions of feminism include the idea that gender roles are at least in part socially constructed, the argument presented by Leo and others is that feminism has claimed that *every* aspect of gender is socially constructed. After totalizing "social roles" as feminism itself, he and others are able to employ the "new outcome" of the John/Joan case to suggest that feminism, again totalized, is intellectually bankrupt. Rather than being seen as an occasion for revision or complication, this becomes an occasion for dismissal.

As has been pointed out many times before, such arguments make one feminism out of multiple feminisms. That is, although one might give a very broad definition of feminism to which a number of people could agree,[25] specific theoretical assumptions concerning the relationships between gender, sex, identity, and behavior are certainly open to a variety of perspectives within different feminist positions, as well as other psychological and philosophical positions. This case represents one more location where feminism as a concept is concretized in popular culture and "performed" by a variety of people, many of whom are not themselves supportive of a feminist position. When one notes the many ways in which feminism is caricatured and dismissed in conversations in the academy and in the public sphere, the need for the careful articulation of any given stance is clear.[26] Indeed, given the tight link assumed between the case and feminism, cultural critics and feminists could do worse in finding a point of articulation over which to struggle for feminism and to complicate its meanings.

Investigating how theories of gender, especially those put forth by John Money, have influenced the way intersexed (hermaphrodite) children are assigned gender by physicians, Suzanne Kessler shows that doctors often make such decisions more on the basis of cultural signification than on the basis of biological concerns. For example, because of a cultural belief that it would be traumatic for a male to go through life with an unusually small penis, a decision might be made to remove the penis of an intersexed child and construct a vagina in its place. While such a decision would be made on the basis of multiple cultural factors, the issue would be presented to the parents, according to Kessler, as a biological one. In essence, Kessler is arguing that physicians, faced with the material bodies of hermaphrodites, see and interpret these bodies, and the possibilities for such bodies, through the same gender culture lens that affects how each of us in the same historical communicative community understands gender and its performance.

By investigating the story of John/Joan, the re-membering of David

Reimer, as it plays itself out on the level of mass mediated discourse (and of its translation from the medical community to mass culture), we are able to perceive some of the ways in which our gender culture is constructed and struggled over. Moreover, we are able to see not only how our gender culture affects the material bodies of intersexed infants but also how it affects and influences our interpretation of others' behaviors and bodies, how we all, to varying degrees, take part in reiterating the norms of gender binarism and normative heterosexuality (e.g., how we monitor the behaviors of others and ourselves, how we discipline that behavior through force, ostracism, taboo, and the reaffirmation of normative gender assumptions). If we take gender culture to be a "society's understanding of what is possible, proper, and perverse in gender linked behavior, and more specifically, that set of values, mores, and assumptions which establishes which behaviors are to be seen as gender linked" (Ramet 2), that is, if gender culture is seen as the rules for gender performance and the morality of performing them well, we find in this case an instance in which the rules governing gender performance are laid bare.

As we have seen, the rules for gender performance in this case are not only surprisingly traditional in form but also fairly rigid—so rigid, indeed, that binary signifiers of gender are employed even by those whose theoretical positions should give no credence to binary theories of gender. The rigidity of the gender binarism is central to the arguments of both constructionists and essentialists, especially when it comes to public perceptions of this case. This rigidity can perhaps be accounted for because it arises in the discursive aftermath of a case in which the foundations of gender are radically placed into question, and, as Alan Hyde notes, it is during such periods that we are most careful in calling forth our definitions of the body (11). Not only do the rules of gender culture and gender performance continue to dictate superficial features such as clothing and hairstyles, but also they prescribe the positioning of the body and its desires on male-female grounds. Indeed, the two themes that were repeated most clearly in every summary of the case in mass mediated journalism were John/Joan's masculinity as seen in her desire to urinate standing up and John/Joan's masculinity as witnessed by his desire, immediately upon surgical reassignment, to aggressively perform heterosexuality through the purchase of a van with a bed and a bar in order to "lasso some ladies" (Angier, "Sexual" A18). To be male or female, then, continues to mean that one performs within a fixed set of constraints. Regardless of the multiple examples that can be given of the plasticity of our culture in terms of gender, and regardless of how much criticism insists that gender behavior is never fully determined in advance, this case illustrates that, at least when mass culture is troubled about gender, "signs" of proper gender behavior are readily called on to stabilize cultural fears about gender ambiguity. The disciplinary mechanisms for holding gender steady are powerful indeed. Regardless of what version of the John/Joan story one believes, regardless of what David Reimer did or is doing now with his body, what matters rhetorically and culturally is the way particular activities and impulses are repeated and reaffirmed in mass media outlets as evidence of gender behavior and misbehavior,[27] for they help provide the contours of our cultural understanding of gender expectations and its links with public morality.

In addition, one can see clearly in these articles how feminism is represented in mass culture and how it is constructed by those who attack it. As I have shown, one particular theory—that gender is purely a cultural construct—gets represented as the main thesis of all feminist theory. Given the articulation of the John/Joan case with feminism, criticism of this case, it is argued, undermines feminism as well, even though one would be hard put to find in that criticism purely discursive theories of gender. Moreover, finding fault with the John/Joan case allows one to fault feminism for the "crime" of this experiment. That feminism so easily fits into these public arguments speaks again for the need for a complicating of feminism on the public level.

Finally, Alan Hyde, in his discussion of the way the body is constructed in legal discourse, says that his purpose is to encourage "an explosion of competing metaphors" of the body, to make a plea "for the multiplication of bodily performance" (80, 123) similar to Gordene MacKenzie's call for the destruction of solid gender concepts and a move to a "transgender nation" (1) and Celeste Condit's call for a gender diversity perspective that would emphasize the ongoing construction of gender; Condit observes that identity categories "will necessarily

be fragmentary and context-bound" ("In Praise" 97).[28] Hyde goes so far
as to assert that this multiplicity of performances is nearly inevitable:
"Attempts to figure a pure or inviolable body, pure because or insofar
as it is 'natural' and 'immutable,' are doomed to fail, are deeply out of
touch, with the complicated circuits of will, control, and power that
condemn the modern body to constant mutability as to weight, appearance, and muscle tone" (129–30). What this case illustrates, however, is
just how strong the constraints against such plasticity, such play, such
indeterminacy can be. I acknowledge that change in representation does
occur and that there are ways in which individuals—in groups and
alone—can resist and rework dominant representations, but such
change is hard-won, if only because of the power, materiality, and common sense of dominant representations. As Susan Bordo notes in both
Unbearable Weight (245–76) and, *Twilight Zones* (107–35), while cos-
metic surgery and other procedures may give the illusion that the body
has become far more "plastic," increasing the number of options for the
public performance of gender, the same options are consistently chosen
and the same body types celebrated. No one chooses reverse liposuc-
tion; no one decides to have their teeth darkened. Instead, though individuals do make choices such as increasing their breast size, they do
so as a matter of, as Bordo calls it, "free choice under pressure" (*Twilight*
44). Rather than being out of touch with "the complicated circuit of
will, control and power" (Hyde 129), perhaps the concept of the "immutable" body is far more in touch with the gender culture we live in
than we care to think. At the very least, we must all take greater responsibility for the fact that the performance of gender continues to be both
tightly constrained and morally suspect, and we must continue to find
ways to complicate those constraints.

Two

Disciplining the Transgendered

Brandon Teena, Public Representation, and Normativity

> How can we have a discussion of how much sex and gender diversity
> actually exists in society, when all the mechanisms of
> legal and extralegal repression render our lives invisible?
> Leslie Feinberg, *Transgender Warriors*

Given the critical success of the 1999 feature film *Boys Don't Cry* and Hilary Swank's Oscar winning portrayal of Brandon Teena, a surprisingly sympathetic telling of a story about a transgendered individual has been etched in the consciousness of the movie going public. Even before the film's release, however, evidence of a growing public fascination with this story was evident as the narrative, or elements of it, were told and retold repeatedly and widely in local newspapers as well as in the *Village Voice* and *Playboy*. The story also became the subject of a true crime book, multiple Web sites, a play, a documentary film (*The Brandon Teena Story*), and the first on-line Guggenheim art project, all before the release of *Boys Don't Cry*.[1]

A review of the story, at least as recounted through mass mediated outlets, might go something like this: Brandon Teena (born Teena Brandon) was a twenty-one-year old woman who moved from Lincoln, Nebraska, where she had been "living as a man," to the smaller town of Falls City, Nebraska, in late 1993.[2] While this move was prompted by a number of brushes with the law as a result of Brandon's forging checks and using other's credit cards without permission, it was also a move that allowed Brandon a fresh start with a male identity in a community where he had no history as a woman. Brandon soon found a circle of friends and, as he had done in Lincoln, began dating several of the women in that circle, some of whom reported later that Brandon was the "ideal man," "the perfect kisser." Brandon continued to have financial problems, however, and was once again arrested for check fraud. While making a court appearance on that charge, Brandon was served with another warrant for a check fraud case in Lincoln. This time, however, the warrant was issued using Brandon Teena's birth name, and he was jailed as a female. It was with this arrest that the Falls City community, most notably Brandon's friends, became aware that Brandon was "really" a woman.

Confusion about Brandon's gender in Falls City persisted, however, if only because there were so many stories circulating about what Brandon "really was," in part because of Brandon's own use of multiple narratives, and in part because so many women claimed intimate knowledge of his "maleness." Perhaps, some argued, Brandon was a hermaphrodite, perhaps he had had an accident as a child, or perhaps he was in the process of a female-to-male transition. Whatever the case, given Brandon's success with the local women, his "true" gender was a matter of great concern to his friends, especially the men. Regardless of what theory people held about Brandon, his presence provided a clear case of gender trouble within a local community, although none of those involved seemed to have had much interest in celebrating gender or sexual fluidity.

Events took a much uglier turn when Brandon was attending a party on Christmas Eve, shortly after having been released by the police. Although most of those at the party were celebrating the holiday, two of Brandon's male friends—Tom Nissen and John Lotter—decided to clear up any ambiguity by forcing Brandon to reveal his genitals. Discovering that Brandon had a vagina, clearly marking him as a woman in Nissen's and Lotter's eyes, the pair forced Brandon to leave the party with them and proceeded to drive to a desolate area of town, where each in turn raped him. Nissen and Lotter then returned to the party with Brandon, threatening to kill him if he reported the rape. Under cover of washing up in the bathroom, Brandon locked the door and escaped through a window, bravely making his way to the local police station to report the crime. A week later, with the rape "under investigation" by local authorities (who were, of course, skeptical of Brandon's story), Nissen and Lotter drove to the farmhouse where Brandon was staying with friends and fatally shot Brandon and two others living in the house. Nissen and Lotter were quickly arrested. In a media-saturated trial, both men were found guilty of murder. Lotter was given the death sentence and Nissen life imprisonment in exchange for testifying against Lotter.

The trial was covered widely in the local and national press both because of its unusual nature and because a large number of transgender activists made appearances inside and outside the courthouse. As a result, the story of Brandon Teena's life and death offers a large body of discourse that reflects public discussions of sex, gender, sexuality, and transgenderism.[3] It is a story that seemingly begs its audience to think through their own gender and sexuality and the possibilities for public performance of gender.[4] Given the topic and the volume of discourse the case produced, it is an ideal public forum for investigating, as Lauren Berlant might say, one area of ideological tension over identities within the American landscape (1, 4).

Historically, cases of gender ambiguity—or gender trouble—brought on by public disclosure of transgenderism or intersexuality have marked ongoing transitions in the meaning of gender within a given cultural context (see, e.g., Garber 11; Holden, "Rape"; Dreger 6). Indeed, Alice Dreger notes that the entire "history of hermaphroditism is largely the history of struggles over the 'realities' of sex—the nature of 'true' sex, the proper roles of the sexes, the question of what sex can, should, or must mean" (15). While the Brandon Teena case is not a case about hermaphroditism[5] (although hermaphroditism is often invoked in mass mediated reports), the quantity of discourse that surrounds the case publicly can be seen as a site for weighing public arguments over the "true" meaning of sex, a location where we might learn something about the struggle over gendered meanings as it takes place in a contemporary, and mass mediated, cultural context.

As I noted in the first chapter, it has become a commonplace in many contemporary discussions, at least since the publication of Judith Butler's *Gender Trouble*, that gender and sexuality are assumed to be potentially fluid, held in check in part by each individual's interpellation into a cultural ideology that works to maintain a series of male-female differences, and through the ideological and cultural mechanisms that help sustain that ideology). Once again, gender will be taken here to be performative, at least within the "forced reiteration of norms" (Butler, *Gender* 94–95). Given the topic of this chapter, I want to note that "drag"—transsexual performance—has been the subject of much critical work that has attempted to understand the ways in which gender is both de- and re-stabilized. For example, Marjorie Garber sees transsexualism as a confirmation of the constructedness of gender and, as a result, as tied to the deconstruction of male-female sexual binarism and of heterosexual normativity (110), while Susan Stryker observes how "transgender phenomena emerge from and bear witness to the epistemological rift between gender signifiers and their signifieds" (147). Aligned with queer politics, Stryker writes, transgendered bodies and transgendered logics can work to deconstruct heteronormative binaries (149).[6] Further, in the introduction to their 1991 volume on cases of gender ambiguity, Julia Epstein and Kristina Straub note that ambiguous gender identities "offer a point at which social pressure might be applied to effect a reevaluation of binary thinking" (4). In such works we are shown how the transgendered phenomenon and queered performances could *potentially* work to loosen, to make fluid, gender binaries and heteronormativity.

While this move to highlight potential disruptions of the gender binary system through drag, transsexualism, and/or transgender identity is indeed a vital project, at times its emphasis on progressive change comes at the cost of a lost or diminished focus on ideological mechanisms that encourage the upholding of bi-gender norms. As a rhetorical and cultural critic of the politics of public argument, I am more interested in the disciplinary side of the coin—the ways in which, in the words of Ronald Greene, public arguments are based on logics of articulation that work materially to make possible "the ability to judge and plan reality" (25).[7] Hence, while drag, transsexualism, and transgenderism obviously have the potential to cause "gender trouble" and disrupt bi-gender normativity, in terms of the "dominant" public arguments

[Chapter Two]

that surround such cases, critics would be well served by thinking through the ways in which their "loosening of gender binarisms" is a potential that goes unrealized for many.[8] Hence, even if we start with the theoretical position (*episteme*) that "personhood is always gendered," as Elspeth Probyn notes (2), echoing Judith Butler, we must still acknowledge and pay careful attention to the fact that, in public discourse (*doxa*), a major assumption still stands that personhood is, rather, always *sexed*. Public arguments and discussions over cases like that of Brandon Teena—indeed, the actions of the young men convicted in Brandon's death—are in part a result of the fact that so many institutions and individuals work to stabilize sex, to reiterate sexual norms, rather than to encourage and explore gender fluidity. Moreover, like all public arguments, this one can serve several masters, working for some to loosen gender norms while working for others to maintain or strengthen them.

As a result, in Butler's words, the discourse surrounding the Brandon Teena incident provides a case study of the public iteration of sexual norms as "a ritualized production, a ritual reiterated under and through constraint, under and through the force of prohibition and taboo, with the threat of ostracism and even death controlling and compelling the shape of the production" of gender and sexuality (*Bodies* 95). Hence, while I do not deny the potential of the case for loosening cultural rules concerning gender, sex, and sexuality, my focus is on the ways in which reactions to the case—including reactions to the film—often reaffirm rather than challenge heteronormative iterations. In this discussion, then, I intend to illustrate how a case in which gender trouble seemingly begs for a transgression of gender barriers and of heterosexual normativity becomes instead an instance in which gender is largely (though not completely) renormalized and re-essentialized, and in which numerous other cultural ideas are reaffirmed within the cultural milieu. In short, while rhetoric is "about" the transformation of public meaning, public discourse is also material and sedimented, as Greene reminds us, reifying norms and stabilizing identities.

As in chapter 1, rather than attempting to comment about "transgendered" subjectivities or the experience of transgenderism, I discuss the case of Brandon Teena as it was represented in a variety of news outlets, focusing primarily on discourses available in common library research databases such as LexisNexis, as well as Aphrodite Jones's *All She Wanted*, a true crime account of the case.[9] My interest is in "dominant" or commercial discourses, rather than marginal or individual ones, for at least two reasons: as I have argued, mainstream discourses illustrate the rhetorically material ways in which those who do challenge dominant ideology are ideologically disciplined, the ways in which gender normativity is upheld and judged. Moreover, while I allow room for individuals to interpret the story of Brandon Teena differently, as a critic reviewing a large volume of discourse, I have been able to trace the general contours of the way Brandon is written into existence as a cultural object. As Kate Bornstein notes, caricatures of transgendered people are "creeping into the arts and media" (59). These are the very caricatures I analyze, asking: What are the ways in which non-transgendered people and mass mediated representations configure transgenderism?

I curtail my claims to mainstream rearticulations of gender norms also because I want to be careful not to suggest that such a study explores transgenderism as a subjectivity. Hence, while I agree in part with Susan Stryker when she says that "it is no longer sufficient (if indeed it ever was) to approach the topic as Marjorie Garber did in *Vested Interests*, where she proceeded solely 'by looking at transsexuals and transvestites and the cultural gaze that both constructs and regards them, with absolutely no concern for transgender subjectivity'" (148), I also assume that some readings of the case are interested in the politics of transgendered subjectivity whereas others, such as this one, focus on the constraints of the public rhetoric *about* transgenderism. In short, I am attempting to utilize the public arguments surrounding this case to understand one dimension of gender ideology in contemporary culture. I am not attempting to understand the position of transgendered people in contemporary culture.[10]

In the remainder of this chapter I provide a critical reading of mainstream discourses and argue that, to a certain extent, the case—especially before the mainstream viewing of *Boys Don't Cry*—is one of ideological discipline in which Brandon Teena's gender is largely tied back into her "sex." Again, regardless of a theoretical assumption that sex is always gendered, in mainstream public arguments a transgendered person becomes a foil for reiterating and reaffirming the gender and sexual norms of contemporary culture, and ritual and taboo operate to ensure this process.

The discourse about the Brandon Teena case works to reify traditional binaristic notions of sex in a number of ways, though allowing room for a complicating of gender. First, by telling the story through a narrative concentrating on *deception*, most news stories prior to the release of *Boys Don't Cry* represent Brandon as a "real" woman who was intentionally posing as a man in order to fool others. Second, the public argument operates to reify the physicality of Brandon Teena's body, including what Brandon does with that body, as conforming to traditional heterosexual activities. In such reports Brandon's body is clearly marked as female, but Brandon's use of that body is marked as a successful performance of masculinity—whether owing to a physical or a wily deception. Third, popular cultural discussions of the causes of Brandon's transgenderism explain the body and/or psyche of Brandon Teena as an abnormality that could have been prevented had Brandon been given proper physical and emotional care as a child. Finally, discussions of Brandon's body as either hermaphroditic or in preparation for a female-to-male surgical transition reveal a cultural impulse to work the body into a traditionally sexed position and to align genitalia with gender.

Each of these themes works by positing Brandon's body and behavior as simultaneously familiar and alien, and in this way the overall representation serves to reify heteronormativity. That is, because Brandon's behavior and appearance are depicted as strikingly and familiarly masculine, women's attraction to him can be configured as a "normal" expression of healthy heterosexuality. And simultaneously, because Brandon's "alien" desires and gender deception are ultimately revealed, the moral of the story is that no one can succeed at fooling the gender binary system. Each of the themes discussed herein thus highlights the ideology of gender and sexuality in contemporary culture, laying bare the ways in which transgenderism and gender fluidity continue to be disciplined back into binary norms.

Nonetheless, in my analysis of the discourse following the release of *Boys Don't Cry*, including reviews of the film, I point out some areas in which gender has been made "messy," left open to question. While such discourse largely continues to reproduce and reiterate traditional understandings of gender/sex, it is clear that the combined impact of the film, the discourse about the film, general interest in the topic, and the work of cultural activists have at the very least complicated the meaning of Brandon Teena in particular and both transgenderism and gender itself on a larger level. Hence, this discussion should be seen as a critical snapshot of a brief moment in the ongoing culture struggle over big-gendered heteronormativity.

DECEPTION IN THE HEARTLAND

Throughout the period of "news" reports about the case, and continuing into descriptions of the films about the case, Brandon Teena's story is told as, at base, a tale of "deception in the heartland," a story of how a young woman deceived others about her gender in the selfish pursuit of her own desires. Even a cursory glance at the titles and subtitles of accounts would starkly make this point. For example, the subtitle of Aphrodite Jones's true crime book is *A True Story of Sexual Deception and Murder in America's Heartland.* The movie poster for the documentary *The Brandon Teena Story* claims that the film is "a true story of love, hate, and revenge in the heartland of America" ("Zeitgeist"). A lengthy report in the *Omaha World Herald* is titled "Romance, Deceit, and Rage" (Burbach and Cordes), while another in the *Des Moines Register* is titled "Charade Revealed Prior to Killings" (Fruhling 1). The *Advocate* used the title "Heartland Homicide" ("Small-town Nebraska life was fine for a 21-year-old man—until everyone discovered he was actually a woman") for its first major article on the case (Ricks) and titled its shorter follow-up report "Deception on the Prairie." A one-act play that deals with the case is called *Murder in the Heartland* (Delmont), and, finally, *Playboy* titled its essay "Death of a Deceiver" (Konigsberg).

When told that one is about to hear a story of "deception," one most likely expects to discover something sinister afoot, a predator who preys on others by keeping them from apprehending the truth. Deception implies the intent to make truth out of appearance. As a result, with regard to this case, "deception" is a term that logically favors fixed notions of sex/gender over an ideology of gender fluidity. There are multiple ways one could logically tell this story so that Brandon's gender would not be seen as deceptive: one could argue, for example, that gender is performative, hence making Brandon male because he performed masculinity; or one could argue a more essentialist line concerning the "reality" of Brandon's "self-identity," in which Brandon was male because he knew himself to be a male "trapped in a female body." Yet the reports of this case—both those that are sympathetic and those that are unsympathetic to Brandon's position—primarily portray the story as one of deception, and the prominence of the deception narrative forecloses other potential ways of thinking about gender and gender identity. To say that Brandon was "deceiving others" (and was caught in the act of deception) is to say that Brandon "knew" he was a woman but wanted others to think of him as a man. That is, the deception narrative implies that Brandon actively lied to other people, hiding what she knew to be her "true" sex. In this way, the deception narrative acts within a traditional iteration of gender norms and desires that ultimately serves to protect and affirm the normative heterosexist ways of making sense of gender and of disciplining gender trouble.[11]

Obviously, the example of a transgendered person like Brandon Teena, who was attractive to self-identified heterosexual women as a sexual partner and to heterosexual men as a friend, could be interesting as a potential case of gender trouble and confusion, one that encourages people to recognize the fluidity of gender, sex, and sexuality. It is on the grounds of familiarity (i.e., she appeared male) and alienation (i.e., we were deceived by her), however, that the story is ultimately told, hence reifying rather than troubling gender norms. In short, rather than making sex and gender identity "messy," the story as told configures Brandon as a woman based on genitalia alone. Aphrodite Jones, for example, quotes Michelle Lotter, sister of one of Brandon's murderers, as saying that she believed Brandon's "deceptive" behavior indicated that she was lesbian and that the two men murdered her because both were "angry after learning about Brandon's deception" (245).[12] Jones further notes that on the *Maury Povich Show*, Brandon was described as a woman who "posed as a man" (258). A press release for the film *The Brandon Teena Story* states that "the catalyst for the murders was the sexual persona of Brandon Teena . . . when it was revealed . . . that Brandon was *actually* female, passing as a male and dating local women" and notes that the murderers were "angry at the lies" ("Zeitgeist"; emphasis added). Chris Burbach and Henry Cordes describe Brandon Teena in the *Omaha World Herald* as "charmingly playing the role of a young man" (1A), and Burbach reports that according to Brandon's mother, Brandon had "started portraying somebody that she wasn't"—a male ("Prosecutor Sees" 1). In a single article in the *Des Moines Register,* Larry Fruhling uses several terms meant to suggest that Brandon Teena's gender was a clear case of deception; he writes that "Brandon's *charade* ended in the bathroom of the small house with her trousers pulled down to her knees," "Brandon's *pretense* began unraveling," "Brandon's *true* identity came to light," and Brandon was "*posing* as a man" (1; emphasis added).

Further, Eric Konigsberg observes in *Playboy* that "posing as a man gave Teena Brandon what she couldn't get as a woman—adoring girl-friends and a fiancée. It also got her killed" (94). Konigsberg does not merely utilize the "female" birth name Teena Brandon throughout the article as Brandon's "real name" but does so in the context of an article which asserts that Brandon was "posing" as male, again emphasizing gender as physically tied to genitalia.[13] Konigsberg's explicitness about Brandon's "deception" is highlighted throughout the article; Konigsberg writes, for example, that "Teena didn't seem to have trouble finding new people to *con,* new women to woo—women who desperately wanted to be charmed by a man who understood their needs. Her relationships were with girls whose ideal of a man had never been realized until they met Teena" (194; emphasis added).[14] He includes portions of an interview with murderer Tom Nissen, who observes that the rape of Brandon was an "ego thing. I felt like I'd been fucked. Me and Brandon had a long conversation that evening, and Brandon started to feed me another line" (197). While by no means offering an apology for the murderers, Konigsberg does make clear that he believes the logic of deception was at work, that Brandon was killed because he had been "feeding lines" to Nissen and Lotter about his "true" gender.[15]

Examples of this deception discourse are widespread. An early report in the *Omaha World-Herald* notes that "Ms. Brandon cross-dressed as a man and was known under male names" until her "true gender became known" (Hammel 9SF).[16] In a lengthy *New Yorker* essay, John Gregory

Dunne remarks early on that the murders were provoked because the two young men became upset once they found out what "everyone else already knew: that Brandon was a woman" (55). Similarly, the *New York Times* reports that Brandon "was a woman who posed as a man" ("Woman" A11). A teaser for ABC's television show *20/20* claims that the story of Brandon Teena was that of a woman "dressing as a man" ("Crossing"). In each case, Brandon is positioned as a *true* woman who posed as a man. Such a rhetorical gesture not only represents Brandon's performance as an intentional deception but also works to essentialize gender to sex or genitalia (i.e., if the body appears female, Brandon is clearly "really" a woman); gender as performance is erased, even as a possibility.

Finally, given that *Boys Don't Cry* was such a mammoth force in the articulation of the "meaning" of Brandon Teena, I want to turn to a few reviews of the film to underscore that, for some, it worked to reinforce this understanding of Brandon as masquerading deceiver. For instance, according to the reviewer John Keenan, the film shows how hard Brandon tried to "make her masquerade work" ("Portrayals" 65). Robert Butler summarizes the film as the story of a Nebraska "woman who passed herself off as a man" and ultimately "paid for that deception with her life" (E6). Similarly, Lorenza Munoz writes in the *Los Angeles Times* that the film features a Nebraska teenager who was murdered after "she had tricked" her killers "into believing she was a boy" (F1). *Newsweek*'s David Ansen writes that the discovery of "deception" led to Brandon's murder, while *Maclean's* review of the film observes that it is the story of "a young woman masquerading as a man" (68).[17] The *Pittsburgh Post-Gazette* notes that the story concerns a deluded woman who thinks she can convince others that she is a man (Vancheri 42), while the *San Diego Union-Tribune* critic summarizes the film as a story of a girl who "pretended to be a boy" (Elliott 7). While other descriptions of the film do emerge, these examples illustrate that the rhetoric of "masquerade" and "deception" has a powerful cultural hold on representations of transgendered people.

The second element of this articulation—the "heartland" in which the deception occurs—works metaphorically and semiotically to heighten the impact of the deception.[18] The coupling of "deception" with "heartland" lends itself readily to a reading of "deception of the heart"—a deception that goes beyond mere trickery into implications of sexual innocence destroyed. Discussions of *Boys Don't Cry*, as well as the semiotics of the film itself, consistently emphasize that the crime took place in the Midwest, suggesting that both Brandon and the homophobia of the Midwest jointly worked to pervert the "family values so often touted as the bedrock of American culture" (Brophy). Roger Ebert writes that the "deception would have worked only in a rural and small town far removed from the idea of gender transitions" (31). Stephen Holden argues that the film "encapsulates the deep-seated fears about gender and sexuality harbored by millions of Americans, especially those living in the heartland" ("Documentary" 7). Such readings seem to imply two aspects of the "heartland" that are somewhat contradictory. First, this discourse suggests that misleading others about our gender is deception of the worst kind, especially among youth, and most especially among "real" midwestern American youth. But the discourse also "others" the heartland by making it the seat of homophobia.[19] As Julianne Pidduck puts it in her reading of *Boys Don't Cry*, "The brutality of *Boys* connects with a widespread cultural articulation of small-town middle America with 'trailer trash' anomie, intolerance, and murder" (100). The discourse implies that although the Midwest is "homophobic," Brandon would have been accepted in other, more enlightened sections of the country, thus limiting homophobia to the "heartland" of America and simultaneously denying it elsewhere.

TEENA'S FEMALE BODY, BRANDON'S MASCULINE PERFORMANCE

Kate Bornstein argues that while there could potentially be "as many types of gender as could be imagined," Western society has culturally taken on "sex" (as in genitalia) as a sign of gender, hence enabling us to utilize visible cultural markers to make assumptions about one another's sex and from there to make judgments about proper public behavior (30). Alice Dreger similarly observes in her history of hermaphroditism that such logic has developed over the last several centuries, with the presence or absence of male or female gonads being determinative of gender/sex in the medical arena and, in the public arena, their assumed presence or absence being the grounds on which appropriate gender behavior is judged. Dreger refers to this as the logic of "one body, one sex": "Regardless of how any given individual might have fused or ambiguous genitalia, this rule, which said that each body must be designated as either male or female, became the magnet rule around which the rhetorical, conceptual, and physical treatment of hermaphroditism hovered" (109).[20] Indeed, rhetorically, gender still works along a male-female binarism in mass mediated accounts. In the discourse surrounding the Brandon Teena case, we see how tightly gender is articulated with genitalia on a rhetorical and ideological level.[21] Discussions of Brandon's body refer to a sex-gender split, with multiple reports pointing to the body of Brandon (i.e., the genitalia) as proof positive of Brandon's "femaleness" while simultaneously observing that Brandon's physical appearance and behavior were marked by masculine signifiers. Whether Brandon is seen as being particularly adept at acting like a "natural man" or his masculine behavior is explained as a psychic or physical defect, Brandon is posited as "physically" a real woman who learns, or is compelled by defects, to perform behaviors that are "naturally" those of men. By pointing out the genitalia that made Brandon "really" a woman and the activities that made Brandon "appear" to be a man, the signifiers of masculinity and femininity are reified, the binarism held intact.

Here, then, I want to pay particular attention to those physical features and behaviors that are employed as evidence of Brandon's "masculinity" or Teena's "femininity." I should emphasize that I am not questioning the veracity of the claims and observations being made—nor, of course, am I verifying them. Rhetorically, what is significant is that particular behaviors and signifiers are consistently reported and reified, whether they actually occurred or not, indicating the importance of these behaviors as elements of the iteration of gender norms in contemporary U.S. culture. Somewhere along the way from Brandon's actual and imagined physical actions, to the reception of these actions by his friends and onlookers, to their comments to news reporters transmitted through the filters of editors, the behaviors described here are those that most clearly resonate with cultural concepts of proper gender behavior. Boiled down, these are the signifiers used to make the case for

Teena Brandon's physical femaleness and Brandon Teena's ability to "deceptively" enact masculinity. I then turn to the discourse that links Brandon's gender and genitalia and outlines Brandon's behavior and aesthetic first as a child, then as an adult, his physical appearance as an adult, and, finally, his (heterosexual) physical activities.

Body, Play, and Clothing

Examples of the coupling of Brandon Teena's "real" gender with Brandon Teena's genitalia are ubiquitous and obviously work hand in hand with the deception metaphors discussed in the previous section. For instance, Aphrodite Jones opens her account of the case by noting that Brandon had told a friend that "he was really a female, that he had female parts" (105). One of the most striking examples of the equation of gender with genitalia occurs when Jones reports that on the night when Brandon was raped, Lotter and Nissen, who had become increasingly dissatisfied with Brandon's explanation as to his gender, and "decided they needed someone to see this guy's cock or else" (208). The *Advocate* report on the case asserts that Brandon was "actually a woman" (Ricks 28); *ID* magazine declares that "he was really a she" (Brucker-Cohen 86), and the *Village Voice* describes Brandon as a "Nebraska girl who had been living as a man" (Huisman 160). Donna Minkowitz observes, also in the *Village Voice*, that Brandon's "true gender" was female (24).[22] In each example, Brandon Teena is posited as having both a "true" gender, which could be evidenced by genitalia (in effect, the lack of a "cock"), and a "deceptive one" insofar as one cannot be male without a penis.

In terms of male/female activities and actions, Brandon's behavior is often examined through references to his/her behavior and dress as a child. In general, when the story of Brandon's youth (as Teena Brandon) is recounted, it is a narrative that suggests that while Brandon was physically a girl and should have developed "feminine behaviors," he developed masculine behaviors as a result of an aberration. For example, when Aphrodite Jones focuses on the story of Brandon's childhood and that of Tammy, Brandon's sister, she sets up a pattern of descriptions that persistently emphasize the contrast between Tammy's femininity and Brandon's masculinity. Tammy's femininity is said to manifest itself in the clothes she liked to wear and the toys she liked to play with. While feminine Tammy decorated her room with stuffed animals and dolls, "Teena collected things—stop signs, beer signs, whatever" (32). One of Teena's favorite activities was to "place snakes in a lunch box and throw the snakes and a collection of bugs at Tammy" (32). While Tammy spent time playing with dolls, Teena "mostly played with sturdy things like Tinkertoys and Lincoln Logs. She liked to construct and destroy. She liked radios and walkie-talkies and spent hours taking them apart and putting them back together to see how they worked" (32). Tammy enjoyed wearing "frilly little flowered dresses and lace ankle socks; Teena was always in T-shirts, jogging shorts, and unsightly boy's tube socks, the kind trimmed with red and blue stripes" (33). Tammy wore makeup but Teena refused (33). Although Teena was forced to wear dresses for pictures, she "tried to tear them off at all other times" (33–34).

The same descriptions are echoed elsewhere. The *Omaha World Herald* observes that as a child, Brandon "preferred playing with a garter snake to playing with a doll. She preferred taking an old radio apart to doing her hair. Rather than dress up, she would just as soon play basketball" (Burbach and Cordes 1A).[23] In similar fashion, *Playboy's* Eric Konigsberg writes that Teena, "awkward and impish," rebelled against her school's dress code by "wearing pants and a tie. She kept her hair short and told people she was allergic to makeup. She was into weight lifting" (94). In the *New Yorker*, John Gregory Dunne repeats the snake story told by Jones and adds that Brandon had a secret desire to become her school's quarterback (50). In each of these descriptions the details powerfully emphasize the signs of masculinity and femininity. It is not just that Tammy wanted to wear dresses; she wanted to wear "frilly little flowered" dresses with lace ankle socks. Brandon did not simply wear shorts and T-shirts but wore jogging shorts and those "unsightly" tube socks with stripes. It is not just that Teena gave up playing with stuffed animals and dolls, but she turned to collecting stop signs and beer signs, snakes and bugs. The masculinity here is one of spiders and snakes and unsightly athleticism versus a femininity of frills and lace, dolls and stuffed animals. Whether offered in support of "essential" or "cultural" explanations of gender, these descriptions provide a crystallization of cultural expectations about gender normativity, and hence ultimately reiterate gender norms.

Descriptions of Brandon as an adult also focus on clothing choices and body movements as signifiers of masculinity. Donna Minkowitz observes in the *Village Voice* that Brandon was physically buried under "men's clothing, wearing her favorite cowboy shirt and black cowboy hat" (24). Ingrid Ricks similarly notes in the *Advocate* that Brandon "dressed in men's clothing, often Western wear, and wore her dark brown hair close-cropped" (29). John Gregory Dunne notes that Brandon died dressed as a man, in "black Jockey-style underwear, sweat shorts, a sweatshirt, a T-shirt and sweat socks" (46). Whether rugged cowboy or jock, Brandon's clothing is consistently used to signify his masculinity.

In addition, Brandon's physical appearance is articulated with specific icons of sexually promiscuous American masculinity. Minkowitz writes that after Brandon arrived in Falls City, every young woman in town was "after this pool player with the jawline of a Kennedy" who gave gifts to women with "Elvis-esque extravagance" (24). She goes on to observe that in one photograph Brandon looks "like JFK, at once serious and mischievously conscious of his good looks" (26). Aphrodite Jones makes a similar observation, noting that when a young woman named Heather had her first kiss with Brandon (then going by the name Billy Brinson), "she was bowled over by his slick crew cut and Kennedy jaw line" (58).[24]

Again, these references to clothing and dress, coupled with the overall characterization of Brandon as deceiver, emerge from a cultural anxiety over being "fooled" about "true gender." Rather than allowing for either gender ambiguity or a configuration in which Brandon was male because Brandon identified as male, we are told that Brandon was able to deceive because "she" so clearly utilized hypermasculine signifiers. As a whole, the authors work to draw out these signifiers of masculinity in order to help explain the gender confusion experienced by those who encountered Brandon Teena. As Marjorie Garber has observed elsewhere: "It is as though the hegemonic cultural imaginary is saying to itself: if there is a difference, we want to be able to see it, and if we see a difference (e.g., a man in women's clothes), we want to be able to interpret it. In both cases, the conflation is fueled by a desire to tell the difference, to guard against a difference that might otherwise put the identity of one's own position in question" (130).

Urination and Bi-gendered Sexuality

This same ideological effort to restabilize gender signifiers is evident in questions about Brandon's physical and sexual behaviors. The physical signifiers of Brandon's masculinity as crystallized in public recountings of the case range from the way he urinated (standing, of course) to his heterosexual behavior with women (i.e., he was like "one of the guys," only more sensitive). Although at times, especially in the post–*Boys Don't Cry* discourse, Brandon is configured as a lesbian ("Fierce" 85), what is important for my analysis is that most discussions about the case provide a lens through which to see the predictable iteration of masculinity and femininity within heterosexual expectations. That is, because the discourse attempts to explain how women were "deceived" by Brandon, it also implicitly works to reassure each of us that our readings of masculinity and femininity are generally correct. Moreover, as I will argue, even those discourses that articulate Brandon as a lesbian maintain a system of bi-genderism.

Observations about Brandon's bodily movements and appearance are centered on the question of how those who were intimate with him were "deceived." For example, Aphrodite Jones, wondering how Lana Tisdel, one of Brandon's last girlfriends, could possibly have thought that Brandon was "really" male, reports that Tisdel claimed in conversations with others that she had felt a penis, albeit a small one, when she had engaged in sexual relations with Brandon, and "she had sworn she'd seen Brandon stand up and pee. . . . Even Tom [Nissen] had seen Brandon stand up and piss at one of the urinals at the Oasis [a local bar], so when John [Lotter] and Tom compared notes, that part of the story seemed real" (209). In the *New Yorker*, Dunne makes a similar observation, again implicitly answering readers' questions as to how Brandon's girlfriends could have been deceived: "Brandon moved from Humboldt into Linda Gutierrez's house, and Lana Tisdel's bed. The sex was good, Lana reported, and Brandon stood up to pee" (54). Further, Minkowitz reports that women told one another that Brandon had a penis because they had "seen him pee!" (28), again indicating that he had stood up to do so.

What is important here is the impulse among those writing about the case to explain how the "difference" between maleness and femaleness was missed. Again, as Lacan remarks about "urinary segregation," despite all the differences among individual males, and despite all the differences among individual females, we have as a culture taken the act of urination, the very way in which our society provides restrooms, to signify that in this act, all men are equal, as are all women (cited in Garber 13–17). That Brandon's "standing up to pee" is so often remarked in the discourse about the case works simultaneously both to destabilize urination as a marker of the essentiality of gender and to reaffirm its status as one way such difference is publicly signified. That is, the evidence is raised to explain how women were fooled, hence destabilizing the sign but simultaneously to reaffirm that it is one way to keep gender straight and binary. Moreover, while Brandon may have been able to use this signifier to "deceive" her peers for a time, in the end, as the story reveals, the truth of gender will win out. A similar dynamic can be noted of the way Brandon's sexual relations with women troubled heterosexual norms.

Dismissing contemporary observations that heterosexuality has "made a comeback" in popular culture, Lauren Berlant writes that "nowhere in the United States has heterosexuality gone into a decline or 'left' in a way that makes the idea of a comeback even remotely possible" (16). The discourse surrounding this case highlights the fact that the assumption of heterosexuality persists as a dominant theme in popular culture. In particular in this case, this is so not because Brandon's sexuality is denigrated but more because one of the primary implied themes in discussions of this case is how to protect the sexual identity—and *sexuality* identity—of those "fooled" by Brandon Teena. In protecting those who were fooled, the discourse protects cultural norms as a whole, assuring all of us that the iteration of gender essentialism and compulsory heterosexuality remains stable regardless of the misidentifications in this particular case. Rather than positioning Brandon and his partners as being engaged in queer sexuality, transgendered sexuality, or sexual behavior and desire based on style rather than sex or gender (Bornstein

32), the public argument persistently confirms that the women who had sexual relations with Brandon were practicing what they thought to be "normal" heterosexuality—and hence in principle they *were* practicing "normal" heterosexuality. Alternative conceptions of sexuality are rarely discussed. Again recalling Garber's claim that the desire to see and know gender differences is an impulse "fueled by a desire to tell the difference, to guard against a difference that might otherwise put the identity of one's own position in question," in explaining how heterosexuals were "fooled" by Brandon, the public discussion upholds normalized iterations of heterosexuality.

While I do not want to discount the possibility that, for particular individuals or groups, the case potentially destabilizes gender identity and sexual desire by recognizing that heterosexual masculinity is always a matter of successful or unsuccessful performance (and hence that all sexual identities are performative), I want to suggest that the case ultimately protects heterosexuality for the majority both by allowing Brandon's "girlfriends" to remain heterosexual and by implicitly emphasizing that Brandon's "lack" ultimately undermines the heterosexual masculine performance. As I will show, Brandon's temporarily successful performance of heterosexual masculinity does not ultimately destabilize gender binarism because it is never permitted to trouble masculinity or femininity; rather, the discourse either reifies the heterosexuality of the participants and/or places homosexuality in an abject position. In these ways, it illustrates a cultural "desire for identity categories to be ontological, dead to history" (Berlant 72).

Garber notes that in public discussions of the case that inspired *M. Butterfly*, the one question that was raised repeatedly, almost obsessively, in the public sphere concerned sexual relations between the two men: "What did they do in bed?" (236). This same fascination predictably follows Brandon Teena and his paramours: not only "What did they do in bed?" but "How were the women persuaded to get into bed with Brandon in the first place?" This question is most generally answered in narrative form, a story that begins with a discussion of Brandon's dating behavior. Repeatedly, Brandon is referred to as the perfect gentleman, the ideal man, these terms repeatedly referring to the ideal within heterosexual romance narratives. For example, Aphrodite Jones quotes Heather, Brandon's first girlfriend, as observing that Brandon would be any woman's dream guy: "He knew how a woman wanted to be treated. . . . He took you out to dinner, bought flowers, roses, just everything" (61). Jones goes on to quote Brandon's next girlfriend, Reana, as observing that Brandon "basically told anybody anything they wanted to hear. He knew what a girl wanted" (88). Finally, Brandon's onetime fiancée asserts that Brandon was the "perfect gentleman," always taking her out to eat, opening doors for her, and never allowing her to pay for anything (100). The *Denver Post* reports that numerous people who knew Brandon described him as "a dream suitor. She [sic] showered them with gifts, showed them respect and swept them off their feet" (Will 10).[25] The *New York Times* notes that Brandon was "courtly and sent flowers and was an excellent kisser" (Holden, "Rape" 85). A *San Francisco Chronicle* story begins by observing, "There wasn't much that Brandon Teena didn't know about pleasing a woman. His girlfriends praised his courtliness, his sweetness, his generosity with flowers and gifts" (Guthman D3). Donna Minkowitz describes a get-together of many of Brandon's former girlfriends, who agreed, while getting tipsy, that Brandon was "the perfect woman's man—every woman's dream" (27). Even Brandon's "less gentlemanly moments" are consistently described as making him "a normal guy"; Jones quotes one of his girlfriends as noting that Brandon "was a pervert, just a regular guy, always making jokes" (126). In the *Advocate*, Brandon's final girlfriend, Lana Tisdel, says that Brandon "was like a normal guy. He talked like one; he acted like one" (Ricks 29). In each report we learn that Brandon was able to seduce women because he performed heterosexual masculinity so successfully—more successfully than most men, in fact.

Because so many women reported having had sex with Brandon, the act itself, and its performance absent the penis, is a matter of obvious conflict throughout the discourse. Once again, Brandon is posited as the perfect man (i.e., his attention was on the women, without pressure or expectations) and simultaneously as not a man. Aphrodite Jones reports that one young woman claimed to have experienced her first orgasm with Brandon during oral sex and quotes others remarking on Brandon's stamina during intercourse (269–70). Eric Konigsberg notes that Brandon evidently provided many of the women with their first answer to the question of "what all the fuss was about," the realization that sex was not simply something they did for their boyfriends (194). He goes on to quote one of Brandon's girlfriends: "I don't think there was a time with him when I didn't come,' the girl said, 'orally, going all the way, even dry humping'" (194). John Gregory Dunne relays stories from women who claimed that they went on the pill because they were having sex with Brandon (51) and others who commented on the high quality of the sex (54). Minkowitz observes that "every former girlfriend the *Voice* talked to said Brandon was 'the best lover' they ever had" (24).

This consistently repeated evidence of Brandon's sexual prowess could obviously be a complication in normative understandings of gender and sexuality. Yet, the irony that the ideal man had female genitalia, an idea that could destabilize gendered meanings, ultimately reifies them instead. That is, rather than stressing gender trouble, the body of discourse consistently suggests that the heterosexual women were fooled only because Brandon performed masculinity so well. It is significant that so many of Brandon's girlfriends are quoted as claiming that Brandon must have been able to deceive them sexually either because he used a dildo, which they neither saw nor touched, or because Brandon performed oral sex without demanding reciprocation. Dunne suggests that Brandon's early girlfriends, who thought he was an expert kisser, could have sex with him and think he was a male because he either "stuffed socks into his shorts" or would "wear a dildo" (50). The problem here once again is that of maintaining strict boundaries between male and female. While an issue such as this one—the sexual success of Brandon Teena—cannot help but trouble gender normativity, the public discourse over the case maintains that the women were fooled and hence were, in their own minds, performing heterosexuality, and that Brandon's deception, his use of appendages and socks, would ultimately have been discovered. In this configuration, gender binarism and heteronormativity can be maintained not just for the women with whom Brandon had sex but for everyone.

The women who had sex with Brandon are allowed to "confess" their heterosexuality after the fact rather than rethinking sexuality and gender as performative. There is an underlying theme in the pre–*Boys Don't Cry* discourse that the women "seduced" by Brandon were not lesbian, that they were in their own minds fully heterosexual. In the clearest example of this configuration, Lana Tisdel is quoted in Minkowitz's article as repeating two mantras to help her understand the experience: "1. When I kissed Brandon, I wasn't kissing a woman, I was kissing a man; 2. Brandon didn't love the way a woman loves a woman, he loved me the way a man loves a women" (27). Minkowitz goes on to note skeptically that while Tisdel cannot explain what such a mantra meant to her, she adamantly wanted to be considered heterosexual (27). Minkowitz also observes that Brandon's former fiancée, Gina Bartu, "freaked out" one time when she was in a gay bar with Brandon because she thought that people might believe she and Brandon were a lesbian couple (26). Roger Ebert, in a film review, asks: "But what about the women Brandon dated? . . . They were not lesbians" (31). The sexual configuration allowed in such discourse is a heterosexual one; there is no fluidity in these descriptions. In a sense, as we have seen throughout this section, the only two options that appear to be allowed are based on gender binarism rather than on, for example, Kate Bornstein's description of stylistic differences, which would configure Brandon and his girlfriends as something other than either homosexual or heterosexual (32).

Although Brandon's girlfriends are protected from the lesbian label by the deception narrative, Brandon's desires could easily be coded as lesbian ones. In pre–*Boys Don't Cry* representations, however, Brandon's fear of, and disgust with, lesbianism is reported continually, reaffirming his own investment in gender binarism. For instance, according to Aphrodite Jones, in a confrontation with her mother over her sexual identity Brandon insisted that lesbians were "disgusting" to her (68–69).[26] Burbach and Cordes in the *Omaha World Herald* quote Brandon's mother observing of Brandon: "She told me she wasn't a lesbian and was very adamant about that. She didn't want to be with a female in that way" (1A). Konigsberg notes that Brandon did not attend "gay parties" if many lesbians were going to be there because Brandon found them disgusting (193). Donna Minkowitz pursues this theme, noting both that a high school classmate reported that Brandon had said that she was "disgusted by lesbians, that she didn't think it was right," and that she was going to "love women like a man" (28). Minkowitz further notes that "the thought of being gay was much more disturbing to her than getting a sex change" (29). It is noteworthy here that all the evidence brought to bear is not situated to work outside of gender binaries; sexual desire and identity are solidly based on heterosexual norms.

I should also point out, however, one very clear reading of *Boys Don't Cry* whereby Brandon and Lana Tisdel are lesbian and ultimately do "come out" to each other. While such a reading can be seen as progressive if one's goal is to encourage public representations and markings of lesbians (even ones in which the lesbian must "fool others" into relationships), the lesbian reading of this text does not render gender itself problematic. Indeed, it works to reify male-female categories. In one of the final scenes of the film, Lana goes to visit Brandon a week after the rape—and, hence, after Lana knows Brandon's "true" gender identity. After a brief discussion, Lana moves her body in such a way as to imply that she is about to perform oral sex on Brandon, and she expresses concern that she will be able to perform properly. Brandon reassures her that she'll probably figure it out. Although some testimony suggests that Brandon "in real life" would never have had relations that positioned her as a woman, this scene, created by screenwriters Kimberly Peirce and Andy Beinen, clearly opens an interpretive door that allows reading the two as now occupying a lesbian relationship. Such an interpretation both refigures Brandon's life "as a man" as fear of her own homosexuality and maintains a gender-as-genitalia equation (Brandon is a lesbian because her body is that of a woman). Indeed, Judith Halberstam, who praises the film for providing a "transgender gaze" throughout much of the narrative, observes of that final scene: "Abruptly, towards the end of the film, Peirce suddenly and catastrophically divests her character of his transgender gaze and converts it to a lesbian and therefore female gaze" (297).

This "lesbian" reading reappears in several reviews of the film. In *Maclean's* we read that, in the film, Brandon "first comes out as a man, a seducer who turns out to be the most sensitive guy these Nebraska girls have ever known. . . . But later, as he gradually surrenders to [Lana], he comes out as a woman, and the final taboo melts away" (Johnson 68). Jay Stone of the *Ottawa Citizen* notes that the film is about a "young lesbian named Teena Brandon" (F10), and similarly, the *Miami Herald* critic writes that the film is "about a young lesbian who passes herself off as a man" (Ingles 4; see also Tong 7). More pointedly, David Elliott of the *San Diego Tribune* asserts that "the film suggests that Brandon was really a lesbian using male camouflage" ("Boys"). In discussions about the plot of the film with a writer for the *Ottawa Citizen*, Peirce supports this interpretation of the film by observing that after Brandon was rebuked by her mother at age fourteen when she tried to identify herself as a lesbian, she decided that the only "proper" way to have sex with women was to act as if she were a man (Laurence C2). In each of these examples, Brandon is either consciously a lesbian or else a lesbian in denial; in either case, she reaffirms the "nature" of bi-gendered thinking.

In short, given the paucity of ways to think, the potentially transgressive and blurred configuration of Brandon's gender/sexuality is made harmless by being forced into binaristic mode, and his sexuality is tied into binarisms as well (i.e., Brandon is homosexual if we take the body as gender and heterosexual if we take into account her self-identity). There is little public blurring of sexuality and identity; it is primarily one or the other for both Brandon and Brandon's partners in the configuration allowed by public argument. What we have seen to be the case with clothing and style, then, is true of sexuality as well: the discourse around Brandon Teena's sexual activities and desires reactivates heterosexual norms.

BRANDON'S BODY: ATTITUDE OF A HERMAPHRODITE

Echoing a large number of gender theorists and cultural critics, Marjorie Garber notes that, paradoxically, transsexuals and transvestites are more concerned with maleness and femaleness than persons who are neither transvestite nor transsexual. Transsexuals and transvestites are often "emphatically not interested in 'unisex' or 'androgyn' as erotic styles, but rather in gender-marked coded identity structures" (110). While I have illustrated this to be true in both the discourse alleged to have been spoken by Brandon Teena and the public discourse about Brandon Teena, another interesting aspect of this case concerns the way Brandon's troubled body is talked about—both by Brandon (reportedly) and by others. In the multiple narratives, stories are consistently recounted of moments when someone "discovered" that Brandon did not have a typical male body, placing Brandon in a position of having to explain "what he was." Whether because Brandon actually thought in these terms or because audience pressure forced him to speak in these terms (or because those reporting the case could work only within certain dynamics), Brandon is reported to have consistently discussed his body in a way that indicates that he clearly saw the penis as the marker of "maleness" or manhood. Brandon's two responses—to position himself either as a hermaphrodite or as a preoperative transsexual—focus on the penis and its importance to being a man. I should point out that while Brandon's own words *as reported* seem more transgressive, at times indicating his own ability to see a disjuncture between body and identity, the reports about the case generally lean back in a direction in which body and identity are necessarily articulated together.

Given a lack of vocabulary to describe oneself as "transgendered," Brandon reportedly described himself on more than one occasion as a hermaphrodite awaiting an operation that would make his body unambiguously male (Dunne reports that Brandon got the idea from of an episode of *Montel Williams* [50]). For example, Aphrodite Jones notes that Brandon told Heather, his first girlfriend, that "he was a hermaphrodite, born with both sexes, that he was raised as a female" and was planning on having an operation to make himself completely male (63; see also Ricks 29). In the *Omaha World Herald*, Burbach and Cordes observe that "when questioned about her sexuality, Miss Brandon told people she was a hermaphrodite, a person with both male and female sex organs" (1A; see also Wheelwright).[27] Dunne also notes that this was the same story Brandon told his earliest girlfriends (50; see also Minkowitz 25), and that each time he made it clear that he would someday become completely male. Alice Dreger shows that modern medicine has developed an attitude about hermaphroditism[28] that forces hermaphroditic bodies into one of the two "natural" sex categories based on what the person "has" (the "one body, one sex" rule).[29] Evidently, in the case of Brandon Teena, this understanding translated into his own need to confine his body to one sex rather than to perceive gender as transitional or as not related directly to the body. If that body were hermaphroditic rather than female, Brandon could adopt the attitude, with others, that his body—despite some aberration—was genuinely male, that is, it came equipped with a "real" penis.

The second explanation Brandon offered concerning his gender was that he was a preoperative transsexual. Jones, for instance, notes that once his first girlfriend had been told by his mother that Brandon was neither male nor a hermaphrodite, Brandon confessed that he felt like a man inside and wanted to have a full sex-change operation (81). Perhaps more telling culturally, many news articles about the case begin with a biography of Brandon Teena which states this preoperative narrative as fact. One story begins, "Brandon Teena, whose birth name was Teena Brandon, was originally from Lincoln, Nebraska, and moved to nearby Humboldt in 1993, shortly after beginning to live full-time as a man in preparation for eventual sex-change surgery"—this despite the fact that Brandon is never reported to have had firm plans to undergo surgery ("Brandon Teena Murderer"). Burbach and Cordes note that Brandon told people "she was a transsexual in the process of getting a sex change" (1A). Ed Will reports in the *Denver Post* that Brandon had told others that she was either "considering or had had sex-change surgery" (10). Konigsberg, who persistently uses the "female" name Teena Brandon, notes on several occasions that Brandon called himself a preoperative transsexual when talking to Gina, his fiancée, and claimed that he was having trouble raising the funds for the operation (see also Minkowitz 26). Jay Carr of the *Boston Globe*, in his review of *The Brandon Teena Story*, takes the claim that Brandon was in the process of a sex change as factual, noting that Brandon had "begun a series of sex-change operations by the time she moved from Lincoln" (D7; see also "Best").

In short, both the hermaphrodite and preoperative discourses focus on the penis as a natural sign of masculinity and maleness, reinscribing the gender-as-sex ideology. Whether positing Brandon Teena as a hermaphrodite or as a preoperative transsexual, reports about Brandon Teena, like Brandon himself, work within the same gender constraints that contain us all. To be male demands the presence of a penis, and Brandon was metaphorically adding one with either rhetorical strategy.

THE CAUSES OF ABERRATION

In her history of hermaphroditism, Alice Dreger notes that while the mothers of hermaphrodites have traditionally been considered by medical personnel to be "poor witnesses with regard to the 'sex' behavior of their 'doubtful' children, they were frequently expected to account for the deformity in their offspring" (71). What is significant, as transgender activists continually point out, is that hermaphroditism *is* natural in the sense that it is the body a person was born with.[30] Hence, surgical changes to that body to make it more closely resemble a male or a female body should logically be seen as acts of deformation rather than repair. Similarly, one could argue that Brandon Teena's identity and desire are as "natural" as anyone else's. Nonetheless, multiple narrative strands configure Brandon's transgendered body as an aberration, as a mistake with a cause that could have been prevented. In general, bodies are forced into male or female categories, and, once in these categories, they must perform properly (i.e., according to gender norms) or else the search is on for the causes of their "malfunction." This is precisely what occurs in discussions of Brandon's body. Although few of the essays and articles surrounding the case make an explicit claim to understand the "cause" of Brandon's sexual identity, it is an underlying theme throughout. Again, one significant point about the search for a cause becomes clear when we observe that while one would never expect to find explanations for the causes of a person's heterosexuality, the "cause" of Brandon's gender and sexuality ambiguity is discussed as a matter of routine.

In the most general terms, Brandon's "transgenderism" is posited as resulting either from a chemical or physical imbalance (e.g., extra hormone shots during his mother's pregnancy) or from psychosexual abuse at an early age. In both instances Brandon's mother is implicated as at least part of the "problem" that led to Brandon's "condition." With reference to a chemical imbalance, Aphrodite Jones suggests that difficulties during Brandon's gestation may have been the cause of his nontraditional desires. Jones quotes Brandon's mother, JoAnn, as recalling that during the early months of her pregnancy with Teena, her uterus was not enlarging at a sufficient rate and had not "tipped" as it was supposed to, so the doctor "gave me hormone shots or something, and they were so thick, a thick serum. . . . I went through this for two weeks, and then she started to grow" (27). As this version of the story unfolds, it becomes obvious that one way of understanding Brandon's aberrant condition is to see it as resulting from a hormonal deficiency. If Brandon had been developing normally, this condition would not have occurred.

There are also a number of intimations that Brandon was sexually abused by a relative as a child, and this abuse is linked to Brandon's eventual transgenderism. For example, Jones notes that Brandon disclosed this sexual abuse to his first girlfriend (63) and that, during a therapy session after a suicide attempt, Teena (Brandon) told the counselors about "hours of sexual abuse in her childhood and adolescence, saying that she felt intimidated by certain men, that she always felt sexually oriented toward women" (83). Donna Minkowitz quotes Brandon's sister Tammy as asserting that Brandon was not happy as a woman because "we were both molested by a male relative when we were little" (29). Brandon's mother, upon learning about the sexual abuse during the counseling sessions, is reported by Jones as declaring that the abusive relative had "destroyed Teena, and that was why Teena wasn't interested in men" (86). Konigsberg also situates the story of Brandon's having been raped and abused at the center of her transgenderism (193). Dunne, in perhaps the clearest example of this form of causal reasoning, makes note of Brandon's sexual molestation and observes that somewhere in this "there might be an early clue, a *first cause*, a reason that would make Teena's subsequent ventures across the gender divide easier to accommodate" (50; emphasis added).

Indeed, among the many contested discourses about Brandon that followed in the wake of *Boys Don't Cry*, the sexual abuse claims are reiterated on multiple occasions. For example, just after Hilary Swank was awarded the Oscar for her performance in the film, JoAnn Brandon held a press conference in which she criticized the film for misrepresenting Brandon's life. She claimed that as a young girl, her daughter was "sexually molested by a man over several years" and began to pretend that "she was a man so no other man could touch her" (Duggan A1; see also "Victim's"). Moreover, she said that she had talked to "Teena" just days before the murder, and it was clear to her that her child saw herself as a woman and was only using her male clothing to keep men away from her (Duggan A1). Similarly, an editorial in the *Omaha World-Herald* criticized the ABC television program *20/20* for leaving out a "major part" of the story. Quoting Dr. Mario Scalora, editorialist Herbert Friedman concludes that the repeated sexual abuse that Brandon suffered as a child "played a role in driving Teena to the life she chose" (19). Another editorial a month later declares that the sexual abuse had kept Brandon from following "her destiny" ("Furthermore" 22), implying a "destiny" more in line with heteronormative expectations.

Rather than taking Brandon's identity as "natural," these accounts all search for the reason, whether chemical or psychological, for the anomaly that led Brandon to live outside the realm of normal behavior. No cause would have been sought if she had not become transgendered (and most sexually abused children do not), but here the search for a simple cause seems vital. If gender operates according to iterated norms, all cases of transgression must be explained. Moreover, whatever the explanation, the mother is implicated as responsible for the problem, either because of the hormones she took during pregnancy or for not having done enough to prevent the physical and sexual abuse.

COMPLICATED POSSIBILITIES

Although I have shown that many readings of the case serve to reaffirm bi-genderism, and most reaffirm heteronormativity, there are readings that complicate gender, that leave cracks in the meaning of gender that trouble its current understanding. I mention a few of them here in order to reaffirm the possibilities of discourse. In such readings, the "meaning" of Brandon, and of Brandon's body, is left troubled, or is simply assumed to be male despite Brandon's female genitalia. That is, such readings, as rare as they are, either accept Brandon as a man based on his reported claims to be a man or else understand Brandon's gender as outside "normal" categories.[31] For example, in the *Omaha World-Herald*, Jim Beckerman agrees with Hilary Swank that there is no "definitive explanation for the real Brandon Teena—who seems to stand outside any of the usual, or even unusual, sexual categories" (4). Vincent Kova explains in *Outspoken* that the story is one of a girl who was fundamentally transformed into a boy as he found his "true self" (24). In

Cineaste, Melissa Anderson criticizes the "lesbian" implication of the end of *Boys Don't Cry* on the grounds that Brandon was indeed a man (55). Francesca Miller refers to Brandon as a "transgendered youth," a "girl-turned-boy" (as opposed to a girl posing as a boy) in the *Gay and Lesbian Review* piece (39). In the *Los Angeles Times*, Mary McNamara observes that the trial and the film have helped teach mass culture and the mass media to refer to Brandon as "him" to match Brandon's own identity (E1; see also Morrison). Finally, in an important outlet for the articulation of Brandon as male, Andrew Arthur criticizes the *Pittsburgh Post-Gazette* in its "Feedback" section for claiming that Brandon was a woman "masquerading as a man"; Brandon Teena, Arthur observes, "was a man; . . . he just happened to be born in a female body" (47).

In short, though much of the discourse articulating Brandon as male (or at least troubling the male/female dichotomy) appears in gay and lesbian outlets, we do see here in embryonic form a notion of gender that indeed troubles bi-gendered heteronormativity. While it seems clear to me that the dominant themes emerging in the discourse about the film and about the case in general remain solidly heteronormative, it is equally clear that critics interested in focusing exclusively on the politics of change have plenty of material to work with here. Although heteronormativity is certainly what John Fiske and John Hartley describe as the "claw back" position, the case does highlight the excessiveness and messiness of signifiers, at least in some limited sense. Indeed, as this "gender trouble" moves into mass consciousness, notions of gender and gender stability may find themselves increasingly open to question.

In *Gender Outlaw*, Kate Bornstein says that one of her purposes was to understand the cardboard characterizations of transgendered people she was witnessing in various arts and media, from poetry and drama to television and cinema, portraits "all drawn by people who were not us, all spoken in voices that were not ours" (59). In part, this study of Brandon Teena attends to those same voices. This has been a study not of "Brandon's voice" but rather of representations of Brandon's voice, representations wrapped in layers of descriptions that are part of a mass cultural discourse concerning gender, sex, and sexuality. It is within these discourses that I have attempted to examine how Brandon Teena is understood, and perhaps the discursive constraints under which Brandon came to understand and negotiate his "self," as well as how transgenderism is understood, and therefore how sexuality and gender are understood in general. A number of observations and suggestions can be drawn from this analysis.

First, I want to make clear that the discourse studied here is part of a cultural ideology that affects all of us; it is a discourse that is defining, disciplinary, even while we negotiate within its boundaries. As Leslie Feinberg notes, everyone is constrained by the same body of public argument; hence, a critical reading of the disciplinary discourses about transsexualism, transgenderism, intersexualism, and so forth helps us all understand our own position within gender and sexual discourses (92).[32] Similarly, those discourses that shape how Brandon Teena was understood by individuals and by mass media reports are the same discourses that shape each of us; they are the same discourses that work to reiterate gender norms and the influence of those norms. Even though I assume that these discourses can be read transgressively or "against the grain," they are clearly also the discourses with which all of us must negotiate and hence should be everyone's shared critical responsibility.

Second, when a subjectivity is either not represented (symbolically annihilated) or represented negatively, those people, including adolescents, who are developing a similar subjectivity are likely to find themselves alone, without support or even the idea that a supportive community or individuals might exist. While this can have tragic implications in cases of adolescent homosexuality, as Alfred Kielwasser and Michelle Wolfe have shown, it is surely even more of a problem with transgendered individuals, as Leslie Feinberg poignantly points out in *Transgender Warriors*. Maturing in a world that either does not acknowledge one's existence, degrades the subject position one wishes to take on, or posits it as an aberration certainly makes one's path a difficult one.[33] Obviously, critical work that draws out the "naturalness" of transgenderism, that highlights the complexity of desire, would help people come to understand their own desires and identities, especially if those desires and identities are outside of cultural norms.

Third, despite the fact that numerous contemporary theoretical voices (and a few public voices) might posit an already existing blurring of gender categories, the Brandon Teena case is one site where the meaning of gender in dominant culture remains fairly constraining. We find that to be true not only in the signifiers of masculinity and femininity that lace this discourse and in the metaphors of "deception," but also, most significantly, in the idea that transgenderism is an abnormality caused either by error or by psychological or physical abuse. We cannot have a useful blurring of gender and sexual categories when that blurring makes sense of a large array of subjectivities only by understanding them as a kind of deformity or when so many discourses continue to discipline transgenderism into a system of bi-genderism and heterosexual desire. Hence, not only is the experience of transgenderism negatively represented, but also gender and sex are "talked about" in ways that are radically limited. As Alice Dreger has illustrated, there continues to be a basic underlying cultural assumption that each body has one gender and that one gender is identified by/on the body itself (whether by gonads or by chromosomes).[34] Thus, when Brandon Teena is situated discursively, he becomes "really" a woman, "really" Teena, because of his "female body." Further, the way that body is allowed to desire works along the same axis of male or female body type (rather than, for example, as Bornstein suggests, style) and along the lines of homosexual and heterosexual desire.

Finally, I am not trying to suggest that "male," "female," and "heterosexual" are useless or out-of-date categories, as it is clear that these remain meaningful to a number of people, including a wide range of queered individuals. Rather, I wish to point out that the discourses surrounding this case—a case very much open to numerous possibilities for refiguring gender and sexuality—instead fold it back into a traditional iteration of heterosexual normativity. As C. Jacob Hale notes in his essay on the Brandon Teena case, we would be wise to recognize that borders and categories are necessary as starting points. In short, while Hale sees the need for categories on which to base identity, he argues that the borders must be kept constantly loose, must be seen as creatively contingent and fluid: "Insofar as sex/gender is hegemonically constructed as nontechnologized and nonperformative, all of us whose sex/gender is explicitly technologized or performative are abjected from the organizing principles of this system at a singular minimum" (338). One of our jobs as critics—at least as a first step—is to continue to add to the metaphors that people have to work with, or at least to continue to encourage creativity within preexisting boundaries, to encourage the production of new taxonomies that would intervene in the hegemonic practice of naming and defining, as Judith Halberstam notes, drawing from Eve Sedgwick (8, 46–47).[35] As Celeste Condit writes: "The goal of gender diversity approaches is to dismantle traditional gender dimorphism without leaving persons identity-less. Both of these moves are necessary for gender liberation" ("In Praise" 97).[36] The first step in making this move, at least in terms of our task as critics and teachers, is to reenvision rhetoric as a constructor of gender rather than as constructed by gender.

THREE

"So Long, Chaps and Spurs, and Howdy—er, *Bon Jour*—to the Wounded Songbird"

k.d. lang, Ambiguity, and the Politics of Genre/Gender

By the early 1980s, [k.d. lang] was belting country music, first as affectionate parody
and then with less and less irony; her voice, with its leisurely swoops and its aching
vibrato, was made for ballads. "I always thought I was delivering emotion," she said.
"But as I grow older I see deeper and more intense ways to deliver emotion and truth."
Jon Pareles, "k.d. lang Leaves Metaphor Behind"

In a section of *Female Masculinity* in which she investigates a "postmodern butch" aesthetic, Judith Halberstam provides a short critique of Percy Adlon's film *Salmonberries*. Halberstam puts her most intense focus on the Alaskan orphan character Kotz, played by k.d. lang. In the midst of a revealing critique of the film, she notes that when Kotz is silent, especially in the early portions of the narrative, the character is complex in ways that bolster and complicate her masculinity, while later in the film, the character's gender and sexuality become far less complicated, easier to interpret through received or "commonsense" categories. As Halberstam puts it, early in the movie lang's Kotz "is brooding, moody, melancholic, violent, sexy, and extremely intense. As you might imagine, things go downhill once lang begins to speak," and the character is simultaneously transformed into a less complicated, more traditional love-stricken girl dyke (224).

While reading this section of Halberstam's argument in the context of working through a number of mass mediated articles dealing with k.d. lang as a recording artist, I could not help but be struck by the ways Halberstam's claim about the character was, and is, to some degree reflected in the public discourse surrounding k.d. lang's sexuality, gender performance, and placement within musical genres and practices. In this chapter, through a critical reading of multiple texts that deal in part with the body, sexuality, gender, politics, and music of k.d. lang, I suggest that the politics of ambiguity that surrounded lang in the early "country music" and closeted portion of her career made for a far messier, far more troubled, far more ambiguous queered representation than the "lesbian chanteuse"–torch singer portion of her career. Through a critical reading of popular articles about lang and her music throughout her career (especially focusing on her transition from country to other genres),[1] I suggest that coverage of lang's musical direction and sexual/gendered persona overlap and intermingle in such a way that the "categorically messy" and ambiguous portion of her career is coupled with the low cultural capital politics of country music, while the torch song and (truth-telling) lesbian portion of her career is coupled with a higher cultural capital construction of her body of work.

I want to make clear at the outset that I do not mean to suggest that the articulation of cultural capital with sexuality and gender performance is in this case causally linked; indeed, the articulation of musical and gender/sexual identity here is based more on the circumstances of lang's career than on cultural necessity, although these circumstances are shaped by ideology and economics. That is, this is not a crass "fandom" argument that lang has "sold out" and hence given up the politics of authenticity by intentionally responding to the call of capital. Rather, regardless of why these changes have taken place (and the pressures of capitalism may indeed be among many overdetermining factors), it seems to me worthy of our attention as cultural critics that we attempt to understand the complex ways in which the politics of cultural capital work in an uneasy alliance with the politics of sexuality and "proper" gender performance.

In brief, I argue, somewhat counterintuitively, that lang's "coming out" as lesbian, because it was coupled with a transition in her musical and performative style—something that is repeatedly mentioned in the discourse about lang—worked to smooth out gender trouble, to create a less queer star text and a more understandable lesbian one, regardless of her intentions. Although ours is no doubt a heteronormative culture, it is also a culture that insists on a clear delineation between male and

Partha is this →

Sloppy argument at KD coming out

female as separate genders, on heterosexual and homosexual as distinctly separate spheres of desire. It is a culture, then, in which knowing where to place someone in the matrix of gender and desire is valued over confusion. That is, while homosexuality may be devalued, it is more highly valued—because it implies a segregated gender system—than a queered sexuality or gender performance that produces anxiety through confusion. In this respect, the analysis of this case is suggestive of Halberstam's reading of *Boys Don't Cry*. Halberstam, as noted in the previous chapter, saw the film as at first providing a transgendered gaze that disrupts normative ways of understanding gender and desire. The turn at the end of the film, however, transforms Brandon's story into a lesbian love story, making it relatively less challenging and disruptive ("Transgender" 297). Here, a sexually ambiguous lang is more discursively troubling than the lesbian chanteuse lang. While representations of lang as an "out" lesbian are certainly one element of a progressive political change in its own right, it comes at the costs of erasing the self-questioning that "gender trouble" encourages within a culture. In short, the "truthful" lesbian is far less troubling than someone who challenges bi-gender semiotics and whose objects of desire are unknown.

K.D. LANG AND POPULAR MUSIC STUDIES

As a popular music persona over which queer and lesbian politics are argued, k.d. lang is clearly not a new subject of critical attention. Indeed, Martha Mockus's "Queer Thoughts on Country Music and k.d. lang" appeared in 1994 in the anthology *Queering the Pitch*. In both Mockus's essay and Keith Negus's summary of work on lang and country music,[2] the primary critical focus is on the ways, in Mockus's terms, in which "the strict gender definition presented in country music provides excellent material for queer drag and butch-femme role-playing among both lesbians and gay men" (260). Mockus and Negus both remark on the ability of gays and lesbians to take up the signifiers of country music and play with them, utilizing them in ways familiar to gay/lesbian and queer understandings in order to critique existing gender and sexual categories, especially in light of the tight normalizing constraints of country music gender ideology. Hence, given the ambiguous, quasi-butch aesthetic of early k.d. lang, the multiplicity of ways lang herself

kd = Portia
country music = model industry

played with gender representation, and the intersection of lang's identity with country music as a genre, some fans were able to queer the meanings and symbols of country music so as to, "in a sense, expose and even undo its homophobic deeds" (Mockus 260). In short, Mockus and Negus focus on how fans of k.d. lang and/or of country music worked with the gender signifiers emphasized and reiterated by country music (and general cultural) ideology, in the sense offered by Judith Butler,[3] in order at least partially to invert and play with those signifiers. Moreover, and more specific to my argument, since lang's sexuality was still a matter of speculation, both gender and sexuality categories were troubled, opened to question by gay/lesbian audiences and to gender anxiety among some heterosexual ones.[4] In short, lang was queer and hence provoked audiences of different subjectivities in different ways. While gay and lesbian audiences were able to place the early androgynous lang into a lesbian narrative, many popular music critics and writers were overtly troubled in their attempts to understand or categorize her.[5]

Further, in the more recent "Mannish Girl: k.d. lang—from Cowpunk to Androgyny," Stella Bruzzi focuses on lang and lang's image throughout her career as itself a text, arguing that lang's move from queer cowpunk to androgynous lesbian chanteuse can be read as politically regressive.[6] That is, through a reading of visual images of lang, coupled with a base of knowledge about her, Bruzzi argues that in the early portion of her career, lang wore so many different types of outfits and espoused so many different ideas that the very "inconsistency" of her image, especially as read through what might be called a country music hermeneutics, queered, challenged, and unsettled numerous ideas about country music, gender, sexuality, and performance. As Bruzzi notes, "In these early years, using drag as her primary mode of self-identification, and drag is manifestly unstable and mocking of any notion of gender identity as Judith Butler suggests, lang's drag, not unlike the function of cross-dressing in other fields of performance, is both concealing and revealing" (197). Bruzzi argues—I think convincingly—that the second part of her career, marked by the release of *Ingenue* (1992), is a move away from androgyny as ambiguity and contingency (accompanied by lang's silence on the question of her sexuality) and toward a period in which lang's androgyny comes to be equated with lang as butch dyke—again, a narrative progression similar to the one Halberstam sees with the character Kotz (*Female* 121). This second artistic period is, significantly for Bruzzi, accompanied by a period of "truth telling" about lang's lesbianism. Bruzzi writes, "By retreating (with few exceptions) from her previously disruptive and troubling images and ostensibly bringing her image and body closer, more 'honestly' together, lang has precipitated, for me, a great loss" (199).

Such an analysis of the style of a popular music artist becomes more interesting, at least metaphorically, if we invoke vocabulary from Jacques Attali. In *Noise: The Political Economy of Music*, Attali argues that we can look at the cultural phenomenon of sound—specifically, the differences between "noise" and "music"—as one site in the shifting relations of power. For Attali, music is tamed, categorizable noise, and noise is the untamed disruption of expected categories. That is, music operates as a structural code that defines the hegemonic ordering of positions of power and difference within the aural landscape of sound. Noise, falling outside the dominant musical code, transgresses and hence challenges the dominant ordering of difference. Music reaffirms dominance, while noise is irritating and ideologically threatening because it operates outside of contemporary codes. Nonetheless, as Attali reminds us—and as we are all aware, owing to our own experiences with new forms of music—what was once noise becomes music as it becomes more familiar; ideology (of sound, gender, desire, etc.), then, is a changing equilibrium. With this in mind, one can read lang's career as a narrative in which lang has become more "easy looking" and "easy listening" as her move to "honest" lesbianism has replaced the more troubling and ambiguous images of the early portion of her career. We might say, then, that lang has moved from the "noise" and messiness of being an ambiguously sexualized/gendered singer in a very unambiguous musical environment to an unambiguous lesbianism coupled with a butch aesthetic within the torch tradition, and this move from a noisy identity within a rigid musical tradition to a musical identity within a different musical tradition has made her more easily accessible and less troubling.

Granting the basics of Bruzzi's argument, I want to move beyond reading k.d. lang's visual image as a text and investigate the broader discursive landscape of lang's representation (and, hence, reception) within the discourse of mass mediated articles about her career and music.[7] As I have already suggested, while much of the discourse surrounding lang's career supports Bruzzi's investigation, I argue that there is simultaneously a link between discussions of lang's sexuality and appeal and discussions of the relative status of the country and torch traditions. This link between gender performance, sexuality, and musical cultural capital proves politically problematic in a number of ways (contingent on one's political commitments and understandings of gender and sexuality) and hence demands critical attention. As I will show, the trouble and ambiguity of lang's early style is situated within a cultural context of low cultural capital, while her later style and articulation of sexual "truth" are read within a musical context of "artistic purity and sophistication."[8] While the combinations of musical and gender/sexuality styles are certainly contingent on a number of issues (e.g., lang's "love" of particular styles, industry pressure, changing popular tastes), these changes have ideological consequences nonetheless. Lang's relatively simultaneous changes in musical style and gender performance ultimately articulate links between ideological clarity and high cultural capital.

DETESTING BORDERS: THE NOISE AND TROUBLE OF K.D. LANG

Even the most cursory glance at feature articles and reviews of the early "country music" portion of lang's career would notice a consistently retold story (largely ignored later in her career), a story that highlights lang's voice, her history as a performance artist who understood how to "play with" the constraints of country music, and the multiple ways in which her status as an outsider (i.e., as a Canadian, an anti-meat activist, a non-Nashvillean, and a stylistic changeling with a strong masculine streak) work to problematize existing categories of gender, sexuality, style, and behavior as understood through a dominant country music paradigm. While the word "androgyny" has been employed throughout her career to describe lang's style and behavior, its meaning during this early moment in her career takes androgyny to signify confusion and trouble in terms of gender, sexuality, and style—androgyny referring here to the multiple ways lang tinkers with image and identity within a genre in which clarity is a virtue. Hence, discourse concerning lang as a country artist consistently emphasizes how she "troubles" the genre in which she performs, literally and figuratively (i.e., in terms of music and in terms of gender and sexuality). Indeed, it is in part because "country" is such a restrained and disciplined genre, at least in its popular manifestation, that lang's "performance" is so productively "troubling."

A profile published in *Maclean's* at the time of the release of lang's *Absolute Torch and Twang* quotes lang declaring, "I detest borders in music" (Mollins 15). This phrase could stand as an aphorism about the ways lang's performance worked within mass mediated discourse regarding genre, style, gender, and sexuality. In the remainder of the *Maclean's* article, as elsewhere, one sees how lang's performance consistently troubles borders of all types—national borders, sexual borders, gender borders, musical borders. In this one profile alone, we find this to be true of almost all of the "markings" by which lang is constituted in other articles, reviews, and profiles. For example, lang is described here as "the Alberta-born singer with the androgynous good looks and smoldering voice" (Mollins 15). The author, Carl Mollins, observes that lang has troubled the country music industry and fan base because no one could trust her "commitment" to country music and her "authenticity" in general. These challenges to authenticity are especially important, as Richard Peterson points out, because country music—at least since the 1950s—has been organized around the concept of authenticity.[9] Lang, Mollins notes, has dressed as both cowboy and cowgirl. Whereas she had once dressed "in cut down cowboy boots and rhinestone studded glasses, with hoop skirts, now, with her short hair and unadorned face, she looks more like a young Elvis Presley than a Dolly Parton" (15). Indeed, the formula of this article, in which lang is described as working against borders by authors who insist on using borders to describe her (e.g., "from Alberta," "more like Elvis than Dolly"), is repeated in numerous others.

First, then, lang's troubling status is signified in terms of her status as a Canadian and as an artist who utilized a recording label and industry outside of Nashville. Virtually every article about lang describes her as "Alberta born" (Guterman; Jennings and Bell 50; Dougherty and John-

son 94; Mollins 15; Hiltbrand 22), a drugstore owner's daughter from
Consort (Jennings and Bell 50), "A Bracing Breeze from Western Canada" (Jennings and Gregor 58), a tomboy from Consort (Appelo 18),
or, more simply, as Canadian (Holden, "Down-Home;" Lee V5; Hochman 77). Moreover, lang's status as an alien in the country music industry is consistently emphasized as a way of explaining some of her other
differences. Hence, the fact that she was signed to Sire Records (Madonna's label, reports emphasize) helped to stress her outsider status (a
non-Nashville label, with non-Nashville producers and musicians). In
one early profile, readers are told the story of lang's first meeting with
Sire chief Seymour Stein. After having her perform a number of canon-
ical country songs, Stein told lang that she was "what country music
would have been if Nashville hadn't screwed up" and signed her immediately (Jennings and Bell 50). Similarly, lang is persistently mentioned
along with performers like Lyle Lovett and Dwight Yoakam, articulated
as a group of people who are revamping country music "from the outside" (Jennings and Bell 50, Bayles 1); lang is referred to in the *Washington Post* as the first of a new breed of "postmodern country singers"
(Harrington, Shales, and Kempley C7). Indeed, collapsing the two
themes, *Maclean's* refers to her as a "bracing breeze from the west who
has helped to invigorate country music" (Jennings and Gregor 58).
Both of these themes clearly situate lang as inside yet outside Nashville
as a geographic location and as an industry. As befits a so-called postmodern singer, her national and industry borders are slippery and in
motion.

Lang's position as campy performance artist is also persistently highlighted as a means of explaining the ways she troubles identity categories and thus troubles her "reading" as a legitimate country artist.
Maclean's observes that lang will have to face concerns about her
"campiness" if she hopes to provide evidence of her seriousness and
stability as a country artist. Indeed, in a rather telling passage, Nicholas
Jennings and Celina Bell observe that in an attempt to move toward
legitimacy, "in concert, she [lang] has even appeared in a blue sequined
evening gown and long white gloves" (50). What would perhaps have
been described by lang herself as a form of drag or performative art is
here discussed as a sincere attempt at legitimacy. A review of lang's

Shadowland notes that her "wacky humor" has often led country music fans to question her seriousness (Jennings and Gregor 58). The same article quotes a reporter from the Nashville *Tennessean*, employing another geographic metaphor, that of borders, in declaring himself troubled by lang's status because "she is in some kind of weird place between artsy new wave and country." The reporter further notes that lang's constantly changing look—from colorful square-dance skirts to dark pantsuits—acts as a stumbling block toward her being understood by the country music audience (Jennings and Gregor 59). Her history as an aspiring roller-derby queen and a truck driver, along with her use of performance props such as wigs and a rocking horse, are cited as additional factors undermining a consistent persona (Jennings and Gregor 59). Carl Mollins notes that most country music purists didn't know if lang was being serious or mocking country music as she changed her look, turning from rhinestone glasses to cowboy boots (15). In a similar vein, many reviews of lang's eventual Grammy-winning *Absolute Torch and Twang* question lang's authenticity as a country artist, even while praising her vocal abilities. One reviewer calls lang's recording a "remolding of the clichés itself" (Cook 48). *People* observes that lang is hammy and "overdoes" the country style (Hiltbrand 22); the *Washington Post* notes that the recording illustrates lang's status as a performance artist whose oddball performances often undermine her genuine country vocals (Swisher C8), while the *New York Times* review recounts lang's history in country music as one of drama, irony, and humor (Holden, "k.d. lang" C12), and the *Los Angeles Times* notes that her music falls "prey to studied effects and calculated corn," undercutting the spine-tingling dynamics of her vocals (Lee, "Lower-Case" V5). Throughout such claims, lang's status as a "true" country artist is persistently questioned precisely because of her constantly troubling use of performance and existing categories. Moreover, while writers reify those categories and norms in describing lang's performance (i.e., "she is between country and new wave"), they clearly find her performance and claims troubling of the categories as adequate containers.

Finally—and, I argue, significantly—lang's gender and sexuality receive constant attention during this early phase of her career; such commentary generally focuses on lang's clothing and mannerisms and com-

Confusing lesbian

parisons of her style or look with that of other performers, especially those in the country tradition. In multiple ways, critics express concern about lang's status within the genre, given her playfulness with masculine signifiers. I want to emphasize again that lang's play with signifiers of gender and sexuality are especially "troubling" (and hence potentially productive change on a cultural level) precisely because this "troubling" takes place within a tradition that requires tightly constrained and stratified gender/sexual categories.[10]

One of the ways this gender trouble is expressed by news outlets and music critics is through a comparison of lang to other performers from country music's past. The most persistent comparison—partially a result of lang's own discourse—is to Patsy Cline, but it is an ambivalent and often undermined comparison that works hand in hand with comparisons to Minnie Pearl, Dolly Parton, and Elvis to trouble lang's style and gender performances. Hence, while she is frequently compared to Patsy Cline both vocally and in terms of attitude (her claims to be the reincarnation of Cline are a dominant theme; see Jennings and Gregor 59; Appelo 18; Adams 1), she is also compared to Minnie Pearl in terms of her playfulness and campiness and to Elvis Presley in terms of her sensuality (Hochman 77). While she may be called a "husky dead ringer for Patsy Cline" in *Rolling Stone* (Guterman 138), she is also called a "high camp" version of Patsy Cline in *Maclean's* (Jennings and Bell 50). How well she fulfills the role of Patsy Cline is debated, generally simultaneously with discussions about her use of "masculine" style signifiers. Hence, lang is often referred to as "boyish" (Jennings and Gregor 58), and her "mannish" appearance is contrasted with the "pronounced femininity" of most female country artists. Lang is described as having "cropped hair" and "male attire" in a review of *Shadowland* (Jennings and Gregor 59). *Savvy* describes her as a tomboy who wears "sawed off cowboy boots and second hand ranchwear" (Appelo 18). While being contrasted to Dolly Parton in the *New York Times*, lang is described as "clad in denims, her hair short and spiky" (Holden, "Down-Home" 221). Similarly, in a review of *Absolute Torch and Twang*, lang is described as a "severe looking young woman" (Cook 48), while a *Rolling Stone* review of the video retrospective *Harvest of Seven Years* notes that "from her blunt cut hair to her shitkicker boots, k.d. lang bludgeons every female country star cliché" (Farber 102).

Although the Patsy Cline comparisons are messy and troubled in and of themselves, the simultaneous move to compare lang to Elvis Presley (and the fact that it is consistently reported that Madonna first made this comparison with approval) also adds to the confusion concerning her style and its meaning in relation to country music and sexuality. For example, the *Los Angeles Times* describes lang as looking "a bit like a poor man's (or make that woman's) Elvis" (Lee V5; see also Wilson). These comparisons to Elvis are accompanied with descriptions of lang's preference for pickup trucks as a form of transportation recreation. A *Vanity Fair* interview metaphorically and semiotically plays with lang's gender by providing her with a forum to discuss different Chevy trucks and their uses beyond "tooling" around Vancouver (evidently, they're useful for hauling grain and drinking beer at bush parties) (Ginsburg 202). Where does one place lang, then, when critics simultaneously articulate her with hypermasculine and hyperfeminine icons and signifiers?

When we couple concerns about lang's gender identity with questions about her "authenticity" as a country musician, we find an artist who troubles gender signifiers, sexual categories, and musical performance norms within country music, problematizing the borders of sound and vision, both within country music as a genre and, through the mass mediated magazines, within dominant culture at large. Indeed, lang exposes the gender, sexual, and musical assumptions (bi-gendered, heteronormative, and based in authenticity) of country music through her play with these categories. As a result, the public discussion and representation of lang exposes not only the stratification of country music norms but also the iterated norms of the dominant culture from which these categories are drawn (i.e., as a genre, country is a hyperarticulation of norms already existing in dominant cultural assumptions). If we return once again to Marjorie Garber, we can expand her claim about the ways in which ambiguous gender signifiers function: "It is as though the hegemonic cultural imaginary is saying to itself: if there is a difference, we want to be able to see it, and if we see a difference . . . , we want to be able to interpret it" (130). Rather than being solely about questions of gender signifiers, lang's public persona and its conjunction with country music as a genre troubled visual and aural categories, leading to a public discourse that struggled to tie lang down: country or new wave? authentic or inauthentic? man or woman? insider or outsider? If categories are to be relatively restabilized—a never-ending process—lang would have to be situated in each of these categories with their borders more clearly defined. If we see the troubling of categories, including gender, sexuality, and authenticity, as politically productive in that such trouble, like Attali's "noise," forces us to see the commonsense meaning of dominant ideology as strange or alien, then we might celebrate this portion of lang's career precisely for helping create a condition in which "common sense" is questioned. As I will suggest, however, simultaneous changes in lang's appearance and musical style, coupled with changes in the public articulation of her sexuality, help reaffirm stable commonsense categories. Further, this reaffirmation is met with praise and ideological affirmation by critics and reporters who have an ideological frame within which to understand her.

THE WOUNDED SONGBIRD AND THE POLITICS OF TRUTH

As noted earlier, Stella Bruzzi argues that lang's "coming out" as a lesbian was articulated along with her move away from a traditional country sound and away from an eclectic and irreverent personal style. Consequently, lang simultaneously moved from a challenging position of androgyny-as-ambiguity to a less challenging one of androgyny-as-lesbian-in-men's-clothes. That is, while the term "androgyny" is applied to lang in both phases of her career, early on it refers to an ambiguity or confusion while later it refers more to a cut-and-paste mixing of "normal" gender signifiers by a person whose gender and sexuality are themselves stratified and unambiguous. In short, in this new phase we witness an example of what John Fiske and John Hartley have referred to as "ideological claw back" (86–87), in which uncomfortable ambiguity (noise, visual and aural confusion) is replaced by a system of sounds, visuals, and social categories that are understandable and familiar, that are "musical." As Bruzzi notes as a spectator and fan herself, "Watching k.d. lang is no longer . . . difficult. She has entered the realm of easy-looking" (203). In her reading, the problem with lang's sound and appearance (and she links the two) after *Absolute Torch and Twang* is that it contains "an enigmatic, vague play on implied lesbian sexuality, but without the inherent danger of the work up to *Torch and Twang* which was informed by the actual absence of any explicit statement by lang about her sexuality" (203). While Bruzzi's descriptions of the changes of sound and position are difficult ones with which to argue, I again want to stress that one's endorsement or criticism of this public move to music over noise, stratified androgyny over troubling ambiguity, is based on one's politics, one's comfort or discomfort with the politics of queered ambiguity over a politics of marked and delineated lesbianism as a politics of truth.

What I want to do now is map out some of the ways in which changes in representations and discussions of lang in print media outlets operate either to reflect or to complicate Bruzzi's reading. In addition to suggesting that much of Bruzzi's argument is reflected in the discourse about lang, I want to trace out the ways lang's move to a "truthful" and unambiguous lesbian identity and butch aesthetic is ideologically (and arguably financially) rewarding because it is coupled with the higher cultural capital genre of the torch singer. While I do not want to suggest that lang's transformation in style and appearance and her shift to a different musical tradition are necessarily linked or even intentional on her part (indeed, the causes of this transition are irrelevant in terms of the changes in meaning that take place in popular culture), I do want to note how transformation works to the ideological benefit of her marking as lesbian.

When k.d. lang's "outing" is discussed in essays published on the release of *Ingenue* and thereafter, it is layered with the politics of "truth" and confession. As Bonnie Dow notes in her analysis of the "coming out" discourse surrounding Ellen DeGeneres, such "truth telling" illustrates both a belief in a stable and core individual identity and the continuing power of what Foucault points to as a confessional ritual for the expression of that "central unambiguous" truth about the self. Lang's "tension reducing" truthfulness about her lesbianism, her "true self," is articulated by both lang and reporters as part of a larger need to disclose completely her "truest beliefs," including her sexual identity and her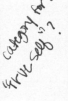

political causes. Hence, the expression of her belief in vegetarianism and her identity as lesbian both operate for lang as an opportunity to be "true to her self." The *New York Times*, for example, observes that "k.d. lang is the type of politically radical vegetarian lesbian defender of wildlife you'd want to bring home to mother" (Specter C1); *Rolling Stone* repeatedly refers to lang as the "proliferating lesbian, feminist, egalitarian" (Udovitch 54),[11] and, more directly, *Mademoiselle* notes that "you'd expect k.d. lang to be a sergeant (at least) in the p.c. police. After all, her two most famous nonmusical performances were denouncing the meat industry and coming out as a lesbian" (Small 104).

Significantly, the discussion of lang's "coming out" is almost always coupled with some discussion—overt or subtle—of the importance of such truth telling in allowing the person to express the *true self*. In the *Los Angeles Times*, Richard Cromelin writes that "after years of 'is she or isn't she' speculation, lang *unburdened* herself in an interview in the June 16 issue of *The Advocate*" (CAL5; emphasis added). In the well-known Cindy Crawford–shaving *Vanity Fair* cover article, we learn the longstanding truth of lang's lesbianism: "There is little doubt which gender her true love will be. Lang knew she was a lesbian before she ever learned the word" (Bennetts 143). Even while lang offers multiple explanations of why one might be lesbian, including both "causal" and cultural factors (she includes choice, genetics, and childhood abuse as some possibilities), the interview persistently emphasizes the naturalness, the *essentialness*, of lang's own sexuality and her "easy relationship" with it (Bennetts 143). Similarly, reviews of Victoria Starr's biography *k.d. lang: All You Get Is Me* repeatedly note lang's "courage" in admitting the truth. Hence, lang is referred to as "the first openly lesbian pop icon" (Stuttaford 76; see also Kuda). In perhaps the clearest statement of this articulation of "outing" with truth, a *New York Times* review of *All You Can Eat* quotes lang claiming that her self-outing "eliminated a lot of unspoken tension. . . . It's really a fantastic feeling. I highly recommend to anybody in this situation to *live in the truth*" (Pareles 37; emphasis added). In short, in multiple ways and in multiple discussions, lang is consistently represented as the lesbian vegetarian who must speak "truth" about her "self."

As Bruzzi notes, the settling of the "Is she or isn't she?" dilemma is coupled with a shift to a less ambiguous and stable form of androgyny, an androgyny that maintains the "truth" of gender semiotics even while lang mixes them, that is, lang is now represented as a woman wearing men's clothes rather than as something more questionable or mysterious. Thus, somewhat ironically in conventional terms, while the question of lang's sexuality was an almost palpable "problem" in the past, it is no longer a cause of trouble; indeed, her sexuality and style almost completely drop out as questionable issues in mass mediated discussions. Instead, her gender "appropriateness" and her sexuality—now truthfully exposed and signified more conventionally—fit snugly within existing categories. When her style was performed as ambiguous, she was rarely represented as sexually attractive. After expressing the "truth" about her lesbianism, however, lang ironically becomes sexually attractive (potentially) to everyone at once. For example, *Vanity Fair* notes that "it doesn't seem to matter whether they're lesbians, gay men, or straight couples: the middle-aged husband next to me is screaming, 'kd—you're beautiful!' His wife is just screaming . . . even Madonna is smitten" (Bennetts 98). Further, the author remarks that while lang used to be open to a wide variety of clothing, "these days lang is most likely to appear onstage in what some describe as 'men's clothes'" (Bennetts 98). Similarly, *Rolling Stone* notes that whereas in her country phase no one was sure what to make of her, "as a chanteuse, her appeal is pansexual. . . . She is a babe. She is one butch babe" (Udovitch 56). In a *Washington Post* review of a concert performance by lang, we read that her "close-cropped hair and mannish appearance" marked a move away from confusion and toward "butch lesbian chic" (Graves WBK8). To summarize, then: stable gender and sexual signifiers provide a much stronger base toward which others can direct and, more important, understand their attraction and desires.

Examples of lang's move to a more pansexual attractiveness are numerous, seemingly articulated with every mention of her. A review of *Salmonberries* notes that "with her fragile shoulders, long arms, and gigantic hands, lang is a ravishing androgyne" (Hinson D7). Later, in an interview after the release of *Drag*, lang observes about her own appearance in *Ellen*'s "puppy episode" that she chose to move away from this "ravishing androgyne" look "to what I think of as a stereotypical dyke. . . . So I had the Mohawk wig and the black leather vest and all those gay buttons" (Gardner F1:4). In an article accompanying a photo shoot in *Vogue*, author Charles Gandee and lang discuss her clothing style, lang observes that whereas she wore a lot of different outfits early in her career as part of her performance, she now has a style that is more directly an expression of her own desires and tastes (147). Finally, in an article in *Maclean's*, the authors note that while lang is now something of a chanteuse and dresses the part, in the past she would mix styles, performing in Nancy Sinatra wigs, as Patsy Cline, and as a lesbian poster girl (Dickie 78). In short, her constantly changing costumes and styles in the past are now seen as part of a "performance," while her current style of dress, like her sexuality, is a more consistent expression of the "self." In each of these articles we, like Bruzzi, find that lang has become "easy looking," easy listening, ideological music rather than noise. Although lang obviously troubles dominant culture simply as an "out" lesbian, the types of trouble she causes, and the way she troubles gender and sexuality as a whole, are clearly different, and clearly tamed. No longer do her "drag" and her sexual ambiguity trouble audiences; now her stably signified androgyny helps make lang appealing to everyone.

To my mind, one of the most interesting aspects of this case, and one rarely commented on, has to do with the links between the changes in lang's style/music/sexual representation and the changes in cultural capital that accrue as a result. Such changes are interesting on any number of levels, but clearly, lang's move to a less ambiguous and less troubling sexual/gender representation, and its accompanying loss of ideological noise, is coupled with a rise in the cultural capital associated with her musical practice. While this move in gender/sexual representation is somewhat distinct from her change in musical style, it clearly accompanies it and works to reinforce her status as a highly cultured chanteuse rather than a low country singer. The relations between the cultural capital of the music and her other changes are articulated together in this case, hence endowing the "truthfulness" of lesbianism with higher capital than the troubling performativity lang had produced within the country genre. Again, while I am not arguing for a causal link, the relative levels of cultural capital granted to the musical genres of country and torch serve to reaffirm the higher status associated with lang's confession of the truth about self.

Before I provide a textual reading of this transition, I want to acknowledge, that how one decides to value this articulation is dependent on one's politics. Clearly, if one wishes to encourage the rhetoric of "truth telling" that fits within contemporary ideologies, one would applaud this link, but if one wishes to highlight instead the discourse of performative gender troubling, one would find this link troubling.[12]

One line from a *Los Angeles Times* article about lang at the time of the release of *Ingenue* is a model of the change in discourse, as is the title *Ingenue* itself. Reporter Chris Wilman notes the transition in lang's musical genres in the following terms: "So long, chaps and spurs, and howdy—er, *bon jour*—to the wounded songbird" (Wilman CAL63). I want to pause for just a moment and compare this remark to one by R. J. Smith about the 1998 Kiss reunion tour: "Kiss went out as cheese," Smith observes, "and they have come back as, well . . . *fromage*" (40). In each case we see a reference to a musical past with little to offer beyond cheeky humor (as distinct from art) and—though marked by a hesitant pause in each case ("Howdy, er . . ." and "well . . . ," respectively)—a present and future of greater artistic value, a transition marked by the employment of French, a language that "commonsensically" signifies high cultural capital. In the case of the band Kiss, they are no longer simple American cheese but a higher cultural capital version—cheese with taste. Similarly, lang moves from a "chaps and spurs" aesthetic that would have been content with a "Howdy" to a wounded songbird who more readily recognizes its French translation.[13] As I will show, this rhetoric of a transition from "campiness" to sophistication is consistently evoked in discussions of *Ingenue* as well as in more contemporary retellings of lang's career.

In reviews of *Ingenue*, critics note that the recording marks a move away from Nashville, from country, from an aesthetic of simplemindedness, from an appeal to the body to an appeal to the mind. Hence, Chris Wilman writes that "the eccentric Canadian songstress is headed well away from Nashville with *Ingenue*, made up entirely of tortured, *philosophical*, very languid pop balladry" (CAL63; emphasis added). *Maclean's* notes that *Ingenue* gives evidence of the "serious singer" who had always lurked behind the "tongue in cheek country exterior" but who had "marred" her earlier music with hoedown humor and country affectations (Jennings S5). The *Washington Post* review, drawing on a metaphor that hierarchizes the written over the aural, calls *Ingenue* a "long, contemplative poem" rather than a simple pop album (Joyce B7). Finally, *Interview* notes that lang has moved from simple country accompaniment to full-scale orchestration (Rogers 34).[14]

Not only is *Ingenue* posited as cerebral and sophisticated rather than visceral and formulaic—highlighting the classic high-low cultural distinction between pleasures of the mind and pleasures of the body—but the contrast between this recording and lang's former country career, as well as country music as a whole, is also highlighted. For example, the *New York Times* notes that the songs on *Ingenue* are "unusually *cerebral and internal*" and that the album is very different from what normally "comes from country" (Schoemer H29, emphasis added; see also Milward 57). In a different and lengthy *New York Times* article, a discussion of lang's offbeat and constantly changing clothing style during her country period contrasts with a discussion of her rise as a singer of a higher style of music. Hence, the performative style of her early career is equated with the lower cultural capital of country music, while her "truth-telling" androgynous phase is articulated with her new musical genre and style: "After more than a decade as a boot stomping cowgirl with a buzz cut and punk pretensions, Ms. Lang, a 30 year old former farmhand from southern Alberta, has suddenly emerged from her rhinestone studded chrysalis as one of pop music's most resonant torch singers." The writer goes on to note her segue from "a life of hoop skirts" to her current role as "an edgy chanteuse" (Specter C1). In the same piece, lang's collaborator Ben Mink notes that lang could never fit into country music precisely because country music is formulaic whereas lang has always been interested in musical expansion and provocation. As Mink notes elsewhere about country music and its fan base, in a clear expression of the mind-body link used here to explain lang's commercial failure in that genre: "They're threatened by what they don't understand . . . people who think a little bit too much and write about that thought in words that aren't blatantly about drinking or cars" (Udovitch 55). Lang herself, quoted in the *Los Angeles Times*, recalls that when she was performing as a country artist, she thought the entire idea was to put on different identities, to make fun of yourself, to make fun of being a hillbilly. When such irony didn't work in Nashville, however, she had no choice but to move back to her earlier influences such as "classical music," which she had "studied" for years (Cromelin CAL5).[15] Finally, in recounting lang's career in 1995, Brian Johnson notes that lang first burst onto the Nashville scene as a kitsch cartoon, a country punk "in spiky hair, sawed off boots and cat's eye glasses with no glass in them" ("Lighter" 68). While her persona changed often in country music, Johnson writes, she ultimately had to leave because country worships only "big hair, big steaks and values" (68).

It is worth emphasizing that even while lang's musical style has continued to change with each recording, the public perception of her career remains consistent. In a *Newsday* review of a Tony Bennett–k.d. lang concert, Steve Matteo observes that lang's set "reflected the maturation process of lang's jazz side. There was little evidence of the campy effects of . . . lang's past"; moreover, the show illustrated "an emphasis on artistry as opposed to personality" (B09). Similarly, the *Daily News* observes that "the singer who first made a splash as a campy, country-fied crooner has transformed herself into a sophisticated singer-songwriter" (Guzman 42). In a number of reviews of, and interviews surrounding, her *Invincible Summer* CD, similar observations and claims are made. First, reviewers consistently emphasize that the CD's title is a portion of a quotation from "French philosopher Albert Camus" (Muther L5).[16] Further, lang herself attests that once she saw that "my life is my art" (Graff 16), she was able to liken her music to something more akin to "sculpting or constructing, being an architect of sound" (Brown 7D), that her music can be compared to an artistic practice like "Meryl Streep's acting" (Nichols 3). Even years after her transition from country to torch and other genres, lang has been moved culturally from campy hack to sophisticated stylist.

An observation in *Vanity Fair* concerning this transition may serve as a conclusion to this discussion. In a lengthy article about lang's career, Leslie Bennetts notes that for lang, *Ingenue* was a bid to break free of all the tightly constrained categories and formulas of country music. What I have been attempting to argue here is that in moving away from the noise lang's performance had produced within the tight constraints of one genre, she moved herself into a domain of higher cultural capital in which her performance is far less challenging, in terms of both music and presentation of the gendered self. Perhaps somewhat ironically, lang's gender/sexual/aesthetic ambiguity was far more troubling in a formulaic genre associated with low cultural capital than in a genre associated with higher cultural capital. While lang may have been breaking free of the categories of country music, the discourse about lang is ultimately able to "make sense of her" only in the process of transition. This is true regardless of how contingent a link these two transitions have to each other. Lang moves from troubling gender, sexuality, and genre categories ("What is she?" "Is she for real?" "Is she lesbian or not?") to reaffirming generic and gender categories ("She is an authentic artist and sophisticated butch lesbian"). While it would be criminal to dismiss the real courage it took for lang to come out as a lesbian, and while it would be negligent to ignore the very progressive politics of her having done so, it is worthy of our attention to note the ways in which gender, sexuality, cultural capital, and ideology all function as part of a matrix that rewards music and disciplines noise.

In the most general terms, I have argued that public representations of k.d. lang's career verify Stella Bruzzi's reading of the k.d. lang star text. The discourse of public culture—the public articulation of k.d. lang— illustrates that lang moved from being a gender- and genre-troubling performer to being both "easy looking" and "easy listening." Again, if noise represents ideological struggle and turmoil, then the trouble lang enacted within the formal structures of country music—both in terms of music and in terms of gender expectations—was clearly noisy. While her music may have fit well within the low capital form of country music, her ongoing play with androgyny as ambiguity ("Who does she sleep with?" "How can she be both country *and* vegetarian?") rather than as style ("She's a woman in men's clothing," "She's a lesbian, a vegetarian, a sophisticated artist") was troubling in terms of sexuality, gender, and aesthetic. Further, for causing noise at this level, lang was disciplined in the ways that "noise makers" always are: press reports note not only the difficulty she had in being understood by mainstream audiences, but also her numerous public difficulties with the country music establishment.

When lang altered her style of sound and her aesthetic—moving from noise within country music to music within the torch tradition, from performative confusion to butch aesthetic—she initially met with both financial and ideological success. Moreover, the discourse about lang addressed the more direct style of her new trajectory, seeing it as one of ideological and musical clarity. In effect, lang's transition from the spurs and chaps of country music to a more sophisticated continental aesthetic is accompanied by clarifications in her presentation of identity. Again, while I do not mean to argue that there is a planned or causal connection between the changes in lang's musical style and her self-presentation, the public articulation of k.d. lang should force us, as critics and political actors, to recognize once again the larger matrix of disciplinary mechanisms that make changes in identity categories and ideology so difficult.

FOUR

The Disciplining of Female Masculinity

Janet Reno as
"the Lesbian Swamp Monster"

[Sojourner] Truth was alternatively and overdeterminedly constructed as either
invisible or visible, constituting either lack or surplus. . . . But as a woman lecturer,
Truth was fully exposed to the public gaze and perceived as unruly and excessive.
Carla Peterson, "Doers of the Word"

When Bill Clinton's first two choices for attorney general were derailed
after news reports exposed that each had legal issues regarding the nannies for their children, Clinton turned to Janet Reno, state attorney for
Dade County, Florida, as his next choice. Not only did Reno have legal
experience and public standing that made her fit for the job, but also,
and significantly, she was childless and therefore had had no cause to
hire nannies of any type. Reno, it was hoped, would come to the public
stage with no hidden baggage to derail her confirmation. Ironically,
however, while Reno's demographic status as childless and unmarried
may have helped her during the confirmation process, when coupled
with what many read as Reno's masculine style or aesthetic, it proved to
present its own types of trouble—especially given her position of public
power—by disrupting gender norms and expectations.

Although this was not the sort of trouble that would lead to a with-
drawal of Reno's nomination, the gender anxiety that was provoked was
widespread enough—and consistent enough—that Liza Mundy would
ask in the *Washington Post Magazine*, as late as 1998, "What is it about
Janet Reno that so fascinates and confounds and even *terrifies* America"
(6; emphasis added)?[1] What is it, indeed, about Reno that proved to be

so aesthetically and politically troubling that it continued to be an issue throughout her tenure as U.S. attorney general and her 2002 primary campaign for the governorship of Florida? While there are certainly a number of viable ways to approach this question, I argue here that Reno's aesthetic, her demographic status, her body, and her position of governmental and public power combined to trouble expectations of gender and sexuality. Hence, the public representations of Reno—the public debate about her—prove telling with regard to our cultural common sense concerning gender, sexuality, and power. Thus, an investigation of the gender/sexual panic that emerged in discourse "about" Janet Reno and Reno's body, especially given her role as a "representative of the republic" of sorts, is simultaneously an investigation of the meaning of gender in our culture's body politic.

Reno is one of a large number of contemporary women cited by Judith Halberstam as examples of "female masculinity" (*Female* 15). Arguing from a performative perspective on gender and sexuality, Halberstam suggests that masculinity is not a style owned by, or *essentially* tied to, men; neither masculinity nor femininity is linked directly to genitals. Observing that "heroic masculinity has been produced by and across both male and female bodies" (2), Halberstam argues that female masculinity is a particularly fruitful site of investigation because it has been "received by heterosexual and homosexual normative cultures as a pathological sign of misidentification and maladjustment, as a longing to be and to have a power that is always just out of reach" (9). Because female masculinity is a form of gender ambiguity that is so troubling to "commonsense" culture, it becomes a key location from which to view the forms not only of modern masculinity and femininity but also of their cultural ties to males and females, respectively, including the articulation of heterosexuality as a norm or expectation.[2] In this way, the study of the public discourse *about* Janet Reno is simultaneously a study of how gender ambiguity is handled in popular culture and public argument and a site of controversy in which we can see the performative expectations placed on contemporary men and women. Reno's case is an especially interesting one because she occupied a role in a nominally representative democracy in an administration that claimed to choose cabinet members and make appointments that reflected the face of the

nation. Hence, because constraint is "the very condition of performativity" (Butler, *Bodies* 95), and because Reno was a public figure who was
implicitly expected at least to *appear* representative of the interests and
"common sense" of the populace at large, the constraints placed on such
a figure are tight indeed. As a result of this constraining context, gender
expectations at the level of popular culture are revealed in this case in a
particularly crystallized manner.

In this chapter I investigate and problematize the ways in which Janet
Reno's masculinity has been understood and articulated in print news
media—the ways in which her masculinity has in effect been "disciplined" or explained out of "normal" existence. Although the comic
sketches that appeared on shows like *Saturday Night Live* clearly indicate that Reno's performance is troubling (i.e., "we" collectively make
fun of her masculinity because it is so alien to our understanding of
proper female performance),[3] I have chosen to look instead at a large
number of newspaper articles that appeared throughout Reno's tenure
as attorney general and during her Florida gubernatorial campaign. My
analysis focuses on Reno's gender performance only as it serves as an
underlying assumption of these news reports as a whole. That is, rather
than explicitly focusing on gender trouble, such news reports and personality profiles claim to provide an "objective" description of Reno
and, in the process, reveal underlying cultural anxieties and assumptions
about gender performance through overt descriptions of her body and
metaphoric descriptions of her actions.[4]

Because a count of individual news articles that discuss Reno
throughout her career would number in the high thousands, I have
limited my analysis to the following topic areas: descriptions of Reno
upon her nomination for, and confirmation as, attorney general; personality profiles of Reno; descriptions of her struggle with Parkinson's
disease; descriptions of Reno after the Branch Davidian standoff in
Waco, Texas; accounts of the Elian Gonzalez case; and accounts of her
failed gubernatorial campaign in Florida.[5] I have chosen these topical
areas for my analysis because these were the areas persistently referred
to in more general preliminary looks at public print discourse about
Reno. As a result, I assume that these are important nodal points for

representations of Reno as a public figure, and hence of the *public fig-uring* of gender and sexuality.

My critical reading of what these essays reveal about contemporary culture's performative constraints on gender and sexuality is played out on the following three grounds. First, I discuss overt descriptions of Reno's physical size, its articulation with masculinity, its meaning in the contemporary cultural context, and the historical role of such descrip-tions as one means of understanding, and ideologically disciplining, women in positions of public power. Second, and relatedly, I turn to discussions of Reno's "toughness," both in terms of attitude and in terms of her physical desires and abilities. In this section, I also discuss the ways in which the advent of Parkinson's disease proves particularly troubling, given the earlier articulation of her physical abilities and their links to masculinity. Finally, given that Reno was said to have been chosen by Clinton in part precisely because she did not have children, I turn to discussions surrounding Reno's family status and presumed (and troubled) sexuality. Here I explore the ways in which discussions of the Elian Gonzalez case worked within discussions of Reno's relationship with children. Ultimately, as Judith Halberstam would have it, in inves-tigating the ways in which Reno troubles femininity and is ideologically disciplined as a result, we learn something about the assumptions that protect the link between masculinity and males, femininity and females, gender and heterosexuality, as well as between men, women, and posi-tions of power.

SIX-FOOT-TWO IN STOCKING FEET

From the first news reports concerning her nomination to those cover-ing her subsequent run for the governorship of Florida, Reno's height is the single most persistent trope invoked to describe her. Moreover, because of its privileged placement in the lead of many articles, it often functions as Reno's most important attribute. Indeed, if one were to read all of the articles about Reno at once, one would be hard-pressed to claim that readers were not obsessed with her height. A number of examples set the tone for this aspect of Reno's representation. Early on, the *New York Times* observes that Reno is "demanding, outspoken, and,

[Chapter Four]

at 6 feet 1½ inches tall, a physically imposing boss" (Rohter A1); the *Los Angeles Times* notes that her "6-foot, 2-inch height in stocking feet made her taller than both President Clinton and Vice President Al Gore" (Ostrow, "Reno" A1); combining references to height with allusions to vigor, the *Washington Post* comments that Reno is "after all, a 6 foot 2 woman who chain saws trees for relaxation" and that her colleagues secretly refer to her by names such as "Bigfoot," "Her Tallness," and "The Tall One" (Blumenfeld B1); *Time* titles a story "Standing Tall"; the *National Journal* refers to her as the "imposing 6 foot 2 Reno" ("Janet Reno"); while the *New York Times Magazine* refers to her as a "6 foot, 2 inch stone wall" (Goldberg 19). Finally, at the beginning of her run for governor of Florida, *Weekly Standard* senior writer Matt Labash refers to Reno's height and then, after noting that people approach her with the subtlety of a Sasquatch sighting, he recalls a moment on the campaign trail when Reno passed out and fell over onstage, "her size 13 gunboats peeping out from behind the rostrum" (21). Moreover, during the gubernatorial campaign, David Wasson of the *Tampa Tribune* artic-ulates Reno's height with her "feminist" personality by noting that Reno had been a "tall, opinionated Miami school girl who refused to back down to men" (A1). In these instances and many more, direct references to Reno's height and the "imposing" nature of such stature provides the reader with a frame through which to understand other comments and observations about her personality and actions.[6]

I should make clear that the issue of Reno's height is not utilized to assert size solely as a matter of public record; rather, such descriptions function as metaphors for the power Reno is seen as wielding over others. For example, in a *Washington Post* piece that is nominally focused on the issue of Reno's integrity (e.g., her unwillingness to accept gifts), we find the following description of Reno after she had been offered a free lunch by a register clerk: "Finally, Reno's large hand emerges from her bag. . . . She tells people she'll pay for her meal. She stamps her foot on 'paying.' It's not a little foot" (Blumenfeld B8). Further, in observing Reno's style as an orator, Lincoln Caplan observes in the *New York Times Magazine* that Reno is "large-boned, and as she looks out at her audi-ence with an intense, darting gaze, she appears to embody the power of the office of Attorney General" (42). In such descriptions, Reno's size is articulated with other aspects of her personality, helping re-produce Reno as larger-than-life, excessive.

What is to be made of such overt references to Reno's size? What is to be made of the fact that such descriptions have followed her throughout her public career? On the one hand, of course, Reno's height is certainly noticeable as a "natural" difference. That is, I do not mean to deny that Reno is empirically taller than the average woman, nor do I mean to deny that this observation is often made by people when they first encounter her.[7] Reno's height and size, however, are more than simply observed; rather, there has been a minor cultural obsession with Reno's height and size, evident in the fact that so many articles not only mention her size but also utilize it as an opening comment. Indeed, when *Saturday Night Live*'s Will Ferrell noted that the entire basis of his caricature of Reno came down to the simple fact "that she's tall" (Mundy 22), it is clear that there is an anxiety-producing connection between height, gender, and Reno's position of power.

We can arguably understand the anxiety about size as operating both within the specific historical moment and as a long-standing theme in U.S. cultural and political discourse. In terms of our current cultural milieu, Susan Bordo argues in *Twilight Zones* that throughout the 1990s—the very period when Reno rose to national prominence—U.S. culture was witnessing the rise of a different aesthetic at a time when some of the benefits of feminism were coming to the fore. "Young women today," she writes, "more seemingly 'free' and claiming greater public space than was available to us at their age, appear especially concerned to establish with their bodies that, despite the fact that they are competing alongside men, they won't be too much" (138). While Bordo's focus is on the preference for smaller bodies and a more "bashful" female aesthetic in positions of power (especially in television and film representations of women in power), the reaction to Reno's height *→ Paper topic??* illustrates the very real ideological and economic danger faced by women who are literally or metaphorically "excessive" and hence are anxiety-producing in terms of the expectations of dominant U.S. gender norms. It is not Reno's height alone that is being pointed to in these reports; it is the size of Reno's physical body coupled with her position of power that makes her height a matter of public concern. Reno's is a large female body occupying a very visible and very powerful public space. That is, while Reno's physical body is the same height regardless of what that body does, its placement in a position of power makes it appear larger, worthy of comment, and thus excessive.

Regardless of its meaning within a temporally local context, the constraints on size and "excessiveness" are also deeply rooted in the discursive material of U.S. history. Indeed, women who have articulated challenges to dominant cultural assumptions regarding race and gender expectations have long been represented as "excessive," as grotesquely large—especially when these bodies do not fit culturally accepted ideas of "the body in power."[8] For example, in her excellent reading of the public representation of Sojourner Truth, Carla Peterson notes that Truth was often ignored in public discussions (i.e., made invisible), or, when discussed, was articulated as "unruly and excessive" (29). While Peterson makes clear that this characterization of Truth was the result of the combination of her physical appearance and the cultural expectations of contemporary culture in terms of race, gender, and public legitimacy, it is this same logic that partially accounts for the commentary about Reno's body. Reno is not just tall but excessively so; when she taps her foot, we are reminded that "it is not a little foot." Reno, we might say, encroaches on public expectations of gender and power "in a big way."

"RENO COMES FROM THE SWAMP"

In addition to (and complementary to) representations that focus on Reno's size, we find persistent representations that articulate Reno with a (masculine) "tough" demeanor and appearance. Through anecdotes about her interpersonal relations and her participation in traditionally masculine activities and descriptions of her background and origins relying on a rustic, self-made myth, Reno is reified as outside the norm of acceptable femininity—at times *monstrously* so. Moreover, as I will illustrate, the articulation of Reno with brash behavior and a proclivity toward traditionally masculine activities and attitudes is concretized through stories about her mother, who is repeatedly discussed as hard-drinking, hardworking, masculine, and eccentric.

In terms of interpersonal behavior and attitudes, the *New York Times*

notes on the occasion of her nomination as attorney general that Reno
had cultivated a reputation as outspoken: "As an example of her willing-
ness to speak her mind, ... she once told a group of juvenile court
judges they were 'dunderheads' and walked out of the convention they
were holding" (Rohter C1). Max Boot observes in the *Christian Science
Monitor* that Reno is known to have a "tough, no-nonsense management style" (8). Similarly, an editorial in *U.S. News and World Report*
claims that Reno is "blunt, strong willed, sometimes unsettling" ("Justice" 28), while a *Los Angeles Times* headline reads, "Janet Reno: The
Blunt Attorney General Speaks Her Mind—As Usual" (Ostrow,
"Blunt" A3), and a Miami lawyer confides to *U.S. News and World Report*
that Reno is "mean as hell" ("Rough" 32). Finally, a description by
Lincoln Caplan in the *New York Times* emphasizes characteristics traditionally associated with masculinity: "In her professional dealings, Reno
... comes across as formal, efficient, and even cold. Her mouth turns
down when her face is at rest and is framed by deep crescents, making
her look dour. Her unanimated look is sometimes called an icy stare"
(46).[9] While each description is interesting in and of itself, it is in combination with other descriptions of her physical activities that a fully
developed mosaic of masculinity appears.

One traditional masculine articulation emerges in representations of
Reno's "outdoorsman" skills and her affinity for animals and nature.
Early in the nomination process, the *New York Times* observes that when
Reno needs time and space to think about a particular issue, "she will
get in a canoe and paddle 30 or 40 miles" (Rohter A22). Further, Reno
chooses kayaking and canoeing over other more conventional pursuits:
"While the capital's elite attended state dinners and fancy fundraisers,
Reno would be out kayaking the Potomac River" (Epstein A4).[10] In a
profile piece during her gubernatorial campaign, we see the interest in
kayaking (and her height) linked to her lack of interest in more traditionally "feminine" pursuits even in her youth: "At 6-foot-1 and more
interested in studying and kayaking than in fashion and homecoming
dances, she wasn't exactly the kind of girl who was going to be chosen
prom queen" (Wasson A1). Moreover it is not simply her adeptness at
and affinity for canoeing which is stressed but also her physical superi-
ority over men. A 1997 piece in the *New York Times* reports how Reno,

in a bright orange life vest, "furiously paddles a kayak down the Potomac to escape the pressures of her office. A panting consort of FBI agents desperately tries to keep up by canoe; unsuccessful, they are ordered into kayak training so their important charge does not elude them in the future" (Johnston and Sontag 1).

Similar tales of her no-nonsense toughness and her connection with nature are widespread. In a feature story, *People Weekly* observes that when a pig once grabbed Reno's niece by the jacket as the girl tried to feed it, Reno "ran out and punched that hog right between the eyes" ("General" 40), and adds that "the 6 foot, 1 inch Florida native has wrestled alligators with Miccosukee Indians" (40). The *Washington Post*, reporting that Reno always makes it to her office regardless of weather conditions or other obstacles, notes that on the severest winter days, Reno could be seen marching "to work in her Everglades boots through a violent blizzard" (Blumenfeld B8). With phrasing that would seemingly fit more readily within the pages of an outdoorsmen's journal, the same writer observes that "Reno swam with water moccasins and alligators" and "slept to the percussive grunt of pig frogs, on ground flecked with shells from an ancient sea. *Reno comes from the swamp*" (Blumenfeld B1; emphasis added). Indeed, John Leo, in a *U.S. News and World Report* editorial, suggests that if her story were an opera, Reno would have to be played by a man (Dan Akroyd being his specific example) (12). In each instance, Reno is situated as excessive, as something more than woman—perhaps a man, perhaps something more exotic—emerging from the shells of the ancient sea. Again, as in Carla Peterson's reading of Sojourner Truth, Reno's position of power, coupled with her brand of masculinity, provides an unacceptable equation, within contemporary U.S. norms, of gender and gender performance.

This articulation of an almost primordial connection to swamps and other signifiers of intimidating masculinity reappears during her campaign for governor, when one headline reads, "Janet Reno Rides Again . . . into the Swamp of Florida Politics" (LaBash 21), and another announces "She's Baaaaack" (Lynch). Further, when Reno drove herself around Florida in a "used red pickup" truck as part of her campaign strategy, it was again highlighted in almost all coverage as a marker of Reno's gendered difference. For example, Matt LaBash notes that the

"Red Truck Tour" seemed designed to emphasize Reno's robust constitution (21), while both the *Economist* ("Enter") and *Newsweek* (Contreras) make note of the "barnstorming" red truck tour and the way it
underscores her image as a blunt and tough straight shooter. Finally,
the *Washington Post*'s Mark Leibovich fashions Reno as the "familiar
odd duck touring Florida in scuffed black shoes and a red Ford pickup"
(C1), while reporter Wes Allison of the *St. Petersburg Times* articulates
the truck with a variety of masculine signifiers in noting that, during
her "red truck tour," Reno "pumps her own gas. She thinks nothing of
changing clothes at a rest area. She drinks beer from a bottle" (1A).

Reno's connection with excessiveness—especially excessiveness not
usually associated with women—is figured genetically through descriptions of her mother, "Jane Wood Reno" (the name, with maiden name
intact, works within its cultural context to evoke thoughts of Hillary
Rodham Clinton). While there are several points at which her father, a
Danish immigrant who worked as police reporter for the *Miami Herald*,
is mentioned, the major story line of Reno's upbringing involves her
mother and the influence she had on her daughter's personality and
demeanor. In the *New York Times*, Larry Rohter describes Jane Wood
Reno as "a coarse-talking, hard-drinking, chain-smoking eccentric until
her death in December [1992] at the age of 79" (A22). Similarly, the
American Bar Association Journal refers to her as "an eccentric who
smoked, drank, swore, and wrestled alligators"; moreover, the journal
notes, Jane Wood Reno built the home the family lived in with her own
hands (Reske, "Reno" 18). These same signifiers are used repeatedly:
the *Washington Post* notes that Reno's mother was "a chain-smoking,
beer-chugging journalist" who built a house but refused to install air
conditioning, fans, an electric washer or dryer, or television (Blumenfeld B8). Lincoln Caplan reports in the *New York Times Magazine* that
Reno's mother built her own house, and that she was "she was a heavy
smoker and drinker, charmingly irascible, known for her short fuse and
sometimes truly antisocial behavior" (43). After the Clinton administration left office, *Newsweek* reports, Reno returned to the house "her
mother built" (Contreras).[11] In addition, in an interview with Reno's
brother, we are introduced not only to their mother but also to two
aunts who are described as "absolutely indomitable," one was a nurse,

"landing with General Patton's army in North Africa," while another was in the Women's Air Force, testing combat aircraft in order to make sure the planes would be safe for their male pilots ("Truth" 22). In each of these cases, the link between Reno and an ancestry of excessive, masculine women works to stress the way in which Reno herself is read.[12]

Because so much discursive work has highlighted Reno's subjectivity as a larger-than-life, masculine character, the reported onset of Parkinson's disease in 1995 acts to trouble this understanding. That is, if the ideal masculine body is one that resists disease, that is not "disabled," then Parkinson's clearly challenges this conception of a hypermasculine body and persona. In the discourse surrounding Reno and discussions of the disease, we see the emergence of signifiers that act as shortcuts to explain, or reassert, her masculinity. For example, when Reno first announced the diagnosis, the *Chicago Sun-Times* reported that "Parkinson's disease is an incurable degenerative illness that causes muscular stiffness and involuntary trembling; it also can alter mood and thinking" (Thomas and Brown 24). The same stress on the physical problems that emerge with Parkinson's appears in the *American Bar Association Journal*, which calls it "an incurable and degenerative syndrome that can lead to a loss of reflexes and a shuffling walk" (Reske, "Unflappable" 16), while *U.S. News and World Report* stresses that some people with Parkinson's "quickly lose so much control of their muscles that they can no longer walk, talk, or eat" (Watson 18). Clearly, one significant aspect of this discourse about Parkinson's is the way that it potentially undermines the masculine imagery associated with Reno. Nevertheless, in Reno's (and her supporters') responses to questions about the effects of Parkinson's on her ability to continue in a professional capacity, we see a reification of the signifiers of power through a persistent rearticulation of the signifiers of "natural" masculinity.

The defense of Reno's ability to maintain her performance as attorney general or, in the future, as governor of Florida, then, hinges discursively on her ability to sustain signifiers of physical masculinity rather than on, say, her leadership abilities or judgment capabilities. For example, in the *Naples Daily News*, Reno asserts that Parkinson's only makes her hands shake but that she still kayaks and enjoys outdoor activities (Spencer). In the *Daily News*, Reno asserts that even with Parkinson's, she will continue to "take her marathon hikes along the Potomac Canal" (Sisk 2).[13] The *Washington Post*'s Mark Leibovich observes that while Parkinson's might cause some minor problems for Reno, she has not abandoned her "regimen" of multiple campaign stops (C1). Leibovich's description of Reno's regimen includes reference to her gubernatorial campaign's "red pickup truck," which once again works as a signifier that ultimately reaffirms Reno's "strength" and masculinity here and in numerous other articles.[14] For example, when Matt Labash writes about Reno's "Red Truck Tour" of Florida, he notes that it was designed as "Reno's shot to prove she is robust enough to be governor" (21). Similar observations are made in the *Economist* ("Enter") and *Newsweek* (Contreras). I do not mean to suggest that Reno doesn't actually enjoy kayaking, hiking, or driving pickup trucks. I am arguing instead that the cultural need to reposition Reno as excessively masculine, given her physical appearance and her position of power, indicates something about how our culture understands the nexus of particular bodies, gender, and power. Moreover, to the degree that a physical ailment re-feminizes that body, the reemployment of particular signifiers (kayaking, "marathon" hikes, a red pickup truck) illustrates some of the semiotics of gender and how they function culturally, regardless of the intent of Reno and her campaign stuff. Indeed, when these signifiers alone are offered as a defense of Reno's strength as a cultural leader, cultural critics—especially those interested in gender—should take notice.

UNMARRIED, WITHOUT CHILDREN

When we couple Janet Reno's status as a childless single woman with her representation as a masculine, excessive female, we have a recipe for a public subjectivity that at the very least potentially troubles some of the basic gender assumptions implied by heteronormativity. That is, in the broadest sense, if the general heteronormative assumption—the "unmarked" person and lifestyle—is that a person in high office is married to someone of "the opposite sex" (with accompanying articulations of male-to-masculine and female-to-feminine signifiers) and has children, Reno's role as a masculine (male-signifying) never-married, childless woman troubles almost *every* aspect of those expectations. In this case, as in all cases of gender trouble (or even minor resistances to gendered expectations), mechanisms and queries work to erase or reduce that trouble. Public discourse assumes and endorses heteronormativity and acknowledges homosexuality but rarely recognizes queered genders or sexualities. Such an erasure, as I have underlined throughout, occurs in two primary ways: either Reno must be defended as a heterosexual or she must be represented as a lesbian. In neither case, however, is gender trouble successfully erased. In the first, Reno as masculine and unmarried female, she does not properly fulfill the demands of heteronormativity. In the second, while the lesbian explanation erases the troubling gender signifiers (i.e., Reno then matches the expectation that a "masculine" female must be lesbian), lesbianism itself—as well as female masculinity—remains troubling to bi-gendered heteronormativity, although, again, as we saw in the case of k.d. lang, it is less troubling than a queered or unrecognizable[15] gender/sexuality.

When Reno was first nominated as attorney general, the fact that she was childless was almost as much of a symptomatic obsession as discussions of her height. The day after her nomination, the *New York Times* emphasized several times that "Ms. Reno has never married or had children" (Rohter A22), while the *Los Angeles Times* observed that Reno is "single and has no children" (Ostrow, "Reno" A1), as did the *American Bar Association Journal* (Reske, "Reno" 18). Barbara Gordon raises the same specter in *Parade Magazine*, noting that "at 54, [Reno] is unmarried, without children" (5).[16] While I again want to make clear that I understand that this obsession derives in part—perhaps in large part— from the problems encountered by the two previous candidates, it is not simply the observation that Reno is childless that is interesting; rather, I am interested in the ways her status not only as childless but also as never married and not currently romantically involved is troubling and hence is "interpreted" by those writing about Reno. That is, in attempting to understand the meaning of Janet Reno, reporters and others act as ideological agents for culture at large in trying to make sense of the ways in which she evades cultural expectations of gendered behavior and gender signifiers.

The first way these writers erase Reno's gender trouble, then, is by stressing that she is a romantic heterosexual despite the ways in which she signifies. That is, when her masculinity and size signify lesbianism and raise a sort of cultural panic, the impulse is to stress her heterosexuality and to explain why it never blossomed "appropriately." Indeed, one of the interesting features of the humor surrounding Reno (e.g., the *Saturday Night Live* skits that represent her as an aggressively desiring heterosexual) is that it works only on the unspoken assumption of her homosexuality. That is, Reno's masculinity and size are humorous precisely because they are discordant with bi-gender expectations. If she is read as lesbian, her "abnormal" sexuality can be seen as consistent with the lack of children, and with her physical and extracurricular activities. As Judith Butler notes, heteronormativity "regulates gender as a binary relation in which the masculine term is differentiated from a feminine term, and this differentiation is accomplished through the practices of heterosexual desire. The act of differentiating the two oppositional moments of the binary results in a consolidation of each term, the respective internal coherence of sex, gender, and desire" (*Gender* 30–31). Hence, if Reno is seen as lesbian, that identity links up with her role as "male" rather than as masculinized female. If she is not lesbian, her very lifestyle must be explained, although no explanation can ever adequately quell gender trouble. Regardless of how she is ultimately read, the question of her sexuality as articulated through her non-married, childless status is evidently a key one in the cultural imaginary.

The reading of Reno as heterosexual, then, hinges first on explaining why she has no children. Second, it works through an expression of regret on Reno's part that she never had children. The operative logic is that if a heterosexual woman does not have children—regardless of the reason—she should express regret. The logic of public heteronormativity does not allow for any satisfactory reason for the lack of reproduction. Again, I want to be clear that I am not suggesting that people are intentionally forcing Reno to express such regret; instead, I am suggesting that this is part of the overall cultural narrative that we collectively expect to unfold and therefore that we collectively *encourage* subtly and overtly. Hence, one way in which the subject is discussed in the overall articulation of Reno is by stressing her interest in legislation concerning children. In one of the first articles discussing Reno as the nominee for attorney general, the *New York Times* notes that "Ms. Reno has also vigorously prosecuted child abuse cases and been a forceful advocate for children's rights" (Berke A22). After also mentioning a long list of Reno's battles for children's rights, *Time* observes that while Reno has no children of her own, "her life is full of them; she is everyone's favorite honorary aunt. Over the years, she has been named in the wills of many friends as legal guardian for their children" ("Truth" 20).[17] There is also an oft-repeated story of a local Miami rapper who wrote and recorded a song about Reno in honor of her efforts as an advocate for children's rights and in forcing divorced and separated fathers to pay child support ("Ask" A4). In such ways, Reno becomes symbolically a "mother," fitting more snugly into the heteronormative matrix.

Reno's handling of the Elian Gonzalez case is another site where her relationship with children is articulated. Here, her concern for, and execution of, a plan to return the child to his father, while applauded by some and seen as misguided by others, is framed in terms of her care for the welfare of children. *Newsweek*'s Donatella Lorch observes that Reno's concern for the child's welfare was so strong that returning the child to his father had become something of a "personal crusade" for her (37). The *Washington Post* suggests that Reno was so worried about the child that she was working fourteen hours a day, and that some observers believed she had become "so deeply and personally" involved in the case that she had lost perspective (Vise A4). Finally, the *New York Daily News* observes that the matter was so personal for Reno that it often brought her to tears (Goldiner 4). In each case, though not intentionally tied to the question of her sexuality and "proper" maternal instincts, the Gonzalez case works rhetorically with earlier claims about her strong desire to protect children.

If her affection for children functions to stress her "maternal instincts," a reaffirmation of her heterosexuality is also approached more directly in a number of descriptions. Laura Blumenfeld makes several direct references to Reno's heterosexuality in her 1993 treatment in the *Washington Post*. First, Blumenfeld retells the oft-repeated narrative of an occasion when Jack Thompson, an anti-pornography crusader running against Reno in Florida, had called Reno a lesbian and asked her to check off a box on a questionnaire indicating once and for all her sexual orientation. Blumenfeld reports that Reno responded by putting her arm around Thompson, saying directly, "Don't worry, Mr. Thompson. I'm not a homosexual. I'm not bisexual. I love big, strong, handsome, rational, intelligent, kind and sensitive men. And I understand why you might be confused" (B8). This response leaves no ambiguity as to Reno's sexuality. Neither homosexual nor bisexual, Reno is completely dedicated not just to men but to "big, strong, handsome" men. Similarly, in *People*, Reno is reported to have "expressed regret that she never married and had children, saying, 'I am just an awkward old maid with a very great attraction to men,'" ("General" 41). The *Washington Post* provides historic (albeit anecdotal) evidence of her heterosexuality, reporting: "Friends and family talk about a male suitor at Harvard Law School. They bring out snapshots of Reno on camping trips with a handsome young man looped through her arm. And they say Reno would have loved to have married and had a family, that it's her life's *greatest regret*" (Blumenfeld B8; emphasis added). Similarly, *Time* provides evidence in the form of a friend of Reno's who explains that "Janet would have loved to have a relationship with a man and have children . . . but she's a very smart woman, and it was difficult to find a man who had both a sophisticated city mind and was an outdoor person—and was not threatened by a successful woman" ("Truth" 27). During her run for the governorship of Florida, a reporter for the *St. Petersburg Times* showed Reno a 1971 newspaper article in which she had stated that she would be happy to trade her political career for a marriage and children (Allison 1A); in revealing the story, the reporter almost overtly asks Reno to explain her childless, unmarried lifestyle.[18] Moreover, there are reports that Reno served as the legal guardian for a pair of twins whose parents had died while the children were in high school (Blumenfeld). What is key in each of these instances is the strident insistence not simply on her heterosexuality but on her "proper" heterosexuality: not only does Reno have a "great affection" for men, but also her "greatest regret" is her lack of a husband and children.[19]

An alternate frame through which Reno's gender may be read that also partially erases the "trouble" her body, power, and sexuality provoke is that which reads her directly as a lesbian, or in a way that assumes lesbianism. As with the discussion of Reno's height and size, this representation is one with deep historical roots in U.S. culture. In an analysis of female sexuality in the nineteenth century, Sander L. Gilman observes that in iconography from that era we may see the roots of an equation that took shape, first, between the "excessive" bodies of African American women and a sexuality that led to "lesbian love," and then eventually between all "excessive" (or large) female bodies and lesbianism (237). That this same connection continues to operate as a generally unspoken assumption is affirmed in the link between Reno's excessive characteristics (her size and behavior) and her sexuality, here assumed as lesbian. For the most part, the question of her sexuality is discussed through either metaphors or implications. *U.S. News and World Report*, for example, predicts that in her confirmation hearing, "some senators may question the never-married Reno about her *lifestyle*" ("Justice" 28; emphasis added). Matt LaBash repeatedly refers to her as looking like a "spinster aunt" (21).[20] The conservative publication *Insight on the News* reports that former Reno opponent Jack Thompson accused Reno, when she was Florida's state attorney, of having forced a suspect named Eliana Fuster—"a shapely 19-year-old woman"—into a confession by having her stripped naked in a cell, then holding her hand throughout the trial. Thompson refers to Reno's behavior in the case as "plain odd" and "possibly perverse" (Timmerman 10). There are also more overt representations of Reno as lesbian. For example, Liza Mundy of the *Washington Post* reports that early in Reno's confirmation process, a videotape about Reno was shipped to the *Washington Post* and to a number of individuals, it was labeled "Janet Reno—Evil Lesbian" (Mundy 9). Further, Jack Thompson suggests that even though Governor Jeb Bush's campaign staff has information about Reno's "lesbian proclivities" and "use of Miami call girls," it was doubtful that they would choose to go public with such information (Timmerman 10).

Ultimately, what we see in these discourses about sexuality (including the implied link between heterosexuality and maternal instinct) are cultural frames for understanding the attempt to erase or diminish the gender trouble evoked by the association of Janet Reno's body, her position of power, and her marital and maternal status. If lesbian, Reno stands outside accepted heteronormativity but fits snugly within the frame of masculine dyke. If heterosexual, though her body and activities continue to work against acceptable versions of femininity, Reno fits more snugly within the frame of traditional heteronormativity. It is as if the culture at large noticed a difference in Reno and forced the question of the meaning or basis of that difference. The narrative response in which her "greatest regret" is that she has no husband and no children implicitly reifies the value of heteronormativity.

In *Gender Outlaw*, Kate Bornstein colloquially explains that gender attribution—our need to know the gender of each person we encounter—working on a heterosexually based binary system, allows a certain level of comfort in that this binary gender system leads us to expect as normal particular behaviors from men and particular behaviors from women (26). As Bornstein notes, however, when any given individual does not match the expected alignment of body, desire, and practice, that person is threatened with "gender terrorism"—Bornstein's term for the ideological, economic, and physical disciplinary mechanisms that go into action against those who trouble categories held by others to be central to identity. In revealing difference, in revealing the ultimate instability of seemingly natural and normal gender expectations, one poses an implicit threat to stability and is hence met with resistance and discipline (71–73).

Although Bornstein's primary focus is on transgendered individuals and the way transgenderism operates in culture, the rhetoric surrounding almost any case of gender confusion leads to the same forms of cultural discipline or terrorism, both by intent and by cultural expectations. Hence, while Reno does not fit any but the broadest definitions of transgenderism (save those that discuss transgenderism as a metaphor for all gender, in that gender is ultimately unstable and performative), the body of discourse surrounding the national career of Janet Reno—especially when she was being "introduced" through the national press—functions in a similar fashion to that which arises whenever any case of gender trouble appears. In this case, a case in which gender boundaries are blurred or broken on multiple levels and in multiple ways, a case in which the gender troubled evoked by Reno's body and behavior is enhanced by her position of public power, cultural mechanisms attempt to reify the borders by explaining Reno in very particular normalized ways. Hence the cultural fixation on Reno's size, her family, her behavior, and, ultimately, the attempts either to understand those characteristics through a reading of Reno as the masculine lesbian of the assumed male-female pair (which assures us that we indeed were right to be confused) or to stress Reno's heteronormativity despite her failure to match expected appearances. As a result, in studying the discourse surrounding Reno—as in the public discussion of gender trouble in general—we find contemporary expectations about gender and gender behavior laid bare, along with some of the ideological means by which these behaviors and expectations are reinforced.

Because I have focused on newspaper reports rather than other depictions such as in comedy sketches or private conversation, we see a more subtle side of gender discipline than we would in mass mediated and vernacular humor and criticism. By drawing out the implied expectations found in the news media, we put on display the cultural "common sense" that holds heteronormativity in place.

FIVE

In Death, a Secret "Finally and Fully Exposed"

Barry Winchell, Calpernia Addams, and the Crystallization of Gender and Desire

> If people insist on appropriating this corpse by locating it definitively within any
> particular identity category, they must explain away multiple inconsistencies,
> ambiguities, and ambivalences in self-identification, self-explanation, behavior,
> and presentation by using concepts of denial, repression, fear, and internalized
> prejudice and shame that all tend to dismiss the agency of the subject once
> animated in that dead flesh.
>
> C. Jacob Hale, "Consuming the Living, Dis(re)membering the Dead"

The July 5, 1999, murder of U.S. Army private Barry Winchell at Fort Campbell, near Clarksville, Tennessee, seemed to provide the same narrative elements that surrounded the ongoing Brandon Teena story, at least as retold in *Boys Don't Cry*. Indeed, given the lengthy "true" accounts presented in *Rolling Stone*, *Time*, the *Advocate*, and the *New York Times Magazine*, in local newspapers, and on television, and given the film projects that were initiated by Turner Network Television, Showtime (*Soldier's Girl*), and a number of independent film production companies,[1] it seems clear that the "gender trouble" of this case, much like that of the Brandon Teena case, piqued the interest of a wide variety of people, raising multiple questions concerning gender and sexuality. That the story was indeed rehearsed through a number of different narrative frames, and that a number of sometimes contradictory positions emerged with regard to numerous elements of the case—especially the "meaning" of the two main characters, Barry Winchell and Calpernia Addams—makes this a story ripe for critical analysis. Again, in light of the obviously gender-troubling elements of the case, its wide coverage, and its partial location within the hypermasculine context of the U.S. Army, it is clearly a site for critical intervention, for rethinking, and for re-troubling normalized reiterations of gender and sexuality.

To tell the story in abbreviated form as I read it in mass mediated representations[2]: Not long after Private Barry Winchell was beaten to death at Fort Campbell by fellow soldier Calvin Glover (encouraged by another soldier, Justin Fisher, who was also Winchell's roommate), army officials were finally forced to acknowledge that Winchell had been the victim of a hate crime, murdered because of Glover and Fisher's belief that Winchell was gay. Winchell, reports noted, had been dating a "female impersonator" who performed at a Nashville club frequented by gays. The performer, whom Winchell had been introduced to by Fisher, was named Cal "Calpernia" Addams,[3] a former navy medic who had served in Operation Desert Storm. Given that Addams described herself as a "preoperative" male-to-female transsexual, newspaper reporters and editors, as well as parents of the victim and gender and sexuality activists, were drawn into public arguments and public self-reflection concerning Addams's gender and both Addams's and Winchell's sexuality. Was Addams a man or a woman? As a couple, were Addams and Winchell gay or heterosexual? Moreover, after Glover had been sentenced to life imprisonment and Fisher sentenced to twelve years, another battle emerged when a *New York Times Magazine* reporter charged the Servicemembers' Legal Defense Network (SLDN) with having encouraged Addams to refer to herself as a gay man in order to simplify public perception of the killing as a hate crime.

In working my way through the multiple documents that recount the story of this case, I could not help but hear the calls of critics such as Leslie Feinberg (x–xi), Sandy Stone (284), and Kate Bornstein, (59), who have noted the necessity for transgendered people to tell their own stories in order to counter the caricatures that emerge in mass mediated reports. Simultaneously, however, as a rhetorical and cultural critic interested in the disciplinary limits of popular culture, I was well aware of the difficulty of those "real" stories "making sense" when articulated through mass mediated outlets. Not only do the characters in mass mediated narratives have to fit within the paradigms and narrative frames that make up the loosely structured "common sense" of mass culture (and hence always get "clawed back" into commonsense ideological understandings),[4] but also there are numerous people and institutions with overt or presumed interests in maintaining the categories that constitute their reality. We all act as ideological agents simply by making interpretations through frames and interests that have necessarily been developed within the context of existing cultural ideologies. Given those assumptions, the best one can hope for is perhaps an image and a representation that allow for at least a troubling of gender and sexual norms. Our job as critics is to enhance and highlight that "trouble."

In the epigraph to this chapter—a quotation I drew upon earlier in this book—C. Jacob Hale observes some of the ways in which the corpse of Brandon Teena, and the gender/sexuality of that corpse, were "frozen" into categories by various groups with competing interests and purposes. As Hale notes, whenever a particular category (e.g., "lesbian," "man") was advanced as "the one" into which Brandon fit, those making that argument, regardless of the perspective from which they began, had to ignore or explain away a multiplicity of ambiguities involving Brandon's life, gender, and sexuality. Moreover, Hale notes, in placing Brandon within a given category, one also had to understand or "read" those women who had relationships with Brandon in certain compatible ways (either as "deceived" heterosexuals or as lesbians). Hence, arguments over the meaning of Brandon's corpse were simultaneously arguments over the meanings of the gender, sexuality, and behavior of others as well, through underlying assumptions about all of us. What is true of the mediated and remembered corpse, then, is true of the public memory of that cultural context: it reflects and partially reifies norms and ideologies.

Turning to the death of Barry Winchell, we find a very similar set of problems, though some are highlighted by the military context. For example, while Calpernia Addams herself seems to be satisfied to understand Winchell's sexuality as in process,[5] mass mediated representations as a whole take a stance on Winchell's sexuality as either homosexual or heterosexual or in teleological progress toward one of those categories. Moreover, arguments over the meaning of Winchell's corpse and Addams's body, because they are read through a bi-gendered matrix, reflect back onto each other; that is, assumptions about Winchell's sexuality determine, or are determined by, whether we read Addams as a man who appears to be a woman or as a woman whose body has the appearance of a man's. Moreover, in line with Hale's observations, different individuals maintain their positions about Addams and Winchell despite the fact that Addams's comments about herself and testimony about Winchell's self-reflection contradict those positions. Indeed, rather than taking Addams at her own word about her identity, observers often perceive both Addams and Winchell as victims of false consciousness, unable to acknowledge publicly what they "really are."

Working through a comprehensive set of print accounts of the case,[6] I outline the signifiers that make up the gender-sexuality matrix through which Winchell is read as either heterosexual or homosexual and through which observations about Addams's body and/or mind are taken to signify "maleness" or "femaleness." Both gender and sexuality are implicated together in this representation. Concerning one of the main cultural puzzles that drove her work, Eve Sedgwick observes the "rather amazing fact that, of the very many dimensions along which the genital activity of one person can be differentiated from that of another . . . precisely one, the gender of object choice . . . has remained as the dimension denoted by the now ubiquitous category of sexual orientation" (8). In one sense, the discussion that follows is a case study of the public reiteration and reification of that dimension, the forces that encourage its reiteration and the implications of its reiteration, and the consistent reification of gender and sexuality as both are articulated around unambiguous genitalia.

Before going further, I should make clear that this is a critique of the struggles over meaning (and constraints on meaning) that take place in mass culture, not a critique of individual speakers. That is, while I of course assume that individuals do hold the opinions I attribute to them, I do not attempt to explain their thoughts or motives; indeed, that is not important to my argument.[7] Nonetheless, it is important to note that in this case, as in all human activities, a variety of forces, all emerging from our culture's heteronormative matrix, encourage different people and institutional representatives to read Addams and Winchell in different ways. Judith Butler wrote *Gender Trouble* in part "to think through the possibility of subverting and displacing those naturalized and reified notions of gender that support masculine hegemony and heterosexist power, to make gender trouble ... through the mobilization, subversive confusion, and proliferation of precisely those constitutive categories that seek to keep gender in its place" (33–34). This case represents the ways in which those categories, once naturalized, become entrenched in law, personal investment, regulations, and vernacular vocabulary to such a degree that everyone who encounters this potentially destabilizing story is under pressure to interpret the actors in the case in very specific stabilizing ways. Hence, both the military's "Don't ask, don't tell" policy and the legal obligations that arise from it emerge from preexisting cultural meanings and ultimately encourage the reification of those meanings.[8] Winchell's friends and family, attempting to re-member him after death, have personal motives, themselves shaped by mass culture and individual experience, to read him in particular ways. Some postoperative transgendered people have had personal experiences within the medical culture that encourage them to read Addams as a "woman," while some gays and lesbians have had experiences that encourage them to read Addams as "really" a man. Regardless of their readings, however, the bi-gendered matrix itself, and the performative stereotypes that accompany it, as well as its resulting sexuality "choices," remain intact.

In the discussion that follows, I work through the assumptions that undergird the different discursive frames through which the case is understood. First, I discuss the matrix within which Winchell is understood as a gay man. I argue that this representation of Addams is held together by the articulation of "maleness" with particular motives, names, and occupations attached to both Winchell and Addams. Second, I turn to the narrative under which Winchell is represented as a heterosexual male, a narrative that works either by focusing on the proper heteronormative performance of "man" and "woman" by Winchell and Addams (regardless of what Addams "is") or by positing Addams as a woman. In either case, the bi-gender norms and the performative acts required by those norms are reiterated by such framings. Ultimately, I suggest that this case—a case that, like others investigated in this book, could lead to a blurring of public understandings of gender and sexuality—takes the corpse of Barry Winchell and the living body of Calpernia Addams and, by ignoring multiple ambiguities, reinforces gender binaries and gender performances regardless of the meanings given those bodies by their owners.

BARRY WINCHELL "FULLY EXPOSED"

In an early article on this case in the *Washington Post*, reporter Sue Anne Pressley observes that Winchell "had a secret that was becoming known among the other soldiers in his unit: He was gay" (A1). Further on, she observes that in death, Winchell's secret was "finally and fully exposed" when, at a memorial service, four people held aloft an American flag while four others "held the rainbow banner, a symbol of the gay rights movement" (A1). The wording here is significant both in that Winchell is figured in this discourse as gay, rather than as queer or as having an "unclear" sexual identity, and that his secret was "fully exposed," as if to indicate that when others proclaimed Winchell to be "gay," that provided full exposure of his identity. There is no room here for his relationship with Addams (who identifies as a woman) to be seen as either a heterosexual relationship based on identity or something much more complicated, a relationship based on styles, perhaps, as Kate Bornstein would have it, rather than on genitalia alone. In short, not only does such a description pose sexuality as clearly based on a genital binary, with no room for contingency, but also it understands the object of genital desire as signifying "full exposure," as if the multiplicity of other aspects of sexual desire and practice (frequency, activity, etc.) were irrelevant to, or completely subsumed by, the category of homosexuality.

Moreover, this configuration of Winchell's identity as homosexual ultimately makes his sexual identity stable not only in the present but also, retroactively, in the past, despite his history of sexual experiences with women. That is, the narrative of Winchell's life and identity has to be retold to work teleologically toward a gay identity. For example, several reporters dismiss his past romantic activities with disclaimers such as, "Although he [Winchell] had dated women exclusively in the past . . ." (Pressley A1; see also Branson, "U.S. Army" 11; "Military Whitewash" 12; Stone, "Soldier" 16A), which assume that he was ultimately gay because of his final relationship, the one with Addams. Further, by pointing out that Winchell had a history of questioning his sexuality "and had been curious about gay life," they read the gay telos as inevitable (Pressley A1; Branson, "U.S. Army" 11). Indeed, I want to make clear that, despite the attempts to trouble public understanding of Winchell's sexuality or identity, the "gay" signifier as assumption continues in the present. For example, in 2002, when the former commander of Fort Campbell, Major General Robert T. Clark, was being considered for a promotion to three-star rank, newspapers such as the *San Antonio Express-News* and the *Atlanta Journal-Constitution* recounted the Addams-Winchell story, referring to Winchell as "a gay soldier" (Christenson 6B; Martz 3A).

In *Sexing the Body*, Anne Fausto-Sterling comments on how such storytelling works to negate entire portions of one's life. After recalling her own history as a girl who at eleven liked to be around bugs more than boys (but also had a painful crush on a male counselor), who at twenty-two married a man "for love and lust" (233), only years later entering into a lesbian relationship, she observes that our culture has become so "genocentric," so dedicated to the notion of understanding gender and sexuality as stable, that men and women who enter into gay relationships in middle age are often forced to ignore or discount the prior history of their lives, declaring that they must have "been gay all along" but never realized it (233–35). In these cases, such storytelling, regardless of the motives of those involved, posits an unchanging and noncontingent sexuality that one "essentially was" from birth to the present. Moreover, it suggests an essential basis to sexuality that is separate from experience and culture. There is, in other words, an overall cultural impulse to name and identify sexuality as stable in a way that reaffirms existing gender categories as the sole basis for sexuality and desire (i.e., to be heterosexual or homosexual implies a "same" and an "opposite" gender). Hence, when it is reported that although Winchell "had dated women" in the past, he was "fully gay," large portions of his history are discounted. Indeed, given that Winchell had reportedly long "questioned his sexuality" and was, according to Addams, still attracted to women,[9] to label him as gay rather than queer, or as attracted to men rather than, for example, to a "femme" style, is to trap him in a single inflexible category.

The discourse that situates Winchell as gay must also, by semantic and cultural logic, rest on the underlying assumption that Addams is a man, based also on a logic in which genitalia equal gender. Although David France, in the *New York Times Magazine*, acknowledges a more complex situation in which Winchell considered Addams a woman but considered himself gay for having sex with her, the possibility of such a conflicted and queered position (or any other conflicted position) is negated by most other accounts of the case. Moreover, as I will show, it is significant that this equation is offered both by those who assume that Addams sees herself as a man as well as by those who assume that she understands herself as a woman. In other words, regardless of how Addams is assumed to identify herself, those who utilize the "gay narrative" logic understand Addams as a man based on genitalia alone, regardless of how she thinks of herself.

One of the primary ways observers situate Addams as a man is by describing her occupation as "female impersonator" or drag performer. Given some of the liberatory and optimistic readings of Judith Butler's comments on drag as potentially gender subversive (*Gender* 136–39),[10] it is ironic that in this case Addams's occupation as a drag performer works only to indicate the marginality of her behavior as a gay man. As Peggy Phelan notes, the "passing" enacted in drag performance does seem to suggest a potential space in which bi-gender boundaries might be broken down. Nevertheless, "fundamental to passing is the binary of the seen and the unseen, the visible and the invisible. This binary functions like the binary of sexual difference" (*Unmarked* 97). Thus, if Winchell is a gay man, Calpernia Addams's body and ontology are marked, made visible, as male. Echoing Marjorie Garber's observation that contemporary cultural politics makes it difficult to imagine a transvestite who is not gay (130), we find that the discussion of Addams's occupation works to erase transgenderism and replace the transgendered Calpernia Addams with the gay male "Cal" Addams. Much as references to Brandon Teena's having "deceived" people into believing that "she" was a "he" are based on the premise of a masking of genitalia, discussions of Addams as an "impersonator" assume that she is a man impersonating a woman. In this way, the possibility of understanding gender at the level of identity (or of understanding gender as potentially unstable at the level of performativity) is undermined. For example, one early report notes that the murder case became far more interesting once "a female impersonator . . . came forward to say he was dating the victim and suspects the killing was an anti-gay hate crime" ("Soldiers" 1). Similarly, Sue Anne Pressley of the *Washington Post* reports that Addams appeared at the trial "dressed as a woman" (A1).[11] Similarly, Francis X. Clines notes in the *New York Times* that Winchell was labeled homosexual by fellow soldiers because he had been dating a "female impersonator" ("Killer's" A18; see also Clines, "For" 33), and a report in *Time* magazine observes that although Winchell had a girlfriend when he went into the army, "he began spending time with a man who performed as a woman at a Nashville, Tenn. nightclub" (Thompson 56). Furthermore, Winchell is said elsewhere to have been ridiculed for falling in love "with a man . . . who worked in a nightclub as a drag queen" (Hackett 5), and Addams is referred to as a "man" who "dresses as a woman" in a voluptuous style with heavy makeup (Sanchez, "Parents" A32). While Addams herself admits that she considers herself a woman but attempts to make the issue of gender complicated in conversations with the press, this "complication" rarely comes across save when Addams or an author is being reflective (see, e.g., Friess, France) about that complication.[12] Again, the persistent discursive specter of Addams as a "man dressed as a woman" testifies to the difficulty faced by those desiring to tell their own stories, as their subjectivity is largely appropriated by the categories most commonly available in popular culture.

Another way in which Addams is configured as male is through editorial decisions regarding pronouns. Judith Halberstam has argued that many narratives of the lives of transgendered people "rationalize them out of existence . . . through misgendered pronouns" ("Transgender" 293), a practice that, coupled with a renaming of Addams, works in this case to situate Addams as male rather than transgendered. The pronoun "he" is employed either because witnesses and reporters themselves assume that Addams is a man, based on the genitalia-equals-gender equation, or because editorial guidelines demand that the pronouns employed be both consistent and, in a sense, invisible to readers. For example, journalist Monica Whitaker of the *Tennessean* observes that although she had used "she" to refer to Addams, her editors forced her to rewrite the article using "he" for the sake of clarity (quoted in Friess 22).

In addition to "misgendered pronouns," the possibility of Addams-as-woman or Addams-as-transgendered is also "rationalized out of existence" through the configuration of her name and nickname in news articles.[13] Given that "Calpernia" is Addams's legal first name, one would usually read the configuration of "real name to nickname" as Calpernia "Cal" Addams (as friends do refer to her as "Cal") rather than Cal "Calpernia" Addams. It is the second configuration, however, that appears most widely as Addams is referred to as "female impersonator 'Cal Addams'" (Clines, "Killer's" A18) or as performer "Cal 'Calpernia' Addams" (Pressley A1; see also Clines, "Killer's" A18). In such a transposition, Addams is transformed from a woman with a nickname derived by shortening her full name into a male who transforms his "real" name into something more feminine when he performs in drag.

Further, Addams's former occupation as a soldier is also invoked in representations of her as a man; indeed, the soldier narrative emerges with regularity when Addams is represented as a gay man and/or female impersonator but less often in discussions of her as transgendered or as a woman. As with the signifiers already discussed, the citation of her past as a soldier works to undermine gender trouble, placing her more in accord with common cultural iterations of maleness. Hence, Addams is referred to as a "former Navy medic who served in the Persian Gulf War" (Pressley A1), "Cal Addams, a former Navy medic" (Clines, "Killer's" A18; see also Thompson 56), "a former Navy medic" who was "a veteran of a gay's travails in the service" (Clines, "For" 31),[14] "a Navy veteran" (Clines, "Mother" A13), a "former Navy medic" working "as a lipsynching entertainer at a gay club" (Friess 22). *Rolling Stone*, drawing together many of these themes, reports that Winchell "had fallen in love with a man—and not just any man, but a veteran of the Gulf War who worked in a nightclub as a drag queen" (Hackett 5).

Discussing attempts to discover the "truth" of gender in the brain and in chromosomes rather than simply on the body through genitalia, Marjorie Garber observes that "essentialism is alive and well; it has just moved inside the body" (108). In this case, while the body itself (i.e., the existence of a penis) remains a physical sign of the essentialism of gender, arguments also imply that if Addams could escape the haze of false consciousness whereby she identifies as female, she would come to understand herself as truly male. The insistence on seeing the penis as establishing Addams as male occurs most overtly in two different on-line debates, both at least partially sponsored by mass media outlets, and both of which assert that Addams is a man regardless of her own thoughts on the subject.[15] In the first instance, which drew numerous responses, gay activist Jim Fouratt widely distributed a criticism of David France's *New York Times Magazine* representation of Addams as transgendered (Morgan).[16] Fouratt insists that transgender theory is simply a move to encourage "gay men and lesbians" to go straight by "endur[ing] painful physical body manipulation and dangerous hormonal injections to take on the topography" of heterosexual men and women. Regardless of how Addams sees himself, Fouratt charges, Addams is a "professional gender illusionist" and a gay man.[17]

Similar arguments are posed by readers responding to a column by Norah Vincent in the *Advocate* ("Cunning Linguists") in which she also suggests that gender-crossing surgery mutilates the bodies of gays and lesbians in order to make them straight. In dozens of on-line responses to the essay, one reader charges that Addams was indeed a gay male because his body was a man's body ("Letters").[18] Moreover, she suggests that had she herself lived in Nebraska as a youth rather than in New York, she would have made the same "mistake" of "false consciousness" made by Brandon Teena, thinking of herself as a male rather than understanding that her body and her desires made her a lesbian. The reader sees Calpernia Addams as a man who has fooled himself into identifying as a woman in order to constitute himself as heterosexual even when having sexual relations with other men. Of such logic Eve Sedgwick argues that "to alienate conclusively, definitively, from anyone on any theoretical ground the authority to describe and name their own sexual desire is a terribly consequential seizure" (26). Here, playing with Sedgwick's terms, we might see just such a consequential seizure occurring in a logic that makes the penis the point of articulation under which Addams is refused the authority to name her own gender and desires.

In sum, when drawing Winchell as a gay man, as he apparently was by the two men prosecuted for his murder, mass mediated reports string together a number of signifiers that work to articulate Addams as a man. I want to make clear here that, regardless of the motives of particular groups, this articulation of Addams works only because it is grounded deep in the ideological assumptions of popular culture and of the institutions that help reiterate and re-cite those assumptions. As we see, the notions of impersonation, occupation, and naming, as well as the (sometimes unspoken) presence of the penis, all serve to reify an assumption of maleness.

THE HETEROSEXUAL MATRIX

In opposition to the representation of Winchell and Addams as gay men is a logic that situates either Winchell as heterosexual, or Winchell and Addams together as a heterosexual couple, that is, as a couple who accurately reflect the roles encouraged by contemporary articulations of heterosexuality. Even though the discourses I draw on in this section are not uniformly consistent in their positions, each one, along with the discourses of homosexuality, works to reify the stability of bi-genderism, and at times the stability of the "proper" iteration of gender. I provide readings, first, of discourses that take Winchell as heterosexual regardless of the status of Addams; second, of those that reaffirm and reiterate heterosexual performative norms; and finally, of those that stabilize the signifiers of gender performance even while equating gender with identity rather than with genitalia.[19]

A Passing Phase

In a variety of interviews and articles, Barry Winchell's parents (mother and stepfather) suggest that Winchell was heterosexual because they saw little evidence that he was gay.[20] For example, Winchell's mother, Patricia Kutteles, knew her son as a confident young man "who told her about several girlfriends" and gave her the impression that his relationship with Addams was simply part of discovering who he was (Clines, "Mother" A13).[21] Illustrating a common theme in which the parents' lack of knowledge of their son's homosexuality is read as indicating his heterosexuality, Wally Kutteles, Winchell's stepfather, notes that Winchell had a girlfriend for years until a breakup just before the murders. Of the letters written by this girlfriend to Barry, which he and his wife had examined, Wally Kutteles observes, "There are no indications that he was gay. They were love letters, just love letters" (Sanchez, "Parents" A32), seemingly asserting a dichotomy between "love letters" and "gay love letters." In the *Advocate*, Patricia Kutteles is reported to be "reluctant to *concede* that Winchell was gay" (Bull 26; emphasis added). Kutteles insists that because she was openly sympathetic to gays, she would have expected Winchell to out himself to her: "I'm not saying that Barry wasn't gay, only that I didn't know him to be gay. He never told me he was gay" (Bull 26). Once again, the search for evidence—in letters, in Barry Winchell's own words—comes up empty. The lack of evidence equals silence, and silence, despite the relationship with Addams, equals heterosexuality.

Finally, in the most telling expression of the Kutteles' belief that Winchell would have felt comfortable discussing homosexuality in their liberal household had he thought himself to be homosexual, Patricia Kutteles suggests that Winchell's silence perhaps "indicates he was simply in a passing phase" (France 29). While one could read the term "passing phase" to indicate a phase of passing as heterosexual just before the moment of outing oneself, or, more radically, as a phase of passing through a number of different identities with no assumed telos, here Winchell's silence, like the silence of the love letters, indicates a temporary phase that was coming to an end—an end that would evidently reestablish Winchell's heterosexuality.

Heterosexual Performativity

Regardless of Winchell's or Addams's self-identity, a number of observers posit Winchell and Addams as a heterosexual couple based on how well they fit the standards of heteronormative performance. That is, while not necessarily concerned with Addams's ontological status, several descriptions of Winchell and Addams, some quoting Addams's words as cited in news reports, accept the two as a male-female couple precisely because they re-mark traditional heterosexuality in such clear terms. In accepting the "commonsense" performances of male and female, these descriptions by necessity reinforce the acceptable contours of such performance. Moreover, regardless of how one might theoretically or practically discuss any form of homosexual coupling as other than a replica or copy of "traditional heterosexual exchange,"[22] the dominant cultural discourse surrounding such coupling—at least in this case—certainly reads that coupling as a replica of heterosexuality.

Hence, an *Advocate* article begins by commenting on the stereotypicality of the Winchell-Addams relationship: "It was, in almost every way, your typical boy-meets-girl story. . . . He timidly admired her auburn hair, her green eyes, her figure. She in turn was attracted to his buzz cut and his quiet and calm demeanor" (Friess 22).[23] After focusing primarily on Addams's appearance and Winchell's demeanor, the author reinforces another set of norms: "The Nashville preacher's daughter wasn't crazy about how much Bud Light he drank, but his full acceptance of her, as she was, helped overshadow that concern. 'He made me feel like a woman,' she says in a voice kissed with a Tennessee twang. . . . 'It's what I look for in life'" (Friess 22).[24] In such a description, in their behaviors and aspirations both Addams and Winchell replicate heteronormativity in a way that many couples do not; indeed, the descriptions of Winchell and Addams as typical (heterosexual) boy and girl clearly represent the goal toward which self-identified "typical" boys and girls strive.

Similarly, in *Rolling Stone*, Thomas Hackett, while understanding the relationship as a gay one, simultaneously configures that relationship as replicating heterosexual norms. Hackett, too, opens with an acknowledgment of the stereotypicality of the story he is about to tell: "Winchell and Addams had found a bond surprisingly old-fashioned: a man in uniform and a country girl" (5). After reporting Addams's desire to "be a housewife in a suburban home, married to a 1950's version of the American man,"[25] Hackett explores how the two fit those roles (5). In outlining their behavior, and quoting Addams on the relationship, Hackett in effect reiterates the expectations of bi-gender heteronormativity: Winchell treated Addams "like a lady, bringing me jewelry and things", Winchell "was the type of man who could undo the jelly jar if it was stuck", the two, like other couples, would "go to the movies, holding hands", and finally, in a retro signifier of maleness, Winchell had "his own car. It had leather seats, and it rode real smooth" (5).

In such statements we observe brief moments of performative acts that signify male and female: on the one hand, opening a jelly jar, a cool demeanor, consumption of beer, a car with leather seats; on the other, her slender "etherealness," her womanly comportment, her eyes, her figure. When welded onto apparent male and female bodies, these markings allow a public space for "holding hands" or going to the movies, "just like a normal couple." Again, my point is not that such signifiers were not part of the "real" performances and lives of Winchell and Addams; instead, I simply want to bring to the foreground the fact that of all the many signifiers and actions that make up human performance, these are the ones listed and cited, reviewed and reiterated, in order to illustrate how Winchell and Addams fit the heteronormative mold. In the rehearsal of that mold in national publications, individual readers are given the opportunity to test themselves, to think about how well they fit the mold of the normal boy and girl, the normal couple. Whereas Monique Wittig rightly argues theoretically that lesbians are not "women," in the story told here through mass media outlets, transgendered women *are* women, acting performatively within the context and vocabulary of heteronormativity.[26]

Heterosexual in the Soul: Body as Birth Defect

Finally, the on-line debates over Jim Fouratt's remarks and Norah Vincent's *Advocate* column provide one other route by means of which the heterosexual norm is defended. Reflecting earlier arguments by Janice Raymond, both Fouratt and Vincent argue that transgenderism (especially via surgery) is a condition that occurs only when gays and lesbians are unable to admit their sexual desires and instead deceive themselves into believing that they are "in the wrong body." The individuals whose responses are worked through here, unlike the articles mentioned earlier, posit an essential male or female identity—a gender of the soul for themselves and for Calpernia Addams.[27] I rehearse these arguments not to question or critique intentions or motives but to highlight a dominant articulation of transgenderism and the implications of this articulation. Moreover, I single out these discourses because the cases of Calpernia Addams and Brandon Teena are often invoked as support for the positions held by the authors.

In these responses there is an articulation of gender identity as based in the "soul" or brain, and of the preoperative body as a birth defect. For example, Kim Cooper argues that when the body has one gender and the soul has another, the body should change: "Why would the body take precedence over the brain/soul?" ("Letters"). Moreover, Calpernia Addams is quoted as claiming that, after the first time she performed in drag, she knew she would "have to either choose to live through the constricted filter of a man's body, or else to try to change that body as much as I could to reflect what I wanted to be, and what I feel like I am" (France 28). In terms of the notion of a "wrong body," one respondent argues that "TS people are not different than those born with a birth defect," while Jessica Kelly asserts that "we transsexuals are only trying to fix a 'cruel hoax' played on us by mother nature" ("Letters"). In each instance there is an overall argument that the transition to the "other" gender was made because the person was already essentially the other, that only a "defect" kept one from one's "natural body." Hence, while such a reading may indeed trouble the idea of equating gender with genitalia, it also works to reaffirm the bi-gender system. Again, as Garber notes, essentialism has not disappeared in such an equation; it has only moved deep inside, and is thus more difficult to dislodge.

In June 2001 it was reported that the number of discharges at Fort Campbell under the "Don't ask, don't tell" policy had jumped from 17 in 1999 to 161 in 2000, the year after Winchell's death, with all 161 discharges resulting from cases of individual soldiers acknowledging their homosexuality ("Military Still" 16A; see also Suro A20). In 2002, the *Cleveland Plain Dealer* observed that the number of voluntary discharges of gay and lesbian soldiers had hit a fourteen-year high, mostly because of the increasing number of gay and lesbian soldiers who asked to be discharged from Fort Campbell, "where soldiers beat Pfc. Barry Winchell to death in 1999" (Koff A2). An editorial in the Nashville *Tennessean* connected the dots, arguing that "the assumption is that many of those soldiers were simply afraid for their lives if such an anti-gay atmosphere were allowed on the base" ("Military Still" 16A). Clearly the situation—the murder itself and the atmosphere allowed to persist on the base—is cause for concern and must be changed. To my mind, however, what this analysis has illustrated is that the problems that encourage such an atmosphere are deep-seated cultural ones, of which events at Fort Campbell are a particular manifestation. Hence, I want to use my conclusions as instruments for reflecting not only on the problematics of military culture but also on the ways in which those problematics emerge and are encouraged by widespread understandings of gender and sexuality.

First, then, the case illustrates how a famous corpse—yet another corpse tied to violence arising from gender trouble—functions as a nodal point around which a number of people articulate their own worldviews, their own understandings of gender and sexuality. Again, just as Hale notes of the body of Brandon Teena, the body of Barry Winchell cannot speak for itself. Instead, a variety of people, with a variety of interests, take over that body, and the history surrounding that body, in order to present their own stories, while ignoring contradictory evidence from Winchell's history as to the self-delusion, internalized prejudice, and fear felt by Winchell when he was alive. As people pick over Winchell's history and body in letters and conversations (he had a history of relations with women, he had a history of thinking about the "gay lifestyle"), they construct Winchell's motives and identity as evidence of the groundedness of their own paradigms. Hence, yet another case that would seem to be ripe for the problematizing of gender and sexuality becomes a point around which different people reinscribe their views of gender and sexuality.

Second, while a number of perspectives on Winchell and Addams have been taken up in terms of Addams's gender and Winchell's sexuality, in one way or another—gay or straight, woman or female impersonator—the norms of gendered performativity are resincribed, heteronormative behavior being marked as most acceptable. Thus the descriptions of Winchell's masculinity (articulated to his maleness) and of Addam's femininity (as either performance or essence) reaffirm and reiterate the norms already established culturally for each gender. As a result, Addams's looks, comportment, and style indicate her successful performance as a woman, while Winchell's demeanor and behaviors reflect and reiterate traditional aspects of maleness, of masculinity.

Moreover, even when they are understood as a gay couple, Addams's successful iteration of femininity makes their relationship a reflection and an imitation of heterosexuality rather than allowing it to be understood on terms located outside heterornormativity, as Judith Butler would have it. That is, because the relationship is constantly referred to as a "traditional boy-meets-girl story," elements of its potential queerness are reinscribed and realigned within the heterosexual matrix.

Third, I want to reemphasize that the pressures exerted on the maintenance of dominant articulations of gender and sexuality emerge from a variety of institutions and arrangements, all of which ultimately lead back to the underlying language of culture. Hence, representatives of the U.S. military, whether resistant to or supportive of the "Don't ask, don't tell" policy, all come to understand and describe Winchell and Addams through a heteronormative paradigm. The soldiers on the base in general, and the murderers in particular, owing both to the "Don't ask, don't tell" policy and, more deeply, to the overall culture of the base, reflect a heteronormative ideology. Winchell's parents, perhaps revealing their disappointment that Winchell had not "outed" himself to them, rearticulate him as probably heterosexual. Some gays and lesbians, perhaps in part because of the confidence required in order to identify as homosexual in a heteronormative culture that disciplines them for that identification, insist on identifying Addams as a gay man. Some transgendered people, perhaps because of personal and public anguish in the aftermath of making their own decisions within that same heteronormative culture in which genitalia are equated with gender, emphasize the essentiality of Addams's "femaleness." Although these factions and positions diverge on a number of levels, for the most part they rearticulate the notion of an essential (physical or mental) bi-gendered identity. Thus this element of our culture's gender/sexual politics functions, emerging from the bricks and mortar of common understandings, as do all cultural politics and disciplinary mechanisms, through multiple locations and sites and through a wide variety of agents. Hence, we are once again reminded that political change can only take place slowly and through long-term commitments to changes in meanings.

Finally, my reference to the slow pace of change is not meant to imply that change is not possible or is not taking place. Indeed, to my mind, this analysis reveals so many institutional and personal ways in which change is resisted precisely because meanings are so unstable, so open to destabilization and change. The point here, as it has been in each chapter of this book, is not to show that change is an impossibility but to highlight the mechanisms by which cases of gender trouble, once publicly articulated, become marginalized and normalized by all of us, simply because, as humans, we have to rely on preexisting meanings and the power of the institutions we have put in place in order to create our own understandings of the present. Nonetheless, the very visibility of this case, as with the others discussed in this book, illustrates that change is ongoing. Once marked, a case like this is constantly being remarked. That is, that so many people do indeed take Addams at her word as a woman rather than a "marginal freak" illustrates that a cultural shift is under way regardless of the relative stability of the performative characteristics of the signifier "woman."

What I hope to have shown in this chapter is that while it is not the critic's job to attempt to unearth the multiple motivations that act upon individuals, encouraging them to understand Winchell and Addams in particular ways, it *is* important for us as critics to remember that such meanings, and the cultural rules enforcing them, are deep-seated ones. As such, they remind us of the profound alignment between institutions, legal structures, personal motivations, and the politics of meaning in mass culture. Hence, such an analysis serves to help us, as critics, understand what we are working with and against as we attempt to motivate changes in culture, changes in the vocabularies and categories of everyday life. While we can never unhinge meanings, making them completely unstable, we can try to fight the politics of stability, to take public cases of gender trouble as ways of furthering that trouble, as ways of working toward an understanding of signifiers as unstable, so that all of us—however we identify ourselves—might be able to follow our own destabilizing urges and desires, finding our movement in life more comfortable and that of others more acceptable.

CONCLUSION

Bringing It All Back Home

No political revolution is possible without a radical shift in one's notion
of the possible and the real.
Judith Butler, *Gender Trouble* (tenth anniversary edition)

Each of these headlines from the 1990s represents a distinct case of
public "gender trouble": "Being Male or Female Is Innate, Study Concludes"; "Tragic Death of a Girl Who Lived as a Guy" (Bernard);
"Straying from Country's Straight and Narrow" (Schoemer); "Janet
Reno Rides Again . . . into the Swamp of Florida Politics" (Labash);
"U.S. Army in the Dock after Gay Soldier Beaten to Death" (Branson).
With each case, we have seen unique domains within which sex, sexuality, and gender are articulated and disciplined in contemporary U.S.
culture. In one case, a physically bodied male who is accidentally cas-
trated is raised as a girl according to the advice of "medical experts." In
another, a transgendered youth meets his death in the Midwest and
becomes a movement's icon. In the third, we observe relationships between the cultural capital of popular music, the politics of "truth," and
sexuality. In the fourth, we discover the focus and discipline gender
trouble receives when it arises in connection with a "public" body. In
the final case, the discursive playing field lies at the crossroads of gender, sexuality, military culture, and popular expectations. Each case is
unique, to be sure. And yet each is one part of a larger cultural mosaic
in which similar themes have emerged and reemerged, providing us

with a sense of the strong consistency of "our" culture's gender and sexual expectations, the strong consistency of the demands of hetero-normativity. As a critic, I hope that one glance at each of the sample headlines allows the reader to bring to bear a larger critical reading frame which has emerged from this analysis. It is my hope that readers will be able to confront other cases of public gender trouble and reflect on, and argue (at least internally) with, the public representations that so strongly hold gender and sexuality in place.

I want to conclude by addressing several of the issues that I raised in the introduction and a few concerns that arose as I carried out and completed this project over the last several years. I want to address first, then, the ways in which a "critical rhetoric" perspective adds to the study of gender/sexuality and some thoughts about how we might reen-vision our world. Second, I comment briefly on the relationship be-tween local or "Americanist" studies of this type and transnational work on gender/sexuality. Finally, I gently push on the tensions this study raises which lie between literalizing and de-literalizing critical projects and conceptions of gender and sexuality.

CRITICAL RHETORIC AND PUBLIC GENDER

Given that the chapters of this book developed from a merging of crit-ical rhetoric with contemporary gender and (trans)gender theory, it might be worthwhile to make one or two observations about the pro-ductivity of such a merger as well as the productivity of critical rhetoric in general to any study of public culture. One of the discussions I have repeatedly found myself in over the last decade with colleagues is one that addresses the question: When rhetorical critics, or critical rhetori-cians, come to the larger interdisciplinary table of cultural studies, what is unique about what we bring? While not providing a technical answer to this question, I hope that in some ways this book offers an example of what critical rhetoricians do and of what we can add to larger discus-sions regardless of the topic area.

When Raymie McKerrow first laid out the critical rhetoric project as one that would gather together fragments of popular culture in order to provide a critical narrative about a given topic, a "rhetoric with an attitude" if you will, the project was clearly ripe for use within the study of gender/sexuality as well as studies of public articulations in general. In each chapter, in each study, I have attempted to put to use the eyes of a rhetorical critic in identifying compelling fragments of discourse that explain, and thereby unhinge, some of the commonsense understandings of dominant culture in terms of gender and sexuality. If successful, a critical rhetoric project such as this one gathers discourse from the public involving gender and sexual norms and the popularly understood "morals" underpinning these norms. In terms of the "critical" portion of "critical rhetoric," I hope that this study has at least suggested the kind of eye for detail that rhetorical studies encourages, as well as the tendency to draw out the presumed (and therefore discursively material) articulations that surround every public debate.

The "rhetoric" side of "critical rhetoric" encourages us as critics to see ourselves as part of the battle over these norms and morals. There is a powerful public rhetoric that underlies gender and sexuality; as critics and activists, we must utilize criticism as a way to envision and encourage other ways of being, other understandings of existing articulations, whether those articulations might involve gender, sexuality, race, occupation, or power. Critical rhetoric forces us not only to function as critics, then, but to function as rhetoricians, to read the material discourse of everyday life and write about it in such a way that our encounters with the world are thereafter altered.[1]

NATIONALISM, TRANSNATIONALISM

The subtitle of this book, *Rhetorics of Sex Identity in Contemporary U.S. Culture*, is meant to acknowledge the limited temporal and cultural boundary of this study. While I of course acknowledge that I mean "dominant mass mediated" U.S. culture rather than all aspects of a much larger struggle over meanings, I also want to make clear that I do not see my analysis indicating much about the meaning of gender and sexuality outside of the understandings and assumptions of mass mediated (mainly print) sources in the United States.

That said, I have in the last few years found myself involved in numerous conversations with colleagues who argue that "our" attention should be directed outside our national boundaries. While I agree with that concern, it seems to me that critics should think as a community rather than as distinct individuals. That is, regardless of what realms or "arenas of meaning" need our critical focus (e.g., production versus consumption, local versus global), it is not the job of every critic to focus on every element in the circuit of meaning. Rather, the critical community as a whole should cover all the elements of the circuit of meaning. Where there is the potential for changing meanings and lives in a productive manner, criticism should find its voice, but not every critic must find his or her voice in every situation. My hope is that this book adds to our understanding of contemporary meanings of gender/sexuality on a local level, within the dominant U.S. mass media.

WHAT KIND OF HOMES?

Finally, over the course of presenting drafts of the chapters of this book at conferences and during lectures, discussing the issues raised by these and other cases of gender trouble with colleagues and friends, and teaching courses dealing with these issues, I found some very familiar problems consistently arising in the inevitable debates that surrounded such discussions—problems that forced me consistently and productively to re-question the politics of a project like this one. For example, when I presented the chapter concerning the case of Barry Winchell and Calpernia Addams at a conference, the panel's respondent, a prominent feminist rhetorical critic, noted that while she applauded my analysis, and the liberal side of her "liberal feminism" approved my tendency to encourage a reading of Addams as occupying a "home"—drawing on Jay Prosser—in the category *woman*, the feminist side was not happy with the kind of passive, stereotypical woman that was represented in the press and reportedly typified by Addams. That is, while she wanted to celebrate the underlying theoretical assumption which disarticulated genitalia from gender, she criticized the way in which my discussion (and Addams) seemingly encouraged gender signifiers to be rearticulated at the level of that "home" identity of male and female.

counter-productive

Another example: In one of the closing scenes of John Cameron Mitchell's film *Hedwig and the Angry Inch*, Yitzhak—Hedwig's bandmate and husband, as played by Miriam Shor—dons one of Hedwig's blond wigs, turns his back to the audience at one of the band's performances, and in a quick moment of cinematic sleight of hand falls back into the audience dressed as, performing as, living as—you choose the verb—a conventionally beautiful woman. She falls, as *Newsday*'s John Anderson would have it, with "a sense of redemption and euphoria" (B3). It was the character of Yitzhak and this moment in the film that as a viewer I found most moving, that I wanted to celebrate, even while knowing that such a celebration would be theoretically and politically suspect. Nonetheless, my sense of celebration emerged from my understanding of the needs and desires felt by Yitzhak. Throughout the film, there are several suggestions that it had always been Yitzhak's desire to be either Hedwig herself or the woman that Hedwig could not be. For example, early in the film Yitzhak tries on one of Hedwig's wigs when Hedwig is out of the room, and at several points we see Yitzhak fetishizing the role of lead singer. Hence, in my reading of the film, I wanted to celebrate Yitzhak's triumph over whatever forces were keeping "him" from being the woman "he" desired to be. When I shared my general appreciation of the film as a whole with a colleague, however, I was surprised—perhaps naïvely so—to find her point to this very scene as the moment at which she found the narrative most problematic. "I don't get it," she said. "An FTM gets to be a woman. What kind of triumph is that?" The trouble had only begun.

As I read reviews of the film, particularly those that mentioned Yitzhak, and as I talked to students to whom I showed the film in my "Rhetoric and Gender" course, I found the Yitzhak character being read in multiple ways and the telos of Yitzhak's journey, at least as far as the film takes us, itself read in ways troubled by viewers' understandings of gender and the politics of performance. So again I found myself asking, How do we negotiate the needs of the individual for what Prosser calls a "politics of home"—the needs of a Yitzhak or a Brandon Teena—to identify fully with a preexisting, perhaps politically problematic category within the heteronormative matrix of a public politics that seeks to queer and disrupt those very categories? What does it mean to celebrate a "Yitzhakian" moment of "redemption and euphoria" when that moment comes at the cost of reifying some very problematic categories?

These are the basic issues at stake in Bernice Hausman's review of transgender theory in *Feminist Studies*. In this essay, Hausman criticizes a number of recent transgender theories and theorists for insisting on gender categories as fundamental ontologies of being while simultaneously allowing for—indeed, encouraging—the infinite expansion of the number of available genders (486). Although one might disagree with Hausman's readings of particular theories, her overall concern deserves the attention of everyone dealing with the issue of gender in that, ultimately, how we talk about gender affects the lives of each of us. Hence, rather than insisting on "gender diversity" (i.e., more gender categories, each of which is read as occupying an *essential* category), shouldn't we rather be working on projects that encourage an evacuation of the concept of gender as a fundamental concept altogether? Shouldn't we, in Hausman's words and in the sentiment of the respondent to my presentation, develop a combined critical project that works toward "the demand for basic human rights and personal dignity and difference" (487). What are the costs and benefits of how we approach these questions? What are the costs and benefits for people living in bodies that they want to claim as male, female, or ambiguous, for people who want to claim themselves as heterosexual, bisexual, homosexual, or queer?

In a sense, if we take Prosser's notion of a "politics of home" seriously, we must very carefully think through the types of "home" categories or identity categories we want to encourage in the public sphere. We must carefully think as critics and activists what our role will be in the way we collectively create shared assumptions about the "essentialism" of a home category, the costs and benefits of our actions. While one might want to encourage the idea of a culture in which, say, Calpernia Addams is able to claim "female" as a home category, one must also take into account the fact that such a category, as an essentialism, comes with its own costs. That is, while it allows a home for a given individual, it also ultimately ties signifiers to that gender category, and these are signifiers that we might ultimately be wise to relinquish.

It is perhaps fitting that I find myself siding in large part with the conclusion of the preface to the tenth anniversary edition of Judith Butler's *Gender Trouble*, a treatise that drives so much of my own project. Butler recalls that the book was originally written "as part of the cultural life of a collective struggle that has had, and will continue to have, some success in increasing the possibilities for a livable life for those who live,

interesting term

or try to live, on the sexual margins" (xxvi). I draw inspiration from, and heartily endorse, this flank of the overall cultural struggle if its meaning is expansive enough to increase the possibilities that all of us envision for our sexual and gendered lives, regardless of margins and borders.

More directly, in her preface Butler reaffirms the idea that cases of gender trouble are ones in which the *reality* of gender is put into a moment of crisis for those who think through their implications (xxiii). While it is indeed true, as I have attempted to illustrate throughout this book, that the ideological impulse of mass culture (and of individuals to the degree that they have been successfully integrated into the common sense of mass culture) is to foreclose that crisis by reaffirming the heteronormative bi-gender system as essential, as ontological, it is also true that these are occasions when we as critics can encourage ourselves and others to "come to understand that what we take to be 'real,' what we invoke as the naturalized knowledge of gender is, in fact, a changeable and revisable reality" (xxiii). Whatever we call such a critical project ("Call it subversive," Butler writes, "or call it something else" [xxiii]), it is indeed part of a long revolution in which our commonsense understandings about gender, sex, and sexuality are disarticulated and rearticulated in more contingent arrangements—arrangements that help increase those "possibilities for a livable life" for everyone.

Ultimately, then, the study of gender trouble is a project that must have both short-and long-term goals, as immediate and long-term needs are often at odds on the battlefields of discursive revolutions. For example, although my immediate goal might be to help shape the collective struggle in such a way that someone like Calpernia Addams or Brandon Teena can comfortably and publicly claim to be female or male, the larger cultural goal might be to help create a discursive cultural context in which Addams, Winchell, Teena, Reno, lang, Reimer, and everyone else understands that while the material body has its shapes and impulses, the understanding of those shapes and impulses, the "naturalized knowledge of gender," is changeable and revisable. These two goals do not have to be at odds with each other if both are seen as impulses within the mosaic of a much larger, much more contentious cultural struggle. Neither of these goals is an "easy" one, as the comfort that is the equilibrium of contemporary gender ideology is necessarily compelling for each individual who faces a situation that seemingly disrupts common sense. As a result, we would do well to develop a critical vision that allows a politics of "homes" that is at once a politics of gender diversity for the present and ultimately a politics that sees gender as existing within the folds of an endlessly changeable and revisable reality. Literalization and de-literalization, freedom and constraint, each must, in different ways and in different critical moments, continue to be a part of the overall critical project.

Notes

INTRODUCTION

1. I want to make very clear that I am not claiming that all readers of such cases read them in a complicitous manner. Rather, I am talking about the overall cultural impulse to contain "gender trouble," in effect to explain the cases within dominant frames of understanding. Certainly there are individuals who read these cases in an oppositional manner, and throughout this book I nod toward such oppositional readings. My focus, however, is on those readings that appear to be preferred within a dominant ideological framework.

2. I do not mean to indicate here that Butler was equating performativity with performance or that she was denying the "materiality" of the body. Although Butler has sometimes mistakenly been read in such a way by some readers (see, e.g., Tim Dean's treatment [218–22]), Butler clarified her position in both *Bodies That Matter* and the preface to the tenth anniversary edition of *Gender Trouble* Regardless of the restraints of "material," it must be understood and worked within a discursive field.

3. Jay Prosser (22–60) provides an interesting reading of Butler's work, specifically focusing on why, given that drag is mentioned relatively briefly in *Gender Trouble*, it became for many readers one of the highlights of the book.

4. Again, I would strongly advise anyone interested in the reception of Butler to read Prosser's engaging analysis in *Second Skins*.

5. Of course, all positions contain a great deal of ambivalence on a multiplicity of issues dealing with transgression and complicity. Certainly none of them fits perfectly in the typology I suggest in this chapter.

6. Judith Butler points in the preface to the anniversary edition of *Gender Trouble* to Rubin's work as her starting point for thinking through the ways of gender is potentially destabilized publicly (xi).

7. Both C. Jacob Hale and Celeste Condit separately make such an observation.

8. A similar concern with and commentary about the complex politics that lie between "home" and fluid identities can be found in Stephanie Turner's investigation of intersexed identities.

9. For more discussions of the way in which the discourse of science constructs a heterosexual bi-gender normativity, even at the cellular level, see both Emily Martin and Bonnie Spanier.

10. For an interesting historical case study of a cross-dresser which shows how such a "transvestite's progress narrative" was employed, see Brookey's analysis of Deborah Sampson Gannett.

11. Critics in the area of gender studies would do well to think through criticisms of transgender theory offered by Bernice Hausman. While Hausman's work has not often received a favorable reaction from transgendered readers, she shares their goal of loosening the constraints on gender as an ontological category.

12. Those rules can be found at http://www.actlab.utexas.edu/~sandy/hale .rules.html.rules.html.

13. Although many of these assumptions may be "old hat" to many readers, I want to outline carefully how I approach these case studies, justifying my choice of documents and my general approach.

14. Indeed, McGee's references to the works of Foucault are some of the earliest uses of Foucault in rhetorical studies.

15. Celeste Condit brilliantly makes this case in terms of "public morality" in a 1987 essay in which she discusses transitions in the meaning of "justice" and related terms in relation to African Americans between 1840 and 1960.

16. A number of readers of a draft of this chapter commented that they found it unusual that I was focusing on mass mediated "dominant" discourses and not including the "vernacular" voices that Kent Ono and I studied with regard to anti-immigration discourse in *Shifting Borders*. To clarify, while I think such a study would prove valuable in understanding how individuals work both with and against the preferred or dominant meanings of terms, I wanted this book to focus exclusively on the tight constraints that the dominant ideology in the United States places on gender and sexuality.

17. See my *Cultural Prison*, "Apology," and "The Parent."

CHAPTER ONE

1. "Reassignment" is the term used by medical professionals to signify that a child has been designated as being of a gender other than that identified at birth. For example, if a child with ambiguous genitalia was first identified as male and a

decision was subsequently made to surgically provide the child with female genitalia or the appearance thereof, the child is said to have been reassigned as female.

2. The case was more readily known as the "Twins" case before the updated account by Milton Diamond and H. Keith Sigmundson appeared in 1997. The first relatively full mass mediated account appeared in an article in *Rolling Stone* by John Colapinto in which the subject of the case remained anonymous. But with the 2000 publication of Colapinto's book *As Nature Made Him* (and the publicity tour that followed), the subject revealed himself to be David Reimer of Winnipeg, Manitoba. Because so many different pseudonyms were used to signify David and his twin brother, Brian, in the varying accounts, I have decided to use the names employed in the article to which I am referring and to put the names David and Brian in brackets next to the pseudonyms when I need to clarify. While the reading of the chapter will sometimes be awkward and difficult, this awkwardness can be instructive. To draw on Joanne Meyerowitz in the introduction to her history of transsexuality, "If the pronouns jar, please consider them a reminder of how deeply we invest our everyday language and lives with constant referents to gender" (*How* 13).

3. At the time of the publication of this book, David would be approaching forty years of age, and if television and newspaper reports provide the correct information, is living with his wife and stepchildren in a "small, nondescript dwelling in a working-class neighborhood of Winnipeg, Manitoba" (Colapinto, *As* xi).

4. I want to make clear that I am using this case, and the discourse that surrounds it, to understand something about the meaning of gender in contemporary culture. I am not using it to understand what it means to be "gender ambiguous" as an experience. I would recommend that anyone writing in the area of gender ambiguity or cases of transgender performance see Jacob Hall's "Suggested Rules for Non-transsexuals Writing about Transsexuals, Transsexuality, Transsexualism, or Trans——." These can be found at http://www.actlab.utexas.edu/~sandy/hale.rules.html.

5. I researched the case by using a variety of databases, including the *Reader's Guide to Periodical Literature*, the University of California's Melvyl system, and Vanderbilt University's Television News Archives. Moreover, in a class I taught in spring 2000 and spring 2001 at Vanderbilt University, students were required to build a full dossier of discussions of the case. Some of their documents, which I had not seen before, are also included here. I also read Colapinto's book as well as multiple reviews of that book.

6. I should state clearly that there is nothing as subtle as Butler's deconstruction of the gender-sex division taking place in public discussions of the case. It is primarily an argument between these two positions. What I am attempting to do is to suggest that the argument about the case illustrates how a specific type of gender performance is reified in this case by all those making public arguments.

7. In the terms of rhetorical studies, my method here amounts to "critical rhetoric," as outlined by McKerrow and refined by McGee and by Ono and Sloop.

I concentrate on pulling together fragments of popular discussions of the case—dominant discourses rather than marginal ones. I realize that I am drawing on only certain types of fragments while not necessarily looking into their use by individuals or within vernacular conversations about the case. Further, I want to make clear that this essay is not about the "real person" John/Joan but about dominant cultural representations of that person and the ways in which these representations are part of our dominant cultural understandings of gender. I do not deny that people can transgressively perform gender "against the grain," or read this case "against the grain." In a sense, I am interested in the constraints we all face in trying to act transgressively.

8. The essay, "The Medical Construction of Gender," is reprinted as a chapter of Kessler's book *Lessons from the Intersexed*. A very good recent history of medical discussions of hermaphrodites is Alice Domurat Dreger's *Hermaphrodites and the Medical Construction of Sex*. For other discussions of the gender ideology of science in terms of medical discussions of male and female bodies, see both Emily Martin and Bonnie Spanier's essays on the medical construction of gender, Anne Fausto-Sterling's thorough *Sexing the Body*, Jennifer Terry's book *An American Obsession*, and Robert Brookey's *Reinventing the Male Homosexual*.

9. In her fascinating history of hermaphrodites, Alice Dreger makes a similar observation and notes that modern medicine, "even when it involves psychosocial theory—in fact remains deeply materialist, reductionist, and determinist in its practical approach to the world, and presumes that a 'successful' female gender requires (and is almost guaranteed by) a certain 'female' sex anatomy, and that a 'successful' male gender requires (and is almost required by) a certain 'male' sex anatomy" (185).

10. In a footnote Kessler raises a point that, while beyond the scope of this chapter, should be reinforced and studied elsewhere, noting that "almost all of the published literature on intersexed infant case management has been written or coauthored by one researcher, John Money," and as a result, "there are no renegade voices either from within the medical establishment or, thus far, from outside" (7 n. 9). The case of John/Joan, as reported in the essay that finally offered a strong challenge to Money's case (Diamond and Sigmundson) and Colapinto's accounts, makes it clear not only that other physicians were hesitant to challenge an established expert in the area, but also that, as a result, Money felt able to report only that evidence that supported his thesis, ignoring evidence that did not support it. Regardless of where one stands on the question of gender fluidity and performance, the case illustrates that, like the humanities, science has a powerful rhetoric and politics that are often outside the rigor that it normally claims. While not a "hoax" like the infamous Sokal affair, cases such as this one, in which reputation makes it impossible to challenge a thesis, are perhaps more dangerous in that others are rhetorically and politically afraid to question a theory that continues to shape decisions about cutting into people's bodies and radically altering their lives. Indeed, H. Keith Sigmundson, one of the co-authors of the follow-up report on the case of

John/Joan which led to the media discussions, claims not to have published an article on the case years before, even though he knew the treatment had been unsuccessful, because "I was shit-scared of John Money. He was the big guy. The guru. I didn't know what it would do to my career" (Colapinto, "True" 92).

11. For some interesting and indeed frightening examples of how tightly thought out gender behaviors and appearances can be for children, especially as revealed in medical discourse, one should see the case studies in Phyllis Burke's *Gender Shock.*

12. Money's case is made in a number of places. I draw primarily on articles written for the lay audience. See, for early accounts, Money, "Sex"; Money and Ehrhardt; Money and Tucker; Money, "Ablatio."

13. Diamond's case is made in a number of places. I would recommend Diamond," "Sexual Identity and Sex Roles"; "Sexual Identity, Monozygotic"; "Sexual Identity and Orientation"; and Diamond and Sigmundson.

14. The evidence taken from scientific reports that is reprinted in mass media publications is significant in that, because the mass media articles are shorter and written for a lay audience, the evidence chosen is that which is deemed to be most convincing to that audience.

15. The examples concerning clothing and shaving appear in numerous venues, including the *Daily Telegraph* (Fletcher), *Chronicle of Higher Education* (Guernsey), *Straits Times* (Branson), *Washington Post* (Murphy), *Ottawa Citizen* (Quan and Laucius), and the *Baltimore Sun* (Bor).

16. It is worth pointing out that while Brenda's desire to pee standing up is presented as evidence that she was "really" a boy and that boys want to urinate standing, there is an entirely different way of reading the story. That is, if one looks at discussions in Money "(Ablatio") or Diamond and Sigmundson, it is possible to assume that the initial surgeries after the accidental removal of the penis created a body in which the "natural" flow of the urine made it easier for the child to urinate standing up. That is, when sitting down, Brenda had to learn to physically (with her hands) force the urine toward the toilet as the surgery had made the urine stream flow awkwardly.

17. Kessler (*Lessons*, 106), drawing on Fausto-Sterling, argues that gender reassignments are made and evaluated on the basis of successful heterosexual performance.

18. In a quick timeline in the *Toronto Star* recounting John's [David's] life, we read that "at 16, he obtained a windowless van with a bed and bar. Girls had crushes on him. At 25, he married a woman several years his senior, adopting her children. 'John can have coital orgasm and ejaculation,' the study says" ("Boys" F8).

19. While I want to stress that heteronormativity in the guise of assumed heterosexuality is at work here, it is also the case that even a homosexual David Reimer would not have led observers to draw very different conclusions. As I illustrate in chapter 5 regarding Calpernia Addams and Barry Winchell, gender is publicly

reified even when the subjects are read as homosexual, although such reification is much more complicated and, hence, allows for "messier" readings of gender and sexuality.

20. I should make clear that while Diamond and Sigmundson see elements of gender being shaped by "nurture," I would classify them as "essentialist" in that Diamond has focused on looking at the ways the body's sex behaves despite cultural forces.

21. For another example which suggests that the David Reimer case is a complete reversal of Money's theory, see "Being."

22. Just to clarify, I am not making an empirical claim that the case was indeed drawn on in large numbers of "feminist" texts. Rather, those who discuss the case link it to feminist texts and use a logic under which all feminisms are the same.

23. I am aware that no bras were actually burned at the event from which the stock image is shown. I am simply pointing to the ways in which the newscast helps rearticulate a particular image of feminism and the myth of bra-burning feminists as relevant to this case. For an analysis of news reports and images of feminism based on this image, see Bonnie J. Dow, "Feminism."

24. For the link of the case with feminism, see also Quan and Laucius A1 and Donahue 7D. Further, Colapinto notes in his book-length account that the case was presented in Kate Millett's "1970 feminist bible" as "scientific proof that the differences between men and women reflect not biological imperatives, but societal expectations and prejudices" (*As Nature* 69).

25. For example, in her analysis of the representation of "feminism" on prime time television shows, Bonnie Dow defines feminism broadly as "a set of political ideas and practices—developed through feminist movements, dedicated to the progress of women and the transformation of patriarchy" (xxiii).

26. What I am advocating here is that cultural critics interested in feminism (or other political projects) have a responsibility when speaking in public to acknowledge that umbrella terms such as "feminism" cover a wide variety of political and pragmatic positions, some of which are at odds with one another.

27. To clarify, while those who study John/Joan and those who know David Reimer would obviously consider his actions and desires to be important, what he "actually" does is not important in terms of how the discourse about the case represents and reifies cultural understandings of gender and gender behavior. That is, this essay is about "John/Joan" as a discursive re-presentation, a public memory of a life, and not about the actual person.

28. One might also be tempted to employ Anne Fausto-Sterling's ("Five," "How") call for recognizing at least five sex categories. While similar, however, Fausto-Sterling's argument does not work in quite the same fashion (as Fausto-Sterling herself observes in *Sexing* 101). As Kessler (90) notes: "The limitation with Fausto-Sterling's proposal is that legitimizing other sets of genitals still gives genitals primary signifying status and ignores the fact that in the everyday world gender

attributions are made without access to gender inspection. There is no sex, only gender." One interesting way to think through the possibility of multiplicities of "humans" on all levels of identificatory discourse, and one that I heartily endorse, is Condit's attempt to understand human beings as "diverse bodies that learn many languages" ("Post-Burke" 355).

CHAPTER TWO

1. The news sources are cited throughout this chapter. The Guggenheim project, titled "Brandon" can be found at http://brandon/guggenheim.org. The film is *The Brandon Teena Story*, directed by Susan Muska and Greta Olafsdottir, distributed by Zeitgeist Films. For discussions of proposed films and plays, see Minge; Moton, "Documentary," "Film," and "Story"; Burbach, "Three Judges"; "Murder"; Delmont.

2. Throughout the chapter I refer primarily to "Brandon Teena," and hence most often use the masculine pronoun. At times, however, when I quote others who speak of Brandon as a woman, or when I discuss Brandon as female (e.g., in stories of her childhood), the feminine pronoun is employed. I mark such moves as clearly as possible. I retell the Brandon Teena story as I would in a face-to-face interaction rather than by looking back at any given article or book. One could refer to any of the sources I cite in this essay for a similar telling of the story. Aphrodite Jones's true crime book is the fullest treatment.

3. Of course, as Leslie Feinberg has pointed out in *Transgender Warriors*, transgender activism has a long and varied history under a number of names. Nevertheless, the Brandon Teena case and the activism surrounding it took transgender activism to a much broader public level, especially given the vocal presence of activists at the trial. A good resource that allows one to follow in narrative form some of the activism that took place around the trial is the FTM International Web site (http://www.ftm-intl.org).

4. This fascination can be seen in numerous references to this case and others. Indeed, in a two-week span during the time when I was researching this case, my attention was directed toward an *Ally McBeal* episode featuring a transgendered person and an incident in Georgia in which a female student was "outed" as male and asked to leave the private school she was attending (Sewell). The Georgia incident seemed to raise a great deal of interest in the local community. Similar cases have attracted heavy news coverage. Marjorie Garber, for example, discusses a case similar to that of Brandon Teena which was also the subject of much media coverage (100). Readers have undoubtedly run into numerous other examples in the wake of the coverage received by *Boys Don't Cry*.

5. The more contemporary term for hermaphrodites is "intersexed." To a large degree, I use the term "hermaphrodite" because it is the term most commonly used in public discussion, and it is the impact and implications of public arguments that I am investigating.

6. If one can point to a celebratory period in Judith Butler's work, it would be in *Gender Trouble*, where she notes the ways in which examples "that fail to comply with the categories that naturalize and stabilize that field of bodies for us within the terms of cultural conventions" significantly upset the meanings that are said to inhere within sexed bodies (110). Another clearly celebratory reader, at least at times, is Kate Bornstein in *Gender Outlaw*. Even here, however, though Bornstein might celebrate the position of gender outlaws (those who are neither man nor woman but remain fluid between positions) in a fashion that makes it appear as if sexual binarism can be easily waved away, she is well aware of the cultural and ideological pressures (and people enacting these pressures—gender defenders) that work to keep our gender binary house in order (71–72). One could also see Judith Halberstam's *Female Masculinity*, in which her interest is in maintaining some of the "spaces in which gender difference simply does not work right now," as "hasten[ing] the proliferation of alternate gender regimes in other locations" (41).

7. Although I do not draw on them by name heavily throughout this chapter, my theoretical assumptions about rhetorical materialism are heavily influenced by the works of Ronald Greene and Celeste Condit 1993. I am also influenced by Lauren Berlant, *The Queen of America Goes to Washington City*, in which Berlant notes that she chooses to study mainstream documents and discourses because she believes that they should be seen not as white noise but as powerful language, not mere fiction but discourse with material effects—often violent ones (13).

8. To put my project in conversation with Elliot and Roen's discussion of the need for both a psychoanalytic take on the "role of the unconscious in the formation of subjectivity" and a historian's approach to the social regulation of subjects, I am clearly pursuing the latter.

9. I searched at Vanderbilt University Library using ProQuest Direct to get access to major publications and resources. I also used LexisNexis to uncover over two hundred newspaper articles dealing with the case, both locally and nationally. To a large extent, I have allowed the combination of ProQuest and LexisNexis to determine what are the "dominant" discourses about the case. I assume that there is some space for argument over these sources, but my overall reading of this discourse, which gives a sense of the dominant themes, is fairly consistent across all of the material with which I worked. Although I also looked at Web resources, I have been more selective in my use of them, as I am trying to get at discourses available in the public sphere through "commercial" outlets. So, though I discuss some of the advertisements for and reviews of *The Brandon Teena Story* found on the Web, I do not discuss the narratives of those transgender activists who attended the trials of John Lotter and Tom Nissen. That discourse, as well as much popular discourse, has been analyzed in a brilliant essay by C. Jacob Hale, "Consuming the Living, Dis(re)membering the Dead."

10. Once again, in large part I take my cues on how to proceed with this analysis from a particularly pointed set of "rules" about writing in this area: C. Jacob Hale's

"Suggested Rules for Non-transsexuals Writing about Transsexuals." One of the points most pertinent to my analysis is Hale's claim that such writing should not attempt to tell transgendered people about transgendered subjectivity but should instead work to explain what the discourse tells about non-transgendered people, about dominant understandings of transgenderism and the way that gender ideology acts in part to constrain all of us, regardless of our gender identities or sexual desires.

11. This is not the case in many of the on-line reports authored by transgender activists who attended the funeral. While they may have had an interest in "essentializing" Brandon as male, as Hale observes, they clearly did not posit what was occurring as a case of deception.

12. For other claims about anger owing to "lies and deceptions," see Fruhling, Keenan ("Brandon"); Strawbridge; Grabrenya; Ebert ("Ignorance").

13. For other examples of "posing" or "masquerade" metaphors, see Burbach and Cordes; Burbach, "Officer," "Jury Told," "Tight Security," "Mothers," "Jury Convicts," "Jury Chosen," "Ex-Girlfriend," "Three Judges"; Powell; "Prison"; "Second"; Moton, "Story," "Film"; Will; Wheelwright; Wade; Boellstorff; "Murder"; "New Trial"; Hartl; Grabrenya.

14. Konigsberg also quotes one of Brandon's former girlfriends as saying, "I just couldn't understand why a girl would trick you into that if she knew you liked the opposite sex," again implying that Brandon was the same sex as the girlfriend (194).

15. Michelle Lotter, sister of one of the murderer's, makes a similar claim in an article in the *Advocate* (Ricks 30). For use of the phrase "true sex" to refer to Brandon Teena as female, see also Burbach and Cordes; "Dateline."

16. Every newspaper report found in my LexisNexis search refers to Brandon Teena as "Ms. Brandon."

17. For other examples of such discourse, see Pearson; "On Video."

18. In addition to the headlines using "heartland" cited earlier, see Will.

19. Lisa Henderson provides an interesting class analysis of the representations of the murder in her essay on *Boys Don't Cry*.

20. Whereas Dreger is discussing the historical treatment of hermaphrodites, Suzanne Kessler has cogently argued that this same logic operates today in that physicians who treat intersexed children often begin with the assumption that these children should be surgically transformed into male or female. There is no space for ambiguity. Furthermore, Dreger begins her history in a period that would follow Thomas Laqueur's period of the "one sex" model, and hence the logic of her history fits well with his.

21. The actual terms "sex" and "gender" may not be employed in discussions of the case, although the notions that they generally represent are certainly put into action.

22. Similar observations are made in the *Los Angeles Times* review of *The Brandon Teena Story* (Thomas F16).

23. Burbach and Cordes go on to note that "Miss Brandon's hair usually was cropped short in front and long in the back. She liked to wear sweaters, turtlenecks, button-down shirts and casual slacks" (1A). Other examples of this clothing-makeup articulation can be found in Wheelwright.

24. For other examples of this masculine icon articulation, see Will; "a Brief Reminder."

25. For other examples of the "dream guy" discourse, see Wheelwright; Bernard; Carr; Taubin; Ebert ("Ignorance"); Atherton; Boone.

26. What is significant is not that Brandon Teena made this statement but that the statement gets worked into every account of the case.

27. For more articulations of Brandon as a hermaphrodite, see Konigsberg 194; Elliott ("Tortural"); Atherton; Boone.

28. In this construction I am playing off of "Hermaphrodites with Attitude," the activist group headed up by Cheryl Chase. For a discussion of the group, see Chase's essay in *GLQ*.

29. Again, for a full account of such thinking among physicians today, I highly recommend Suzanne Kessler's *Lessons from the Intersexed*.

30. See Cheryl Chase and Suzanne Kessler (*Lessons*) on this point.

31. While my interest is in mass mediated and popular culture representations of the case and the film, there are clearly a number of academic readings of the film that see the case as providing a progressive or sympathetic reading of transgenderism. As noted in the text, Judith Halberstam sees the film doing this through a "transgender gaze." Others who provide liberatory readings of the film include Michele Aaron, Brenda Cooper, and Patricia White.

32. Similarly, Kate Bornstein tells the story of a heterosexual man who remarked after one of Bornstein's book readings that while he had no idea what it felt like to feel transgendered, her presentation forced him to think about the pressures that constrained him as a man—the point being that critiques of any public representations of cases concerning gender/sexuality are useful to everyone, regardless of gender and sexuality.

33. As Feinberg puts it, "Every single child today—no matter how their sex or gender is developing—needs to know about these militant battles and the names of those who led them" (81).

34. Similarly, Kate Bornstein notes that it is not that transgendered people are "trapped in the wrong body" but rather "that there is a shortage of metaphors for how to talk about what we are and a culture that forces us to think of the body as right or wrong" (66). Sandy Stone similarly notes that while "the wrong body" is not an appropriate metaphor in most cases, it "has come, virtually by default, to define the syndrome" (297).

35. Such "encouragement" may come in the form of the de-naturalization of existing categories and metaphors.

36. She goes on to note: "The sexual discourse we have settled for is woefully

inadequate when it comes to accounting for the myriad practices that fall beyond the purview of homo and heteronormativity. The development of a new sexual vocabulary and a radical sexual discourse is happening already in transgender communities, in sexual subcultures, in clubs" (139). Similar calls for an enlarged public vocabulary can be found in Feinberg (102) and Stone ("*Empire*" 297).

CHAPTER THREE

1. After searching both LexisNexis and ProQuest databases, I obtained and analyzed 258 full documents in mass mediated publications that discussed k.d. lang at some length.

2. Negus works with Victoria Starr's biography of lang, a conference paper by Louise Allen, and two anthology essays (Ainley and Cooper, and Andermahr) in his brief analysis.

3. In short, I am analyzing gender and gender behaviors as performative in the sense of seeing each as "a ritualized production, a ritual reiterated under and through constraint, under and through the force of prohibition and taboo, with the threat of ostracism . . . compelling the shape of the production, but not . . . determining it fully in advance" (Butler, *Bodies* 95).

4. Obviously, neither gay/lesbian audiences nor heterosexual audiences read lang in such universal and constrained ways. I am trying to point to a general inclination.

5. In a way, the reactions of different audiences regarding lang could be said to parallel the reactions of various audiences to *Star Trek*, as discussed by Henry Jenkins. While marginalized and disempowered audiences could rework that text to serve their own interests, "dominant" audiences and subjectivities read the text— a fairly untroubled one—in untroubled and traditional ways.

6. Obviously, the phrases "politically progressive" and "politically regressive" are contingent on one's politics. The "lesbian chanteuse" is regressive only if one privileges a politics of "messiness" over a politics of public representations of lesbians.

7. In short, Bruzzi mainly reads k.d. lang as a text from her theoretical perspective. That is, lang acts as a traditional literary text with Bruzzi as critic. I instead provide a "discourse" analysis, focusing on arguments and discussions about lang rather than reading from the lang text as it appears to me. Further, I want to make clear here that I am not holding k.d. lang "the person" at fault. Her decision to change musical genres and to refer to her sexuality as she wishes is clearly not only her right but also praiseworthy in that "coming out" is never an easy process and more commonly entails personal and financial costs. Instead, I want to focus on the ways in which the cultural assumptions about gender and sexuality always tend to eradicate trouble. In this case, if lang is "different," we want to know why and how. In effect, to figure out how she troubles such categories is to place her back within an accepted understanding of male and female, hetero- and homosexual.

8. I of course do not take "high" and "low" cultural capital to be natural phenomena, but, rather, I recognize them as socially crafted categories that work to the advantage of some and the detriment of others, with the link between the labels "high" and "low" culture or aesthetic being a historically and culturally contingent one.

9. Peterson brilliantly illustrates how "authenticity," a contingent and constructed concept, becomes central to many industry and fan conceptions of country music.

10. For clarity's sake, I am not suggesting that anyone was confused about lang's gender; I am suggesting that lang's appearance was a site of gender anxiety for many because she employed so many "culturally proper" signifiers of masculinity in her public presentation.

11. For other examples of this configuration, see McKenna Fl; Johnson, "sex" 68; Helligar 37; Ali 40.

12. I am obviously troubled by the politics of this issue myself. While I lean toward celebrating representations that trouble and destabilize gender and sexuality, especially at this historical moment, I also find myself persuaded, in particular at the level of the individual, by arguments that provide zones of comfort or "home places" of identity. Perhaps the job of the cultural critic is to trouble both ends of this continuum, to keep the question open.

13. For a reading of the discourse surrounding this transition in the reception of Kiss (as well as the Sex Pistols), see Sloop, "Emperor's."

14. For similar descriptions of this and later recordings by lang, see Rogers 34; Handelman 304; Bennetts 95; Cromelin CAL5; Walters 112; Sischy 140.

15. One recalls here Robert Walser's discussion of how the notion of "study" operates in the politics and cultural capital of guitar playing and musical genres.

16. See also Harrington N11; Soeder 1E; Vaziri 37; Vivinetto 29W; Nichols 3.

CHAPTER FOUR

1. Mundy's piece is a nice analysis of the humor, both jokes and television skits, that centered on Reno's sexuality and gender once she took office. The article includes interviews with Reno's staff and with comedians who have portrayed her.

2. While gender itself is a category that could use troubling, here I am interested in investigating how the concepts of masculinity and femininity are tied to bodies that are commonly understood as being male and female.

3. I place "we" in quotation marks to indicate that I am referring to general cultural assumptions, not necessarily those of all people living in that culture and speaking that cultural language.

4. I am working with liberal, conservative, and moderate sources. I am not claiming that these sources do not at times contradict one another. Of course they do. Nor am I claiming that their readings are non-ideological. Of course they are. Rather, if each source is presented as if its perspective were "correct," then taken as

a whole, they illustrate some of the common underlying assumptions about gender/ sexuality in U.S. culture.

5. I conducted this search by using a combination of terms in a search of LexisNexis sources. For example, in one search I combined the terms "Reno" and "Parkinson's." While I include numerous examples of each claim, I do not cite all of the over five hundred articles I read for this analysis.

6. For other examples, see Mundy 22; "General" 40; Gordon 4; "Rough" 32; Caplan 42; Ruth 2; Allison 1A.

7. Indeed, some reports cite observers mentioning Reno's height in a way that seems to function as an excuse for the reporter to mention her size.

8. I am indebted to Kirt Wilson for providing me with the idea for this parallel.

9. See also Berke A22, Meddis 4A.

10. See also Allison A1.

11. Mentions of the house "her mother built" are nearly ubiquitous in reports about Reno's gubernatorial campaign. See, for example, Epstein, "Reno" A4; Dahlburg 12; Baxter 1A; Allison 1A; and Leibovich C1.

12. See also "General" 41; Blumenfeld B8; Gordon 5; "Standing" 46; Ostrow, "Blunt" 32; "Gambling" 44.

13. See also Kondracke for a discussion of hiking and outdoor activities after the Parkinson's diagnosis.

14. While I would not want to stress the parallels too strongly, it is interesting to note, in reference to my analysis of the discourse about k.d. lang, that the signifier of the pickup truck appears in both cases.

15. I mean "unrecognizable" within the current cultural discursive regime.

16. For other examples of this configuration, see Berke A1; "Truth" 20; Mundy 11.

17. For other examples, see "Justice" 28; Blumenfeld B8; Gordon 4; Moss 36; "Gambling" 44, "Can" 370; Reske, "Unflappable" 17; Goldberg 18.

18. Reno's response—basically that she never found the right person—is less interesting here than the fact that a reporter virtually demands that she explain why she is single and childless.

19. Further, in an explanation of the humor surrounding Reno and her sexuality, the *Washington Post* reports the existence of multiple Web sites that refer to Reno's sexuality and suggests that "a sensuous beast" lurks "within the Attorney General's wacky two piece cotton blend suits" (Mundy 9). See also Rohter A22.

20. See also Contreras.

CHAPTER FIVE

1. My understanding of these productions comes from a variety of sources, including Sanchez ("Officials" B3) and discussions with Calpernia Addams. It is my understanding that the Showtime project was the only one to complete production. That project, *Soldier's Girl*, was screened at the 2002 Sundance Film Festival.

2. I stress that I am retelling the story in the terms in which I generally read it, not in the terms I would use were I telling the story. My analysis includes every public document on the case I could find. For a relatively "full" account of the narrative, see Thompson; Hackett; Bull; France.

3. The ordering and relationship of name to nickname used here, which I discuss later in the chapter, is significantly different from that employed by Calpernia Addams. The same is true, of course, with regard to the pronouns used in this retelling of the "mass mediated" story and the way I would use pronouns in my own telling.

4. I refer again to John Fiske and John Hartley's discussion of ideological "claw back" in *Reading Television*. While this point has been made by a variety of critics and theorists and in a number of ways, their discussion remains for me one of the most satisfying metaphorically.

5. I discuss Addams's perspective later in the chapter.

6. I used LexisNexis, Proquest Direct, a variety of Web searches, and conversations with Addams to uncover the documents on which I build my argument. Conversations with Addams were used to clarify particular points that she had made in print about her life and understandings of self. I do not employ them as equivalent to the mass cultural discourse I critique in this chapter, nor do I claim them as evidence of the "real" thoughts of Calpernia Addams.

7. As should be clear, too, this is a "discourse" analysis in which I am looking at overall cultural knowledge and understandings rather than those of individuals. Even when I quote individuals who are cited in news reports, I am treating their words as *examples* of particular ways of configuring cultural knowledge. Again, while I sometimes employ conversations I had with Addams to clarify her understanding of her own gender/sexuality, for the most part, these quotations refer to the way she was quoted by others, and hence show how those quotations reflect cultural assumptions.

8. For an insightful example of the constitutive and reifying effects of law, see Vicki Schultz's now classic "Women 'Before' the Law."

9. Addams observed this in print as well as in a conversation with me. While labeling Winchell "bisexual" continues to maintain the gender binary system, it is a recognition that there was something more going on than "full gayness."

10. I want to emphasize that I do not mean to attribute a "liberatory" position to Butler, but instead, as she does in the preface to *Bodies That Matter*, I only observe that others took her discussion of the performativity of gender to imply that gender was easily taken off and put on and that drag was clearly a subversive deconstruction of the citationality of gender. Instead, Butler was discussing the potential subversiveness of certain campy styles of drag, fully realizing that drag could also play into hegemonic structures of meaning.

11. I am assuming that the point is clear here. She would not have observed that

a woman was "dressed as a woman." Such an observation would be made only if the person was assumed not to be a woman.

12. In conversation Addams noted that although she has a "preference" to behave like a "traditional" woman and to date a "traditional" man, she realizes the multiple complications involving identity and gender.

13. This certainly harks back to the arguments over the use of "Brandon Teena" versus "Teena Brandon" in the popular press, among Brandon's friends and family, and among transgender activists. See Hale, "Consuming" 312–15.

14. In conversation, Addams indicated that she was not a gay male while in the navy, at least in terms of practice.

15. Addams is referred to as "biologically male" in an *Advocate* essay (Friess 22) and in David France's critique of the SLDN, in which France indicates that the SLDN considered that the penis made Addams a gay man (26). My argument here is not only that one could argue that the hormone treatments had already given Addams a "biologically female body" if we take the focus off of the penis as the sole signifier but also that the body is used here as signifier par excellence, more important than identity.

16. I have cited the Riley Morgan Web document because it is a location where one can find the original text of the Fouratt E-mail message as well as editorial commentary critical of it. For information on Jim Fouratt and his historical importance in the gay rights movement, see Duberman.

17. Fouratt also refers to Brandon Teena as a "baby butch lesbian."

18. Because they received so many responses to Vincent's essay, the *Advocate* claims to have published every response (and a reprint of Vincent's essay) on its Web site. The letters are published unedited, however, and in no particular order. Hence, they sometimes have authors' names attached to them but sometimes do not. I have cited each as carefully as possible.

19. Some of the references in this section are drawn from the same essays cited in the first section. This is not to suggest that there are contradictions within individual articles; it illustrates instead that people representing different discursive assumptions about gender and sexuality are cited in those articles.

20. Again, I claim no knowledge of what his parents "really" thought about Barry Winchell's sexuality, nor am I making claims about what they currently believe. Rather, I simply comment on how their observations were reported in the popular press.

21. Winchell is apparently assumed here to have been shifting back to heterosexualism after this "discovery" process.

22. I am of course referring to Butler's celebrated discussion in *Gender Trouble* (156–58). I of course agree with Butler's position; once again, I am simply reiterating the notion that cultural constraints continue to reify an understanding of all relationships as mirrors of the heterosexual model.

23. Similarly, elsewhere we read that Addams had "a woman's hands, a woman's comportment, a woman's slender etherealness" (France 26) and that Addams "has a certain Gypsy Rose Lee quality of vulnerability" (France 27). I am not discounting the possibility that such a description was meant to be read as "camp," although I do not think so given the context. In addition, it is interesting that the wording of this piece is so close to that of the *Rolling Stone* article discussed later in this chapter.

24. Elsewhere, Addams asserts that Winchell "treated me just like a normal girl, and that was the most wonderful feeling, to have an attractive, masculine, nice man treat me like a woman, like I wanted to be treated" (France 26).

25. In reading this, one cannot help but recall a similar statement by Venus Xtravaganza in *Paris Is Burning*. The fact that both instances involve murders that occurred in relation to transgenderism should provide impetus for cultural reflection.

26. Wittig of course meant that lesbians are not women if we understand "woman" to have meaning only according to heterosexual systems of thought and heterosexual economic systems. The descriptions of Addams as a "typical girl" clearly place her within those heterosexual systems of thought and economics.

27. While I am not discussing the "cause" of this articulation of transgenderism as living "in the wrong body," I do want to recall Sandy Stone's (288) remark that this articulation arises in part because transgendered individuals in the United States understand that they must make this argument to align themselves with the accepted transgender diagnosis if they are to get approval for gender surgery. Here again we see how cultural understandings of gender work both in commonsense terms and through institutional power. See also Shapiro 254.

CONCLUSION

1. Critical rhetoric owes its debt here to Michel Foucault's notion of "history of the present" (30–31). For a much larger discussion of how critical rhetoric might function, as well as its relationship to contemporary theory, see the introductory chapter of Ono and Sloop, *Shifting Borders*.

WORKS CITED

Aaron, Michele. "Pass/fail." *Screen* 42 (2001): 92–96.

Adams, James Ring. "Country Music Foundation: Mecca with a Mission." *Wall Street Journal*, 1 September 1988: 1.

Ainley, Rosa, and Sarah Cooper. "'She Thinks I Still Care: Lesbians and Country Music." In *The Good, the Bad, and the Gorgeous: Popular Culture's Romance with Lesbianism*. Ed. Diane Hamer and Belinda Budge. London: Pandora, 1994. 41–56.

Ali, Lorraine. "k.d. lang." *Rolling Stone*, 30 November 1995: 40.

Allen, Louise. "k.d. lang and the White Lesbian Body." Paper presented at the British Sociological Association Conference, 28–31 March 1994.

Allison, Wes. "Be It Beltway or Backwoods, Folksy Image Is No Façade." *St. Petersburg Times*, 1 September 2002: 1A.

Andermahr, Sonya. "A Queer Love Affair? Madonna and Lesbian and Gay Culture." In *The Good, the Bad, and the Gorgeous: Popular Culture's Romance with Lesbianism*. Ed. Diane Hamer and Belinda Budge. London: Pandora, 1994. 28–40.

Anderson, John. "'Hedwig' on Film." *Newsday*, 20 July 2001: B3.

Anderson, Melissa. "The Brandon Teena Story/Boys Don't Cry." *Cineaste* (March 2000): 54–56.

Angier, Natalie. "Sexual Identity Not Pliable After All, Report Says." *New York Times*, 14 March 1997: A1, 18.

———. "X + Y = Z." *New York Times Book Review*, 20 February 2000: 7.10.

[Works Cited]

Ansen, David. "Walk Like a Man, Talk Like a Man." *Newsweek*, 11 October 1999: 85.

Appelo, Tim. "Is k.d. lang Really Patsy Cline?" *Savvy* (July 1988): 18.

Arthur, Andrew Jacob. " 'Boys Don't Cry' Coverage Belittles a Martyr's Life." *Pittsburgh Post-Gazette*, 7 April 2000: 47.

"Ask a Rapper: Reno Is 'Bad.' " *Atlanta Journal and Constitution*, 12 February 1993: A4.

Atherton, Tony. "A Poignant Story of Brutal Intolerance." *Ottawa Citizen*, 1 May 1999: E5.

Attali, Jacques. *Noise: The Political Economy of Music*. Minneapolis: University of Minnesota Press, 1985.

Baxter, Tom. "Florida Primary." *Atlanta Journal-Constitution*, 8 September 2002: 1A.

Bayles, Martha. "TV: Failed Pilots, Pretty Teens, Weary Bikers." *Wall Street Journal*, 21 July 1988: 1.

Beckerman, Jim. "Actress Swank Transforms Herself to Play Role." *Omaha World-Herald*, 13 February 2000: 4.

"Being Male or Female Is Innate, Study Concludes." *Toronto Star*, 16 March 1997: C2.

Bennetts, Leslie. "k.d. lang Cuts It Close." *Vanity Fair* (August 1993): 94–98, 142–46.

Berke, Richard L. "Clinton Picks Miami Woman, Veteran State Prosecutor, To Be His Attorney General." *New York Times*, 12 February 1993: A1, 22.

Berlant, Lauren. *The Queen of America Goes to Washington City: Essays on Sex and Citizenship*. Durham: Duke University Press, 1997.

Bernard, Jami. "Tragic Death of a Girl Who Lived as a Guy." *Daily News*, 23 September 1998: 48.

"Best Bets." *Detroit News*, 8 February 1999: C4.

"Biological Imperatives." *Time*, 8 January 1973. 34.

Blumenfeld, Laura. "Janet Reno, in the Fires of Justice." *Washington Post*, 21 April 1993: B1, 8.

Boellstorff, Leslie. "Nissen's Lawyer Says Juror Misconduct Tainted Trial." *Omaha World Herald*, 3 December 1996: 13SF.

Boodman, Sandra G. "A Terrible Accident, a Dismal Failure." *Washington Post*, 29 February 2000: Z07.

Boone, Mike. "A Chilling Tale of Rural Ignorance." *Montreal Gazette*, 1 May 1999: C9.

Boot, Max. "Justice Nominee Reno Offers New Priorities." *Christian Science Monitor*, 18 February 1993: 8.

Bor, Jonathan. "Little Boy Lost." *Baltimore Sun*, 10 February 2000: 1E.

Bordo, Susan. *Twilight Zones: The Hidden Life of Cultural Images from Plato to O.J.* Berkeley: University of California Press, 1997.

———. *Unbearable Weight: Feminism, Western Culture, and the Body*. Berkeley: University of California Press, 1993.

Bornstein, Kate. *Gender Outlaw: On Men, Women, and the Rest of Us*. New York: Vintage, 1994.

"Boy or Girl?" *Prime Time Live*. ABC News. 22 July 1998.

"Boys Will Be Boys, Report Says." *Toronto Star*, 23 March 1997: F8.

"Brandon Teena Murderer Sentenced." http://data.club.cc.cmu.edu/~julie/teenarage.html.

Brandon Teena Story. Dir. by Susan Muska and Greta Olafsdottir. Zeitgeist Films, 1998.

Branson, Louise. "This 'Girl' Always Knew 'She' Was a Boy." *Straits Times*, 17 March 1997: 2.

———. "U.S. Army in the Dock after Gay Soldier Beaten to Death." *Scotsman*, 12 August 1999: 11.

"A Brief Reminder of Hate." *Toronto Star*, 30 April 1999.

Brookey, Robert Alan. *Reinventing the Male Homosexual: The Rhetoric and Power of the Gay Gene*. Bloomington: Indiana University Press, 2002.

———. "Keeping a Good Wo/man Down: Normalizing Deborah Sampson Gannett." *Communication Studies* 49 (1998): 73–85.

Brophy, Stephen. "The Brandon Teena Story." http://www.stephenbrody.org/review/queer/documentary/b_teena.htm.

Brown, Mark. "k.d. Kicks Back." *Denver Rocky Mountain News*, 15 August 2000: 7D.

Brucker-Cohen, Jonah. "Brandon." *ID* (September–October 1998): 86.

Bruzzi, Stella. "Mannish Girl: k.d. lang—From Cowpunk to Androgyny." In *Sexing the Groove: Popular Music and Gender*. Ed. Sheila Whiteley. New York: Routledge, 1997. 191–206.

Bull, Chris. "Life after Death." *Advocate*, 25 April 2000: 24–28.

Bunn, Austin. "Fanning the Fame." *Village Voice*, 21 July 1998: 33.

Burbach, Chris. "Ex-Girlfriend Testifies Lotter Threatened One Victim Earlier." *Omaha World Herald*, 19 May 1995: 13SF.

———. "Jury Chosen for Lotter Murder Trial." *Omaha World Herald*, 11 May 1995: 15SF.

———. "Jury Convicts Nissen in Slayings of Three at Humboldt Farmhouse." *Omaha World Herald*, 4 March 1995: 1.

———. "Jury Told How Bodies Found: Triple-Slaying Trial Begins." *Omaha World Herald*, 21 February 1995: 11SF.

———. "Mothers of Three Victims First to Testify in Slaying Trial." *Omaha World Herald*, 22 February 1995: 15SF.

———. "Officer: Sheriff Delayed Falls City Suspects' Arrest." *Omaha World Herald*, 27 October 1994: 17SF.

———. "Prosecutor Sees 'Intent' in Three Killings." *Omaha World Herald*, 16 May 1995: 1.

———. "Three Judges to Decide Lotter's Fate." *Omaha World Herald*, 19 November 1995: 1B.

———. "Tight Security Planned for Triple-Murder Trial." *Omaha World Herald*, 21 February 1995: 1.

Burbach, Chris, and Henry J. Cordes. "Romance, Deceit, and Rage." *Omaha World Herald*, 9 January 1994: 1A.

Burke, Phyllis. *Gender Shock: Exploding the Myths of Male and Female.* New York: Anchor, 1996.

Butler, Judith. *Bodies That Matter: On the Discursive Limits of "Sex."* New York: Routledge, 1993.

———. *Gender Trouble: Feminism and the Subversion of Identity.* New York: Routledge, 1990.

———. *Gender Trouble: Feminism and the Subversion of Identity.* 10th Anniversary Edition. New York: Routledge, 1999.

Butler, Robert. "She Found Her Man." *Kansas City Star*, 22 February 2000: E6.

"Can Reno Be the People's Lawyer?" *Nation*, 21 March 1994: 370.

Caplan, Lincoln. "Janet Reno's Choice." *New York Times Magazine*, 15 May 1994: 42–46, 70.

Carr, Jay. "Denial and Death in Falls City." *Boston Globe*, 15 January 1999: D7.

Chase, Cheryl. "Hermaphrodites with Attitude: Mapping the Emergence of Intersex Political Action." *GLQ* 4 (1998): 189–212.

Christenson, Sig. "A Soldier's Murder Clouds S.A. General's Promotion." *San Antonio Express-News*, 17 November 2002: 6B.

Clines, Francis X. "For Gay Soldier, a Daily Barrage of Threats and Slurs." *New York Times*, 12 December 1999: 33.

———. "Killer's Trial Shows Gay Soldier's Anguish." *New York Times*, 9 December 1999: A18.

———. "Mother Sees No End to Ordeal in Slaying." *New York Times*, 10 January 2000: A13.

Colapinto, John. *As Nature Made Him: The Boy Who Was Raised as a Girl.* New York: HarperCollins, 2000.

———. "The True Story of John/Joan." *Rolling Stone*, 11 December 1997: 55–73, 92–97.

Condit, Celeste. "Crafting Virtue: The Rhetorical Construction of Public Morality." *Quarterly Journal of Speech* 73 (1987): 79–97.

———. "Hegemony in a Mass-Mediated Society: Concordance about Reproductive Technologies." *Critical Studies in Mass Communication* 11 (1993): 205–30.

———. "In Praise of Eloquent Diversity: Gender and Rhetoric as Public Persuasion." *Women's Studies in Communication* 20 (1997): 91–116.

———. "Post-Burke: Transcending the Sub-stance of Dramatism." *Quarterly Journal of Speech* 78 (1992): 349–55.

Contreras, Joseph. "Janet versus Jeb." *Newsweek*, 5 September 2001: Web exclusive.

Cook, Richard. "Music: Cowpoke in the Eye." *Punch*, 2 June 1989: 48.

Cooper, Brenda. "*Boys Don't Cry* and Female Masculinity: Reclaiming a Life and Dismantling the Politics of Normative Heterosexuality." *Critical Studies in Media Communication* 19 (2002): 44–63.

Cromelin, Richard. "For k.d. lang, It's Bye-Bye, Patsy—Hello '*Ingenue*.'" *Los Angeles Times*, 2 August 1992: CAL5.

"Crossing Over." *20/20*. ABC News. 1 August 1997.

Dahlburg, John-Thor. "The Nation." *Los Angeles Times*, 18 September 2002: 12.

"Dateline Iowa." *Des Moines Register*, 8 May 1998: 7.

Dean, Tim. *Beyond Sexuality*. Chicago: University of Chicago Press, 2000.

"Deception on the Prairie." *Advocate*, 8 February 1994: 16–17.

Delmont, Jim. "'Murder' Vividly Portrays Shocking Triple Killings." *Omaha World Herald*, 24 May 1997: 61SF.

Diamond, Milton. "Sexual Identity, Monozygotic Twins Reared in Discordant Sex Roles and a BBC Follow-Up." *Archives of Sexual Behavior* 11 (1982): 181–86.

———. "Sexual Identity and Sex Roles." *Humanist* (March–April 1978): 16–19.

———. "Sexual Identity and Sexual Orientation in Children with Traumatized or Ambiguous Genitalia." *Journal of Sex Research* 34 (1997): 199–211.

Diamond, Milton, and Keith Sigmundson. "Sex Reassignment at Birth: Long-Term Review and Clinical Implications." *Archives of Pediatric and Adolescent Medicine* 151 (1997): 298–304.

Dickie, Mary. "Drag." *Maclean's*, 25 August 1997: 78.

Donahue, Deirdre. "The Triumph of Nature over Medical Hubris." *USA Today*, 23 March 2000: 7D.

Dougherty, Steve, and Kristina Johnson. "Quirky k.d. lang Steps Out as Country Music's Latest Hit Kicker." *People*, 4 July 1988: 94.

Dow, Bonnie J. "Ellen, Television, and the Politics of Gay and Lesbian Visibility." *Critical Studies in Media Communication* 18 (2001): 123–40.

———. "Feminism, Miss America, and Media Mythology." *Rhetoric and Public Affairs* 6 (2003): 127–60.

———. *Prime-Time Feminism: Television, Media Culture, and the Women's Movement since 1970*. Philadelphia: University of Pennsylvania Press, 1996.

Dreger, Alice Domurat. *Hermaphrodites and the Medical Invention of Sex*. Cambridge: Harvard University Press, 1998.

Duberman, Martin. *Stonewall*. New York: Plume, 1993.

Duggan, Joe. "Mom Outraged over Oscar." *Lincoln Journal Star*, 28 March 2000: A1.

[Works Cited]

Duggan, Lisa. *Sapphic Slashers: Sex, Violence, and American Modernity.* Durham: Duke University Press, 2000.

Dunne, John Gregory. "The Humboldt Murders." *New Yorker,* 13 January 1997: 45–62.

Ebert, Roger. "Ignorance Spawns Murder in 'Teena' Documentary." *Chicago SunTimes,* 5 March 1999: 31 (Weekend Plus).

Ebert, Teresa L. *Ludic Feminism and After: Postmodernism, Desire, and Labor in Late Capitalism.* Ann Arbor: University of Michigan Press, 1996.

Elliott, David. "'Boys Don't Cry' a Sorry Rendering of a Sad Tale." *San Diego Union-Tribune,* 21 October 1999: 7.

———. "A Tortured Soul Sinks into the Bleak Landscape of 'Brandon Teena Story.'" *San Diego Union-Tribune,* 26 March 1999: E10.

Elliott, Patricia, and Katrina Roen. "Transgenderism and the Question of Embodiment: Promising Queer Politics?" *GLQ* 4 (1998): 231–62.

"Enter Ms. Reno." *The Economist,* 8 September 2001: 55.

Epstein, Julia, and Kristina Straub. "Introduction: The Guarded Body." In *Body Guards: The Cultural Politics of Gender Ambiguity.* Ed. Julia Epstein and Kristina Staub. New York: Routledge, 1991. 1–28.

Epstein, Keith. "Reno Took the High Road, Lost Map along the Way." *Tampa Tribune,* 13 September 2002: A4.

Evans, Nicola. "Games of Hide and Seek: Race, Gender, and Drag in *The Crying Game* and *The Birdcage.*" *Text and Performance Quarterly* 18 (1998): 199–216.

Farber, Jim. "Music Videos—Harvest of Seven Years (Cropped and Chronicled) Featuring k.d. lang." *Rolling Stone,* 17 October 1991: 102.

Fausto-Sterling, Anne. "The Five Sexes." *Sciences* (March–April 1993): 20–24.

———. "How Many Sexes Are There?" *New York Times,* 12 March 1993.

———. *Sexing the Body: Gender Politics and the Construction of Sexuality.* New York: Basic Books, 2000.

Feinberg, Leslie. *Transgender Warriors: Making History from Joan of Arc to Dennis Rodman.* Boston: Beacon, 1996.

"Fierce Flicks." *Ms.* (September–October 1998): 85.

Fiske, John, and John Hartley. *Reading Television.* New York: Methuen, 1978.

Fletcher, David. "Boy Raised as Girl after Surgical Accident: 'I Wanted to Climb Trees, Not Wear Dresses.'" *Daily Telegraph,* 15 March 1997: 3.

Flick, Larry. "Singles—*Sexuality,* a Single by k.d. lang." *Billboard,* 10 February 1996: 68.

Foucault, Michel. *Discipline and Punish: The Birth of the Prison.* Trans. Alan Sheridan. New York: Vintage, 1979.

France, David. "An Inconvenient Woman." *New York Times Magazine,* 28 May 2000: 24–29.

[Works Cited]

Friedman, Herbert J. "Teena Brandon Still Being Abused." *Omaha World-Herald*, 25 February 2000: 19.

Friess, Steve. "Insult and Injury." *Advocate*, 1 February 2000: 22–23.

Fruhling, Larry. "Charade Revealed Prior to Killings." *Des Moines Register*, 9 January 1994: 1.

"Furthermore. . . ." *Omaha World-Herald*, 29 March 2000: A22.

"Gambling on Reno." *National Review*, 15 November 1993: 44.

Gandee, Charles. "Cross-Dressing for Success." *Vogue* (July 1997): 146–49.

Garber, Marjorie. *Vested Interests: Cross-Dressing and Cultural Anxiety*. New York: Routledge, 1992.

Gardner, Elysa. "A Plucky Strike." *Los Angeles Times*, 10 June 1997: F1:4.

"General Janny Baby." *People Weekly*, 29 March 1993: 40.

Gilman, Sander L. "Black Bodies, White Bodies: Toward an Iconography of Female Sexuality in Late-Nineteenth Century Art, Medicine, and Literature." In *"Race," Writing, and Difference*. Ed. Henry Louis Gates Jr. Chicago: University of Chicago Press, 1985. 223–61.

Ginsburg, Mark. "Cars: Tuckin'." *Vanity Fair* (April 1990): 202–6.

Goldberg, Jeffrey. "What Is Janet Reno Thinking?" *New York Times Magazine*, 6 July 1997: 16–21, 39–40, 48.

Goldiner, Dave. "Emotional Reno Is Seared by Heat from Hometown." *Daily News*, 31 March 2000: 4.

Gordon, Barbara. "Will She Be a Force for Change?" *Washington Post Parade Magazine*, 2 May 1993: 4–7.

Gorman, Christine. "A Boy without a Penis." *Time*, 24 March 1997: 83.

Grabrenya, Frank. "Tale of Masquerade, Murder Should Spark Conversation." *Columbus Dispatch*, 7 January 1999: 4.

Graff, Gary. "lang Rekindles Her Muse." *Plain Dealer*, 27 July 2001: 16.

Graves, Tom. "k.d. lang." *Washington Post*, 21 August 1994: WBK8.

Greene, Ronald Walter. "Another Materialist Rhetoric." *Critical Studies in Mass Communication* 15 (1998): 21–40.

Guernsey, Lisa. "Researchers Challenge Idea of Sexual Neutrality." *Chronicle of Higher Education*, 28 March 1997: A18.

Guterman, Jimmy. "Records—Angel with a Lariat." *Rolling Stone*, 16 July 1987: 136–138.

Guthman, Edward. "'Brandon' Makes Simple Plea for Compassion." *San Francisco Chronicle*, 19 February 1999: D3.

Guzman, Isaac. "By Request, a Trip Down Memory Lang." *Daily News*, 13 December 2000: 42.

Hackett, Thomas. "The Execution of Private Barry Winchell: The Real Story behind the 'Don't Ask, Don't Tell' Murder." *Rolling Stone*, 20 March 2000: 5–8.

[Works Cited]

Halberstam, Judith. *Female Masculinity*. Durham: Duke University Press, 1998.

———. "Transgender Butch: Butch/FTM Border Wars and the Masculine Contin-uum." *GLQ* 4 (1998): 287–310.

———. "The Transgender Gaze in *Boys Don't Cry.*" *Screen* 42 (2001): 294–98.

Hale, C. Jacob. "Consuming the Living, Dis(re)membering the Dead in the Butch/FTM Border Wars and the Masculine Continuum." *GLQ* 4 (1998): 311–48.

Hale, Jacob. "Suggested Rules for Non-transsexuals Writing about Transsexuals, Transsexuality, or Trans———." http://www.actlab.utexas.edu/~sandy/hale.rules.html.rules.html.

Hammel, Paul. "Relatives Say Victim Was Threatened by Two Men." *Omaha World Herald*, 3 January 1994: 9SF.

Handelman, David. "In Brief—Ingenue by k.d. lang." *Vogue* (April 1992): 304.

Harrington, Richard. "k.d. lang; Basking in the Sun." *Washington Post*, 25 August 2000: N11.

Harrington, Richard, Tom Shales, and Rita Kempley. "k.d. lang: Harvest of Seven Years (Cropped and Chronicled)." *Washington Post*, 3 October 1991: C7.

Hartl, John. "Seattle International Film Festival." *Seattle Times*, 7 June 1998: M1.

Hausman, Bernice L. "Recent Transgender Theory." *Feminist Studies* 27 (2001): 465–90.

Hawkes, Nigel. "Boy Raised as Girl Discovers Happiness as a Man." *Times*, 15 March 1997:

Helligar, Jeremy. "Movable Feast." *People*, 13 November 1995: 37.

Henderson, Lisa. "The Class Character of *Boys Don't Cry.*" *Screen* 42 (2001): 299–303.

Hiltbrand. "Absolute Torch and Twang." *People*, 19 June 1989: 21–22.

Hinson, Hal. "lang's Piquant '*Salmonberries.*'" *Washington Post*, 26 August 1994: D7.

Hochman, Steve. "The Next C&W Legends?" *Los Angeles Times*, 1 April 1990: 77.

Holden, Stephen. "Documentary Traces Killing of Transgendered Teen." *New York Times*, 22 January 1999: 7.

———. "Down-Home Postcards from Two of Country's Frontier Women." *New York Times*, 28 May 1989: C21.

———. "k.d. lang's Special Brand of Balladlike Country Rock." *New York Times*, 14 August 1989: C12.

———. "A Rape and Beating, Later Three Murders and Then the Twist." *New York Times*, 23 September 1998: B5.

hooks, bell. *Ain't I a Woman: Black Women and Feminism*. Boston: South End Press, 1981.

Huisman, Mark J. "Docfest." *Village Voice*, 2 June 1998: 160.

Hyde, Alan. *Bodies of Law*. Princeton: Princeton University Press, 1997.

Ingles, Ken. "Girls' Right." *Miami Herald*, 20 April 2000: 4.

[Works Cited]

"Janet Reno." *National Journal*, 14 June 1997: 1231.

Jenkins, Henry. "*Star Trek* Rerun, Reread, Rewritten: Fan Writing as Textual Poaching." *Critical Studies in Mass Communication* 6 (1988): 85–107.

Jennings, Nicholas. "Unchained Melodies: *Ingenue* by k.d. lang." *Maclean's*, 16 March 1992: S5.

Jennings, Nicholas, and Celina Bell. "Riding High on a Down-Home Revival." *Maclean's*, 3 August 1987: 50–51.

Jennings, Nicholas, and Anne Gregor. "A Bracing Breeze from Western Canada." *Maclean's*, 30 May 1988: 58–59.

Johnson, Brian D. "A Lighter Side of lang." *Maclean's*, 6 November 1995: 68–70.

———. "Sex, Love, and Human Remains." *Maclean's*, 1 November 1999: 68.

Johnston, David, and Deborah Sontag. "In Control." *New York Times*, 23 November 1997: A1.

Jones, Aphrodite. *All She Wanted: A True Story of Sexual Deception and Murder in America's Heartland*. New York: Pocket Books, 1996.

Joyce, Mike. "Straight from the Heart." *Washington Post*, 18 March 1992: B7.

"Justice, the Janet Reno Way." *U.S. News and World Report*, 15 March 1993: 28.

Keenan, John. "'Brandon Teena' a Chilling Documentary." *Omaha World-Herald*, 21 October 1998: 45.

———. "Portrayals Illuminate 'Don't Cry.'" *Omaha World-Herald*, 19 February 2000: 65.

Kessler, Suzanne J. *Lessons from the Intersexed*. New Brunswick: Rutgers University Press, 1998.

———. "The Medical Construction of Gender: Case Management of Intersexed Infants." *Signs: Journal of Women in Culture and Society* 16 (1990): 3–26.

Kielwasser, Alfred P., and Michelle Wolf. "Mainstream Television, Adolescent Homosexuality, and Significant Silence." *Critical Studies in Mass Communication* 9 (1992): 350–73.

Koff, Stephen. "Military Discharge of Gays, Lesbians Hits Fourteen-Year High." *Plain Dealer*, 14 March 2002: A2.

Kondracke, Morton. "Cruel and Unusual." *Washingtonian* (April 1996): 74.

Konigsberg, Eric. "Death of a Deceiver." *Playboy* (January 1995): 92–94, 193–99.

Kova, Vincent. "Stranger in a Strange Land: Brandon Teena." *Outspoken* 4 (2000): 24.

Kuda, Marie. "Gay and Lesbian Books: They're Everywhere." *Booklist*, 1 June 1994: 1735.

Labash, Matt. "Janet Reno Rides Again . . . into the Swamp of Florida Politics." *Weekly Standard*, 25 March 2002: 21.

Laqueur, Thomas. *Making Sex: Body and Gender from the Greeks to Freud*. Cambridge: Harvard University Press, 1990.

Laurence, Charles. "The Boy Who Never Was." *Ottawa Citizen*, 2 April 2000: C2.

[Works Cited]

Lee, Craig. "Lower-Case lang's Torch 'n' Twang." *Los Angeles Times*, 2 September 1989: V5.

Lee, Gretchen. "Homophobia in the Heartland." *Curve* (September 1998): 16–17.

Leibovich, Mark. "Knock-Knock: Janet Who?" *Washington Post*, 9 September 2002: C1.

Leo, John. "Boy, Girl, Boy Again." *U.S. News and World Report*, 31 March 1997: 17.

———. "Elian: The Opera." *U.S. News and World Report*, 8 May 2000: 12.

"Letters to Norah." Retrieved 27 November 2000. http://www.advocate.com/html/stories/816/816_norah.html.

Lorch, Donatella. "Janet Reno's Last Crusade." *Newsweek*, 24 April 2000: 37.

Lynch, Tim. "She's Baaaaack!" *National Review Online*, 5 September 2001.

MacKenzie, Gordene Olga. *Transgender Nation*. Bowling Green: Bowling Green State University Popular Press, 1994.

Martin, Emily. "The Egg and the Sperm: How Science Has Constructed a Romance Based on Stereotypical Male-Female Roles." *Signs: Journal of Women in Culture and Society* 16 (1991): 485–501.

Martz, Ron. "General Faces a Battle for Third Star." *Atlanta Journal-Constitution*, 16 October 2002: 3A.

Matteo, Steve. "Partners in the American Songbook." *Newsday*, 1 October 2001: B09.

McGee, Michael Calvin. "A Materialist's Conception of Rhetoric." In *Explorations in Rhetoric: Essays in Honor of Douglas Ehninger*. Ed. Raymie E. McKerrow. Glenview, Ill.: Scott-Foresman, 1982. 23–48.

———. "Text, Context, and the Fragmentation of Contemporary Culture." *Western Journal of Speech Communication* 54 (1990): 274–89.

McKenna, Kristine. "A Farm Gal Trades the Spotlight for the Sunshine." *Los Angeles Times*, 10 October 1995: F1.

McKerrow, Raymie E. "Critical Rhetoric: Theory and Praxis." *Communication Monographs* 56 (1989): 91–111.

McNamara, Mary. "Transgender Artists, Works Gaining Acceptance." *Los Angeles Times*, 28 February 2001: E1.

Meddis, Sam Vincent. "For Reno, a Rocky First Year." *USA Today*, 28 January 1994: 4A.

Meyerowitz, Joanne. *How Sex Changed: A History of Transsexuality in the United States*. Cambridge: Harvard University Press, 2002.

———. "Sex Change and the Popular Press: Historical Notes on Transsexuality in the United States, 1930–1955." *GLQ* 4 (1998): 159–88.

"Military Still Wrong on Gays." *Nashville Tennessean*, 7 June 2001: 16A.

"Military Whitewash." *Advocate*, 14 September 1999: 12–14.

Miller, Francesca. "Putting Teena Brandon's Story on Film." *Gay and Lesbian Review* 7 (2000): 39.

[Works Cited]

Milward, John. "Recordings—*Ingenue* by k.d. lang." *Rolling Stone*, 30 April 1992: 57.

Minge, Jim. "Film to Depict Triple Murder." *Omaha World Herald*, 21 October 1995: 61SF.

Minkowitz, Donna. "Love Hurts." *Village Voice*, 19 April 1994: 24–30.

"The Mirror Has Two Faces." *Dateline NBC*. 23 March 2001.

Mockus, Martha. "Queer Thoughts on Country Music and k.d. lang." In *Queering the Pitch: The New Gay and Lesbian Musicology*. Ed. Philip Brett, Elizabeth Wood, and Gary C. Thomas. New York: Routledge, 1994. 257–71.

Mollins, Carl. "New Fame for a Soaring Superstar." *Maclean's*, 26 December 1988: 14–15.

Money, John. "Ablatio Penis: Normal Male Infant Sex-Reassigned as a Girl." *Archives of Sexual Behavior* 4 (1975): 65–71.

———. "Sex Reassignment as Related to Hermaphroditism and Transsexuality." In *Transsexualism and Sex Reassignment*. Ed. Richard Green and John Money. Baltimore: Johns Hopkins University Press, 1969. 91–114.

Money, John, and Anke A. Ehrhardt. *Man and Woman, Boy and Girl*. Baltimore: Johns Hopkins University Press, 1972.

Money, John, and Patricia Tucker. *Sexual Signatures: On Being a Man or a Woman*. Boston: Little, Brown, 1975.

Morgan, Riley. "Permission Granted to Forward This Email to Other Lists/Persons." Retrieved 27 November 2000. http://www.koan.com/~1bear/alert.html.

Morrison, Benjamin. "The Life and Death of Brandon Teena." *Times-Picayune*, 25 July 1999: T5.

Moss, Debra Cassens. "A Popular AG Is Lesson in Image." *ABA Journal* (October 1993): 36.

Moton, Tony. "Documentary Only the First." *Omaha World Herald*, 22 October 1998: 41.

———. "Film Tracks Murder Case." *Omaha World Herald*, 13 October 1996: 1E.

———. "Story Inspires Filmmakers." *Omaha World Herald*, 5 November 1995: 1E.

Mundy, Liza. "Punch Lines." *Washington Post Magazine*, 25 January 1998: 6–11, 21–25.

Muñoz, Lorenza. "'Boys' Is Proving to Be a Hard Sell." *Los Angeles Times*, 8 March 2000: 1F.

"Murder Case Inspires New Play." *Omaha World Herald*, 18 May 1997: 11.

Murphy, Caryle. "Can an Infant's Sex Be Changed?" *Washington Post*, 18 March 1997: Z07.

Muther, Christopher. "After Some Time Down, k.d. lang Gets Happy." *Boston Globe*, 27 August 2000: L5.

Negus, Keith. *Popular Music in Theory: An Introduction*. Hanover, N.H.: Wesleyan University Press, 1996.

[Works Cited]

"New Trial Sought in Triple Killing." *Des Moines Register*, 8 May 1998: 7 (Metro).

Nichols, Natalie. "Her Castles in the Sand." *Los Angeles Times Calendar*, 11 June 2000: 3.

Ono, Kent A., and John M. Sloop. "Commitment to Telos: A Sustained Critical Rhetoric." *Communication Monographs* 59 (1992): 48–60.

———. *Shifting Borders: Rhetoric, Immigration, and California's "Proposition 187."* Pittsburgh: Temple University Press, 2002.

"On Video." *St. Petersburg Times*, 21 April 2000: 14W.

Ostrow, Ronad J. "The Blunt Attorney General Speaks Her Mind—As Usual." *Los Angeles Times*, 4 July 1993: M3.

———. "Reno Gets High Marks for Her Drive, Integrity." *Los Angeles Times*, 12 February 1993: A1, 15.

Pareles, Jon. "k.d. lang Leaves Metaphor Behind." *New York Times*, 8 October 1995: H37.

Pearson, Mike. " 'Boys' an Intense Drama." *Denver Rocky Mountain News*, 21 April 2000: 14D.

Peterson, Carla. *"Does of the Word": African-American Women Speakers and Writers in the North (1830–1880)*. New York: Oxford University Press, 1995.

Peterson, Richard A. *Creating Country Music: Fabricating Authenticity*. Chicago: University of Chicago Press, 1997.

Phelan, Peggy. *Mourning Sex: Performing Public Memories*. New York: Routledge, 1997.

———. *Unmarked: The Politics of Performance*. New York: Routledge, 1993.

Pidduck, Julianne. "Risk and Queer Spectatorship." *Screen* 42 (2001): 97–102.

Powell, Joy. "Lawsuit against Former Sheriff Dismissed in Humboldt Case." *Omaha World Herald*, 11 August 1995: 18.

Pressley, Sue Anne. "Hate May Have Triggered Fatal Barracks Beating." *Washington Post*, 11 August 1999: A1.

"Prison Term in Death of Cross-Dresser." *Des Moines Register*, 1 September 1995: 7.

Probyn, Elspeth. *Sexing the Self: Gendered Positions in Cultural Studies*. New York: Routledge, 1993,

Prosser, Jay. *Second Skins: The Body Narratives of Transsexuality*. New York: Columbia University Press, 1998.

Quan, Douglas, and Joanne Laucius. "Why Brenda Wanted to Be a Boy Again." *Ottawa Citizen*, 10 February 2000: A1.

Ramet, Sabrina Petra. "Gender Reversals and Gender Cultures: An Introduction." In *Gender Reversals and Gender Cultures: Anthropological and Historical Perspectives*. Ed. Sabrina Petra Ramet. New York: Routledge. 1–21.

Raymond, Janice. *The Transsexual Empire: The Making of the She-Male*. Boston: Beacon, 1979.

Reiner, William. "To Be Male or Female—That Is the Question." *Archives of Pediatric and Adolescent Medicine* 151 (1997): 224–25.

[Works Cited]

Reske, Henry J. "Reno Called Tough, Honest." *American Bar Association Journal* (April 1993): 18.

———. "The Unflappable Janet Reno." *American Bar Association Journal* (February 1996: 16.

"Rethinking Gender Identity." *Maclean's*, 24 March 1997: 31.

Rich, Adrienne. "Compulsory Heterosexuality and Lesbian Existence." *Signs* 5 (1981): 631–60.

Ricks, Ingrid. "Heartland Homicide." *Advocate*, 8 March 1994: 28–30.

Roan, Shari. "The Basis of Sexual Identity." *Los Angeles Times*, 14 March 1997: E1, 8.

Rogers, Ray. "Sound Advice—*Ingenue* by k.d. lang." *Interview* (April 1992): 34.

Rohter, Larry. "Tough 'Front-Line' Warrior." *New York Times*, 12 February 1993: A1, 22.

"Rough Rider." *U.S. News and World Report*, 7 June 1993: 32–33.

Rubin, Gayle. "Thinking Sex: Notes for a Radical Theory of the Politics of Sexuality." In *American Feminist Thought at Century's End: A Reader*. Ed. Linda S. Kauffman. Cambridge: Blackwell, 1993. 3–63.

Ruth, Daniel. "Reno Lacks Glitter for Political Gamble." *Tampa Tribune*, 23 May 2001: Nation/World 2.

Sanchez, Mary. "Officials Meet with Slain Soldier's Parents." *Kansas City Star*, 28 July 2000: B3.

———. "Parents Speak Out after Son Beaten to Death in Army." *Kansas City Star*, 19 March 2000: A32.

Schoemer, Karen. "Straying from Country's Straight and Narrow." *New York Times*, 12 April 1992: H26, H29.

Schultz, Vicki. "Women 'Before' the Law: Judicial Stories about Women, Work, and Sex Segregation on the Job." In *Feminists Theorize the Political*. Ed. Judith Butler and Joan W. Scott. New York: Routledge, 1992. 297–340.

"Second Trial in Killing of Three Begins Today." *Des Moines Register*, 15 May 1995: 2.

Sedgwick, Eve Kosofsky. *Epistemology of the Closet*. Berkeley: University of California Press, 1990.

Sewell, Dan. "Student 'Invited to Withdraw' from School for Cross-Dressing." *Athens Daily News*, 30 October 1998: 4B.

"Sex: Unknown." *Nova*. PBS. 30 Nov. 2001.

Shapiro, Judith. "Transsexualism: Reflections on the Persistence of Gender and the Mutability of Sex." In *Body Guards: The Cultural Politics of Gender Ambiguity*. Ed. Julia Epstein and Kristina Staub. New York: Routledge, 1991. 248–79.

Sischy, Ingrid. "k.d." *Interview* (September 1997):138–42.

Sisk, Richard. "Reno Has Mild Parkinson's." *Daily News*, 17 November 1995: 2.

[Works Cited]

Sloop, John M. "'Apology Made to Whoever Pleases': Cultural Discipline and the Grounds of Interpretation." *Communication Quarterly* 42 (1994): 345–62.

———. *The Cultural Prison: Discourse, Prisoners, and Punishment.* Tuscaloosa: University of Alabama Press, 1996.

———. "The Emperor's New Makeup: Cool Cynicism and Popular Music Criticism." *Popular Music and Society* 23 (1999): 51–74.

———. "'The Parent I Never Had': The Contemporary Construction of Alternatives to Incarceration." *Communication Studies* 43 (1992): 1–13.

Small, Michael. "k.d. lang Loves It Up—*All You Can Eat* by k.d. lang." *Mademoiselle* (November 1995): 104.

Smith, R. J. "It's Alive." *Spin* (August 1996): 44–52, 112.

Soeder, John. "Summer of Love; for k.d. lang." *Plain Dealer*, 19 August 2000: 1E.

"Soldier's Murder Draws Attention of Gay Community." Associated Press. 9 August 1999.

Spanier, Bonnie. "Encountering the Biological Sciences: Ideology, Language, and Learning." In *Writing, Teaching, and Learning in the Disciplines.* Ed. Anne Herrington and Charles Moran. New York: MLA, 1992. 193–212.

Specter, Michael. "Patsy Cline Meets Judy Garland." *New York Times*, 23 July 1992: C1.

Spencer, Terry. "Janet Reno Says She May Run for Governor." *Naples (Florida) Daily News*, 19 May 2001. http://www.naplesnews.com/01/05/florida/d635687a.htm.

"Standing Tall." *Time*, 10 May 1993: 46–47.

Stone, Andrea. "Soldier Admits Killing Gay Man." *USA Today*, 8 December 1999: 16A.

Stone, Jay. "Acting Like Someone Else—The Good and the Devilish." *Ottawa Citizen*, 21 April 2000: F10.

Stone, Sandy. "The *Empire* Strikes Back: A Posttranssexual Manifesto." In *Body Guards: The Cultural Politics of Gender Ambiguity.* Ed. Julia Epstein and Kristina Staub. New York: Routledge, 1991. 280–304.

Strawbridge, Patrick. "Judge Dismisses Federal Suit in Slaying of Teena Brandon." *Omaha World Herald*, 10 November 1998: 21.

Stryker, Susan. "The Transgender Issue: An Introduction." *GLQ* 4 (1998): 145–58.

Stuttaford, Genevieve. "Nonfiction—*k.d. lang: All You Get Is Me* by Victoria Starr." *Publishers Weekly*, 23 May 1994: 75.

Suro, Roberto. "Military's Discharges of Gays Increase." *Washington Post*, 2 June 2001: A20.

Swisher, Kara. "k.d. lang." *Washington Post*, 10 August 1989: C8.

Taubin, Amy. "Splitting Image." *Village Voice*, 29 September 1998: 128.

Terry, Jennifer. *An American Obsession: Science, Medicine, and Homosexuality in Modern Society.* Chicago: University of Chicago Press, 1999.

[Works Cited]

Therborn, Göran. *What Does the Ruling Class Do When It Rules?* London: Verso, 1980.

Thomas, Kevin. "Outfest '98 Saves Its Best for Last." *Los Angeles Times*, 18 September 1998: F16.

Thomas, Pierre, and David Brown. "Reno Has Parkinson's, but Will Stay on Job." *Chicago Sun-Times*, 17 November 1995: News 24.

Thompson, Mark. " 'Why Do People Have to Push Me Like That?' " *Time*, 13 December 1999: 56–58.

Timmerman, Kenneth R. "Reno Redux in Florida." *Insight on the News*, 29 October 2001: 10.

Tong, Kelvin. "Looking for Love in All the Wrong Places." *Straits Times*, 10 March 2000: 7.

"Truth, Justice, and the Reno Way." *Time*, 12 July 1993: 20.

Turner, Stephanie S. "Intersexed Identities: Locating New Intersections of Sex and Gender." *Gender and Society* 13 (1999): 457–79.

Udovitch, Mim. "k.d. lang." *Rolling Stone*, 5 August 1993: 54–58.

Vancheri, Barbara. "As Rough as It Gets." *Pittsburgh Post-Gazette*, 21 April 2000: 42.

Vaziri, Aidin. "Q&A with k.d. lang." *San Francisco Chronicle*, 30 July 2000: 37.

"Victim's Mother Blasts Swank's Oscar Speech." *Chicago Sun-Times*, 29 March 2000: 45.

Vincent, Norah. "Cunning Linguists." *Advocate*, 20 June 2000: 120.

Vise, David A. "For Reno, Elian Case Is Extremely Personal." *Washington Post*, 19 April 2000: A4.

Vivinetto, Gina. "k.d. lang, Invincible Summer." *St. Petersburg Times*, 21 July 2000: 29W.

Wade, Gerald. "Author Hopes Crime Books Can Make a Difference." *Omaha World Herald*, 27 May 1996: 33SF.

Walters, Barry. "Recordings—*All You Can Eat* by k.d. lang." *Rolling Stone*, 16 November 1995: 112.

Walser, Robert. "Highbrow, Lowbrow, Voodoo Aesthetics." In *Microphone Fiends: Youth Music and Youth Culture*. Ed. Andrew Ross and Tricia Rose. New York: Routledge, 1994. 235–49.

Wasson, David. "Political Baggage Weighs on Reno." *Tampa Tribune*, 1 September 2002: A1.

Watson, Traci. " 'I Feel Fine Now.' " *U.S. News and World Report*, 27 November 1995: 18.

Wheelwright, Julie. "The Boyfriend." *Guardian*, 20 February 1996: T6.

White, Partricia. "Girls Still Cry." *Screen* 42 (2001): 217–21.

Will, Ed. "Murder in a Small Town." *Denver Post*, 6 March 1994: 10.

Williams, Raymond. *The Long Revolution*. New York: Columbia University Press, 1961.

[Works Cited]

Willman, Chris. "k.d. lang, Sans the Twang." *Los Angeles Times*, 15 March 1992: CAL63

Wilson, William. "Roni Horn and the Art of Abstraction." *Los Angeles Times*, 22 April 1990: C91.

Wittig, Monique. "The Straight Mind." In *Out There: Marginalization and Contemporary Cultures*. Ed. Russell Ferguson et al. New York: New York Museum of Contemporary Art, 1990. 51–58.

"Woman Who Posed as a Man Is Found Slain with Two Others." *New York Times*, 4 January 1994: A11.

"Zeitgeist Films: The Brandon Teena Story: The Crime." http://www. zeitgeistfilms.com/current/brandonteena/brandoncrime.html.

Index

Aaron, Michele, 160n. 31
abuse, 76–78, 81, 96, 118
Adams, James Ring, 92
Addams, Calpernia, 5, 123–41, 145,
  148, 155n. 19, 163n. 1, 164nn. 2–3,
  164nn. 5–7, 164n. 9, 165n. 12,
  165nn. 14–15, 166nn. 23–24, 166n.
  26
Adlon, Percy, 83
Ainley, Rosa, 161n. 2
Akroyd, Dan, 112
Allen, Louise, 161n. 2
Ali, Lorraine, 162n. 11
Allison, Wes, 113, 119, 163n. 6,
  163nn. 10–11
Althusser, Louis, 20
American culture, 2, 6, 14, 33, 52, 57,
  60–62, 65, 67, 99, 105–7, 109–10,
  112, 115, 117, 120, 128, 136, 142–
  45, 152n. 16, 159n. 18, 163n. 4,
  166n. 27
Andermahr, Sonya, 161n. 2
Anderson, John, 146

Anderson, Melissa, 79
androgyny, 86, 88–89, 94–95, 97–98,
  100, 102
Angier, Natalie, 26, 32, 35–36, 39, 41,
  48
Ansen, David, 60
Appelo, Tim, 90, 92
Atherton, Tony, 160n. 25, 160n. 27
Arthur, Andrew, 79
Attali, Jacques, 87, 94

Baxter, Tom, 163n. 11
Bayles, Martha, 90
Beckerman, Jim, 78
Beinan, Andy, 72
Bell, Celina, 89–90, 92
Bennett, Tony, 101
Bennetts, Leslie, 96–97, 101, 162n. 14
Berke, Richard L., 118, 163n. 9, 163n.
  16
Berlant, Lauren, 2, 26, 52, 67–68,
  158n. 7
Bernard, Jami, 142, 160n. 25

Blumenfeld, Laura, 108, 112–13, 118–19, 163n. 12, 163n. 17

Boodman, Sandra G., 35

Boellstorff, Leslie, 159n. 13

Boone, Mike, 160n. 25, 160n. 27

Boot, Max, 111

Bor, Jonathan, 155n. 15

Bordo, Susan, 49, 109

Bornstein, Kate, 9, 11, 55, 61, 67–68, 71, 79, 81, 121, 124, 128, 158n. 6, 160n. 32, 160n. 34

Boys Don't Cry, 50, 55–57, 60–61, 66, 70–72, 77, 79, 85, 123, 157n. 4, 159n. 19, 160n. 31

brain, 26, 30, 40–42, 132, 138

Brandon, JoAnn, 59, 76–78

Brandon, Tammy, 63–64

Brandon, Teena. *See* Teena, Brandon

Brandon Teena Story, The, 4, 50, 57–59, 157n. 1, 158n. 9, 159n. 22

Branson, Louise, 128–29, 142, 155n. 15

Brinson, Billy, 65

Brookey, Robert, 14, 152n. 10, 154n. 8

Brophy, Stephen, 61

Brown, Mark, 101

Brown, David, 114

Bruce/Brenda. *See* John/Joan

Brucker-Cohen, Jonah, 63

Bruzzi, Stella, 86–88, 94–96, 98, 102, 161n. 7

Bull, Chris, 135, 164n. 2

Burbach, Chris, 57, 59, 64, 71, 74–75, 157n. 1, 159n. 13, 159n. 15, 160n. 23

Burke, Phyllis, 155n. 11

Bush, Jeb, 120

butch, 7, 11, 83, 85, 87, 95, 97, 102, 165n. 17

Butler, Judith, 1, 6, 7, 8, 22–23, 25–30, 36–37, 43, 52–54, 86, 106, 117, 126–27, 130, 140, 147–48, 151nn. 2–4,
152n. 6, 153n. 6, 158n. 6, 161n. 3, 164n. 10, 165n. 22

Butler, Robert, 60

Camus, Albert, 101

Caplan, Lincoln, 108, 111, 113, 163n. 6

Carr, Jay, 75, 160n. 25

Chase, Cheryl, 160n. 28, 160n. 30

Christenson, Sig, 129

chromosomes. *See* genetics

Clark, Major General Robert T., 129

class, 14, 35, 98–100, 102, 144. *See also* cultural capital

Cline, Patsy, 92–93, 98

Clines, Francis X., 131–32, 134

Clinton, Bill, 104, 107–8, 113

Clinton, Hillary Rodham, 113

Colapinto, John, 26, 32–33, 35–36, 40, 42, 45, 153n. 2, 153n. 5, 154n. 10, 156n. 24

Condit, Celeste, 22, 48–49, 82, 152n. 7, 152n. 15, 157n. 28, 158n. 7, 160n. 36

Contreras, Joseph, 113, 115, 163n. 20

Cook, Richard, 91–92

Cooper, Brenda, 160n. 31

Cooper, Kim, 138

Cooper, Sarah, 161n. 2

Cordes, Henry, 57, 59, 64, 71, 74–75, 159n. 13, 159n. 15, 160n. 23

Cromelin, Richard, 96, 101, 162n. 14

cross dressing. *See* transvestitism

cultural capital, 98–100, 102, 142, 162n. 8

Dahlburg, John-Thor, 163n. 11

Dean, Tim, 151n. 2

deception, gender, 23, 56–61, 63, 65–72, 81, 125, 130, 159n. 12. *See also* passing

DeGeneres, Ellen, 95, 97

Delmont, Jim, 57
Diamond, Milton, 30–33, 35–39, 41, 44, 153n. 2, 154n. 9, 155n. 13, 155n. 16, 156n. 20
Dickie, Mary, 98
"Don't ask, don't tell," 127, 138, 140
Dougherty, Steve, 89
Dow, Bonnie, 95, 156n. 23, 156n. 25
drag, 5, 6, 7, 12–13, 53, 85–86, 90, 98, 124, 130–33, 138–39, 151n. 3, 164n. 10. *See also* transvestitism
Dreger, Alice, 14, 39, 52, 61–62, 74, 76, 81, 154nn. 8–9, 160n. 25
Duberman, Martin, 165n. 16
Duggan, Joe, 77–78
Duggan, Lisa, 14
Dunne, John Gregory, 59–60, 64–66, 70, 74, 77

Ebert, Roger, 61, 71, 159n. 12
Ehrhardt, Anke A., 34, 37, 155n. 12
Elliot, Patricia, 16
Elliott, David, 60, 73, 158n. 8, 160n. 27
Epstein, Julia, 1, 10–11, 53
Epstein, Keith, 111, 163n. 11
Evans, Nicola, 6, 12

Farber, Jim, 92–93
Fausto-Sterling, Anne, 129, 154n. 8, 156n. 28
Feinberg, Leslie, 10, 80, 124, 157n. 3, 160n. 33, 161n. 36
female impersonation. *See* drag
feminism, 3, 13, 28, 41, 43–46, 48, 96, 108–9, 145, 156nn. 22–26
femme, 7, 11, 85, 129
Ferrell, Will, 109
Fisher, Justin, 5, 124
Fiske, John, 79, 94, 164n. 4
Fletcher, David, 35, 155n. 15

Foucault, Michel, 6, 17, 19, 21, 95, 152n. 14, 166n. 1
Fouratt, Jim, 133, 137, 165nn. 16–17
France, David, 130–31, 133, 138, 164n. 2, 165n. 15, 166n. 23
Friedman, Herbert, 78
Friess, Steve, 131–32, 136, 165n. 15
Fruhling, Larry, 57, 59, 159n. 12

Gandee, Charles, 98
Gannett, Deborah Sampson, 152n. 10
Garber, Marjorie, 15, 34, 41, 52–53, 55, 65–66, 68, 73, 93, 130, 132, 138, 157n. 4
Gardner, Elysa, 98
genitalia, 2, 14–16, 25, 29, 38, 40–42, 45–46, 51, 56, 59–63, 66–67, 69–70, 72, 74–75, 78, 81, 105, 126, 128, 130–34, 138, 145, 152n. 1, 154n. 9, 155n. 16, 156n. 28, 165n. 15
genetics, 29, 38, 41, 81, 96, 113, 132, 152n. 9
Gilman, Sander L., 120
Ginsburg, Mark, 93
Glover, Calvin, 5, 124
Goldberg, Jeffrey, 108, 163n. 17
Goldiner, Dave, 118
gonads. *See* genitalia
Gonzalez, Elian, 106, 118
Gordon, Barbara, 116, 163n. 6, 163n. 12, 163n. 17
Gore, Al, 108
Gorman, Christine, 26, 32, 35–36, 41, 45
Grabrenya, Frank, 159nn. 12–13
Graff, Gary, 101
Gramsci, Antonio, 22
Graves, Tom, 97
Greene, Ronald Walter, 20–23, 53–54, 158n. 7
Gregor, Anne, 90–92

Guernsey, Lisa, 35, 155n. 15
Guterman, Jimmy, 89, 92
Guthman, Edward, 69
Guzman, Isaac, 101

Hackett, Thomas, 131, 136, 164n. 2
Halberstam, Judith, 10, 16, 23, 27, 72, 82–83, 85, 87, 105, 107, 131, 158n. 6
Hale, C. Jacob, 16–17, 81–82, 123, 125–26, 139, 152n. 7, 153n. 4, 158nn. 9–10, 159nn. 10–11, 165n. 13
Hammel, Paul, 59
Handelman, David, 162n. 14
Harrington, Richard, 90, 162n. 16
Hartl, John, 159n. 13
Hartley, John, 79, 94, 164n. 4
hate crime, 124, 131
Hausman, Bernice, 146–47, 152n. 11
Hawkes, Nigel, 42
Hedwig and the Angry Inch, 145–46
Helligar, Jeremy, 162n. 11
Henderson, Lisa, 159n. 19
hermaphroditism. *See* intersexuality
Hinson, Hal, 97
Hochman, Steve, 90, 92
Holden, Stephen, 52, 61, 69, 90–92
home, politics of. *See* politics of home
hormones, 25, 38–39, 41, 76–78, 133, 165n. 15
Huisman, Mark J., 63
Hyde, Alan, 10, 25, 47–49

Ingles, Ken, 73
intersexuality, 10, 14–15, 29, 38–39, 46–47, 51–52, 56, 61–62, 73–76, 80, 154nn. 8–10, 157n. 5, 159n. 20, 160nn. 27–30

Jenkins, Henry, 161n. 5
Jennings, Nicholas, 89–92, 100

John/Joan, 2, 3, 12–13, 23, 25–49, 142, 148, 153nn. 2–7, 154n. 7, 154n. 10, 155n. 10, 155nn. 12–13, 155n. 16, 155nn. 18–19, 156nn. 19–24, 156n. 27
Johnson, Brian, 72, 89–90, 101, 162n. 11
Johnston, David, 112
Jones, Aphrodite, 54–55, 57–58, 63–66, 68–69, 71, 74–77, 157n. 2
Jorgensen, Christine, 21, 33
Joyce, Mike, 100

Keenan, John, 60, 159n. 12
Kelly, Jessica, 138
Kempley, Rita, 90
Kessler, Suzanne, 15, 29, 46, 154n. 8, 154n. 10, 155n. 17, 156n. 28, 159n. 20, 160nn. 29–30
Kielwasser, Alfred, 23, 80
Kiss, 99, 162n. 13
Koff, Stephen, 138
Kondracke, Morton, 163n. 13
Konigsberg, Eric, 57, 59, 64, 69–71, 75, 77, 159n. 14, 160n. 27
Kova, Vincent, 78
Kuda, Marie, 96
Kutteles, Patricia, 134–35
Kutteles, Wally, 134–35

Labash, Matt, 108, 112–13, 115, 120, 142
Lacan, Jacques, 34, 67
Laclau, Ernesto, 17
Lacquer, Thomas, 14, 159n. 20
lang, k.d., 4, 83–103, 116, 142, 148, 161nn. 1–2, 161nn. 4–7, 162nn. 8–10, 162n. 14, 163n. 14
Laucius, Joanne, 155n. 15, 156n. 24
Laurence, Charles, 73
Lee, Craig, 90–91, 93
Leibovitch, Mark, 113, 115, 163n. 11

Leo, John, 40, 45, 112
Lorch, Donatella, 118
Lotter, John, 51–52, 58–59, 63, 66, 158n. 9
Lotter, Michelle, 58, 159n. 15
Lovett, Lyle, 90

MacKenzie, Gordene Olga, 10, 48
Madonna, 90, 93, 97
Martin, Emily, 14–15, 152n. 9, 154n. 8
Martz, Ron, 129
Masters and Johnson, 44
Matteo, Steve, 101
McGee, Michael, 18–19, 152n. 14, 153n. 7
McKenna, Kristine, 162n. 11
McKerrow, Raymie, 17–18, 143, 153n. 7
McNamara, Mary, 79
Meddis, Sam Vincent, 163n. 9
Meyerowitz, Joanne, 14–16, 21, 33, 153n. 2
Miller, Francesca, 79
Millett, Kate, 156n. 24
Milward, John, 100
Minge, Jim, 157n. 1
Mink, Ben, 100
Minkowitz, Donna, 63, 65–67, 69–72, 74–75, 77
Mitchell, John Cameron, 145
Mockus, Martha, 85–86
Mollins, Carl, 89–91
Money, John, 3, 25, 30–34, 37–38, 40–44, 46, 154n. 10, 155n. 12, 155n. 16, 156n. 21
Morrison, Keith, 44, 79
Moss, Debra Cassens, 163n. 17
Moton, Tony, 157n. 1, 159n. 13
Mouffe, Chantal, 17
Mundy, Liza, 104, 109, 120, 162n. 1, 163n. 6, 163n. 16, 163n. 19
Munoz, Lorenza, 60

murder, 4–5, 8, 23, 52, 54, 57–61, 123–24, 127, 131, 134–35, 138–40, 142
Murphy, Caryle, 155n. 15
Muther, Christopher, 101

Negus, Keith, 85–86
Nichols, Natalie, 101, 162n. 16
Nissen, Tom, 51–52, 59, 63, 66, 158n. 9

Ono, Kent, 152n. 16, 153n. 7, 166n. 1
Ostrow, Ronald J., 108, 111, 116, 163n. 12

pansexuality, 97
Pareles, Jon, 96
Parton, Dolly, 89, 92
passing, 9, 15, 59–60, 65–66, 73, 79, 130, 135, 159n. 13
Patai, Daphne, 45
Pearl, Minnie, 92
Pearson, Mike, 159n. 17
Peirce, Kimberly, 72–73
penis. See genitalia
Peterson, Carla, 104, 110, 112
Peterson, Richard, 89, 162n. 9
Phelan, Peggy, 33, 130
Pidduck, Julianne, 61
politics of home, 1, 11–12, 145–49, 152n. 8, 162n. 12
postmodernism, 83, 90
poststructuralism, 17, 19
Powell, Joy, 159n. 13
Presley, Elvis, 89, 92–93
Pressley, Sue Anne, 128, 131–32, 164n. 11
Probyn, Elspeth, 36–37, 54
Prosser, Jay, 1, 8, 11–12, 145–47, 151nn. 3–4

Quan, Douglas, 155n. 15, 156n. 24
queer sexuality, 6, 10–11, 67, 85–86, 95, 128–30, 140, 146–47

Ramet, Sabrina Petra, 16, 28, 47
rape, 3, 4, 51–52, 59, 63, 72, 77
Raymond, Janice, 9, 137
Reimer, David. *See* John/Joan
Reiner, William, 41
Reno, Janet, 4, 5, 23, 104–22, 142,
    148, 162n. 1, 163nn. 5–20
Reno, Jane Wood, 113–14, 163n. 11
Reske, Henry J., 113–14, 116, 163n.
    17
Rich, Adrienne, 36
Ricks, Ingrid, 57, 63, 65, 69, 74, 159n.
    15
Roan, Shari, 26, 32, 35–36, 40, 42
Roen, Katrina, 16, 158n. 8
Rogers, Ray, 100, 162n. 14
Rohter, Larry, 107–8, 111, 113, 116,
    163n. 19
Rubin, Gayle, 8–9, 152n. 6
Ruth, Daniel, 163n. 6

Salmonberries, 83, 97
Sanchez, Mary, 131, 135, 163n. 1
Saturday Night Live, 4, 106, 109, 117
Scalora, Mario, 78
Schoemer, Karen, 100, 142
Schultz, Vicki, 164n. 8
Sedgwick, Eve, 82, 126, 133
Sewell, Dan, 157n. 4
Sex Pistols, 162n. 13
sexual abuse. *See* abuse
sexual reassignment, 2, 3, 9, 15–16, 25,
    29–33, 35, 37–40, 44–49, 51, 56,
    61, 72, 74–76, 124, 127, 133, 137–
    38, 152n. 1, 155nn. 16–17, 159n.
    20, 166n. 27
Shales, Tom, 90
Shapiro, Judith, 15
Sigmundson, Keith, 30–33, 35–36, 39,
    41, 44, 153n. 2, 154n. 10, 155n. 13,
    155n. 16, 156n. 20
Sischy, Ingrid, 162n. 14

Sisk, Richard, 115
Sloop, John, 152n. 17, 153n. 7, 162n.
    13, 166n. 1
Smith, R. J., 99
Snyderman, Nancy, 41
Soeder, John, 162n. 16
Soldier's Girl, 123, 163n. 1
Sontag, Deborah, 112
Spanier, Bonnie, 14–15, 152n. 9,
    154n. 8
Specter, Michael, 96, 100
Spencer, Terry, 114–15
Starr, Victoria, 96, 161n. 2
Stein, Seymour, 90
Stone, Andrea, 128
Stone, Jay, 72
Stone, Sandy, 9–10, 15, 124, 160n. 34,
    161n. 36, 166n. 27
Straub, Kristina, 1, 10–11, 53
Strawbridge, Patrick, 159n. 12
Streep, Meryl, 101
Stryker, Susan, 10, 53, 55
Stuttaford, Genevieve, 96
Suro, Roberto, 138
Swank, Hilary, 50, 77–78
Swisher, Kara, 91

Taubin, Amy, 160n. 25
Teena, Brandon, 3, 16, 23, 50–82, 85,
    123, 125, 130, 133, 137, 139, 142,
    146, 148, 157nn. 1–5, 158n. 9,
    159nn. 11–19, 159nn. 21–22,
    160nn. 23–27, 160n. 31, 165n.13,
    165n. 17
Terry, Jennifer, 14, 154n. 8
Therborn, Goran, 20
Thomas, Pierre, 114, 159n. 22
Thompson, Mark, 131–32, 164n. 2
Thompson, Jack, 118–20
Timmerman, Kenneth R., 120
Tisdel, Lana, 66, 69, 71–72
Tong, Kelvin, 73

transgenderism, 4, 8, 9, 10–13, 16–17, 21, 23, 48, 50–82, 121, 124, 127, 130–33, 137, 140, 142–43, 146–47, 152n. 11, 153n. 4, 157nn. 3–4, 159nn. 10–11, 160nn. 31–34, 165n. 13, 166n. 27
transnationalism, 143–45
transsexuality, 5, 9–10, 14–16, 53, 55, 73, 80, 124, 138, 146, 153n. 4, 159n. 10
transvestism, 9–11, 15–16, 55, 59–60, 73, 86, 92, 97, 102, 130–31, 152n. 10. *See also* drag
Truth, Sojourner, 104, 110, 112
Tucker, Patricia, 34, 38, 155n. 12
Turner, Stephanie, 152n. 8

Udovitch, Mim, 96–97, 100
United States. *See* American culture
urination, 34, 36, 42, 47, 66–67, 155n. 16

vagina. *See* genitalia
Vancheri, Barbara, 60
Vaziri, Aidin, 162n. 16

Vincent, Norah, 133, 137, 165n. 18
Vise, David A., 118
Vivinetto, Gina, 162n. 16

Wade, Gerald, 159n. 13
Walters, Barry, 162n. 14
Walser, Robert, 162n. 15
Wasson, David, 108, 111
Watson, Traci, 114
Wheelwright, Julie, 74, 159n. 13, 160n. 23, 160n. 25
Whitaker, Monica, 131–32
White, Patricia, 160n. 31
Will, Ed, 69, 75, 159n. 13, 159n. 18, 160n. 25
Williams, Raymond, 19
Wilman, Chris, 99
Wilson, Kirt, 163n. 8
Wilson, William, 93
Winchell, Barry, 5, 123–42, 145, 148, 155n. 19, 164n. 9, 165nn. 20–21, 166n. 24
Wittig, Monique, 137, 166n. 26
Wolfe, Michelle, 23, 80

Yoakam, Dwight, 90

John M. Sloop (Ph.D., University of Iowa) is associate professor of communication studies at Vanderbilt University in Nashville. He is the author of *The Cultural Prison* in addition to journal articles and book chapters, coauthor with Kent A. Ono of *Shifting Borders: Rhetoric, Immigration, and California's Proposition 187*, and the coeditor of two books. He is a past winner of the Karl Wallace Award and was the 2002–2003 Jacque Vogeli Fellow and codirector of the Fellows Program at the Robert Penn Warren Center for the Humanities.